PLEASURE AND
THE GOOD LIFE

PLEASURE AND THE GOOD LIFE

CONCERNING THE NATURE, VARIETIES, AND PLAUSIBILITY OF HEDONISM

Fred Feldman

CLARENDON PRESS · OXFORD

OXFORD

UNIVERSITY PRESS

Great Clarendon Street, Oxford OX2 6DP

Oxford University Press is a department of the University of Oxford.
It furthers the University's objective of excellence in research, scholarship,
and education by publishing worldwide in

Oxford New York

Auckland Bangkok Buenos Aires Cape Town Chennai
Dar es Salaam Delhi Hong Kong Istanbul Karachi Kolkata
Kuala Lumpur Madrid Melbourne Mexico City Mumbai Nairobi
São Paulo Shanghai Taipei Tokyo Toronto

Oxford is a registered trade mark of Oxford University Press
in the UK and in certain other countries

Published in the United States
by Oxford University Press Inc., New York

© Fred Feldman 2004

The moral rights of the author have been asserted
Database right Oxford University Press (maker)

First published 2004

British Library Cataloguing in Publication Data
Data available

Library of Congress Cataloging in Publication Data
Data available

ISBN 0-19-926516-X

1 3 5 7 9 10 8 6 4 2

Typeset by Newgen Imaging Systems (P) Ltd., Chennai, India
Printed in Great Britain
on acid-free paper by
Biddles Ltd., King's Lynn, Norfolk

ACKNOWLEDGMENTS

I have been thinking about the topics of this book for about thirty years. During that time I have enjoyed and benefited from conversations with very many people. I think here primarily of students who took various courses with me and colleagues who commented on my work. Although I know that many friends made very many useful contributions, it is not easy for me to recall, after all these years, precisely who said what. So I start with thanks and an apology. I thank all of those who made comments or suggestions about hedonism. I apologize to those whose names I have neglected to mention.

Several people read complete (or nearly complete) versions of the manuscript. Some of them gave me detailed and useful critical commentary on a variety of topics. I am especially grateful to Chris Heathwood, Jens Johansson, Andrew Moore, Wayne Sumner, Eva Bodanszky, and Owen McLeod for their generous and helpful criticism and suggestions. I am also grateful to Dick Godsey for comments and encouragement. Quite a few years ago I had the honor and pleasure of directing Earl Conee's doctoral dissertation. His topic was 'Pleasure and Intrinsic Value'. I learned a lot from the enjoyable conversations I had with Earl, and with Eva Bodanszky around the same time. In the spring of 1997 I taught a seminar on hedonism. Many students made very useful contributions. I recall in particular the contributions of Eddie Abrams, Ty Barnes, Clay Splawn, Jean-Paul Vessel, and others. Irwin Goldstein visited UMass at that time and gave a useful and provocative presentation in the seminar.

I learned a lot about the concept of intrinsic value from exchanges with some of the people already mentioned, as well as with others. I think here especially of Ben Bradley, Roderick Chisholm, Shelly Kagan, Noah Lemos, Erik Wielenberg, and Michael Zimmerman.

The overall structure of this book corresponds to the structure of my article 'Hedonism', which appears in *The Encyclopedia of Ethics*, 2nd edition, edited by Lawrence Becker and Charlotte Becker. I thank them for permission to use material from that article.

Many of the ideas at the core of this book can be found as well in my paper 'The Good Life: A Defense of Attitudinal Hedonism'. That paper was presented at a memorial conference in honor of Roderick Chisholm that was held at Brown University in November 2000 and was subsequently published in *Philosophy and Phenomenological*

Research. My commentator at the memorial conference was Michael DePaul, who raised several interesting objections, for which I thank him. The paper (or slightly revised versions) was also presented at several other places, including Arizona State University, the University of California at Davis, and Western Washington University. Several friends made useful comments and suggestions. I think here of Tom Blackson, Peter de Marneffe, Greg Fitch, Peter French, Michael Jubien, Ned Markosian, Elinor Mason, and Connie Rosati. I thank *Philosophy and Phenomenological Research* for permission to use material from that paper as well as from my reply to DePaul.

In the spring of 2002 I had the pleasure of presenting a talk on 'Attitudinal Hedonism and the Shape of a Life' at Oxford University, the University of Lund, and the APA Pacific Division Meetings in Seattle. In Oxford I enjoyed a very enlightening and pleasant conversation with Gustaf Arrhenius in the lovely garden behind John Broome's office. I enjoyed meeting and receiving criticism from John Broome, Krister Bykvist, Roger Crisp, Bob Frazier, and several others. At Lund I met (for the first time) my dear old friend Ingmar Persson as well as several of his colleagues, including Johann Brannmark, Dan Egonsson, Wlodek Rabinowicz, and Toni Rønnow-Rasmussen. My visits to Oxford and Lund are surely to be counted among the most enjoyable experiences of my academic life.

My commentators at the Pacific Division Meetings in Seattle were Connie Rosati and Elinor Mason. I thank them for their helpful commentaries on that occasion. I also thank Peter DeMarneffe who helped to organize the session and who subsequently raised (and continues to raise) lots of interesting and difficult questions for a hedonist like me. My interest in the puzzle about the shape of a life started many years ago when I read a paper on that topic by David Velleman. I am grateful to him for generating my interest in the question and for continuing to raise insightful questions about additive forms of hedonism.

Quite a lot of the material in Chapter 8 was included in a paper 'But is it Really Hedonism?' that I presented at the Cambridge Moral Sciences Club and then again at the University of Copenhagen in the spring of 2002. In Cambridge I enjoyed many useful discussions with Edward Craig, Jane Heal, Serena Olsaretti, and others. In Copenhagen I met Kasper Lippert-Rasmussen, who raised a number of helpful points.

I am grateful to Ty Barnes, Kristen Hine, and Clay Splawn for their insightful contributions to my understanding of the hedonism of Epicurus. I have relied on Splawn's paper on this topic, 'Updating Epicurus's Concept of Katastematic Pleasure'.

During the spring of 2003 I attended meetings of a discussion group devoted to Stephen Darwall's *Welfare and Rational Care*. Some of the material in Appendix D benefited from those discussions. I am grateful to Chris Heathwood, Kristen Hine, Jens Johansson, Kris McDaniel, Jason Raibley, and others who participated.

For Elizabeth

CONTENTS

Introduction

The central aim of this book is to defend hedonism as a substantive theory about the Good Life. I try to show that, when carefully and charitably interpreted, certain forms of hedonism are plausible and defensible. They give an account of the amount of welfare, or well-being, that an individual enjoys, and they do this by appeal to the notion that pleasure is the Good. On this view the Good Life is the pleasant life.

Before I can attempt to defend my thesis, I have to explain more precisely how I understand it. This involves first explaining more exactly how I understand talk of "the Good Life". As I interpret this, it means something like 'the life that is good in itself for the one who lives it', or 'the life high in individual welfare'. Clarification of this concept is the topic of Chapter 1. I turn next to a discussion of the nature of hedonism. This is complicated by the fact that many of the received formulations of the doctrine are confused and incoherent. I am inclined to think that quite a lot of the controversy about hedonism arises in part because of this confusion. In Chapter 2 and Appendix A I discuss some typical formulations of hedonism and explain why they are unacceptable. I present a simple form of sensory hedonism—I call it 'Default Hedonism'—that provides a kind of starting point for all the other forms of hedonism to be discussed in the book.

Another of my aims in the book is to provide critical accounts of some historically important forms of hedonism. I begin this project in Chapter 2 with a discussion of the hedonism of Aristippus. I acknowledge that my account of Aristippean hedonism is somewhat speculative.

In Chapter 3 I present a catalogue of classic objections to hedonism. The objections come from a variety of sources, ancient and modern. The first of these concerns the idea that some pleasures are base or disgusting or unworthy. Hedonism, it is alleged, goes wrong because it says that a life full of such pleasures would be a good one, when in fact it would be a bad life. I focus on versions of the argument due to Aristotle, Broad, Moore, Brentano, and Brandt. In section 3.2 I discuss an objection based on the notion of "false pleasure". This is also an ancient objection, going back perhaps to Plato. I discuss versions of the argument due to some contemporary philosophers—Kagan, Nozick, and Nagel.

In section 3.3 I turn to a passage from Plato's *Philebus*. In this passage Socrates tries to show that pleasure without knowledge is worthless—or at least worth a lot less than pleasure combined with knowledge. Section 3.4 focuses on objections to hedonism based on alleged problems about measurement. In an amusing passage, Brentano claimed that it is absurd to suppose that there is a precise mathematical relation between the amount of pleasure one gets from smoking a good cigar and the amount of pleasure one gets from listening to a symphony of Beethoven. This allegedly shows that hedonism is false, since hedonism presupposes that there is a uniform scale of measurement for all pleasures. Many other philosophers, including Rawls, have raised similar objections.

In section 3.5 I discuss an argument that is perhaps not exactly a "classic". It is based on the idea that we can imagine lives that seem pretty good for the ones who live them *even though they don't contain any pleasure*. I describe one such possible life and try to make it seem plausible that (a) it contains no pleasure, but (b) it is nevertheless a pretty good life. I call the objection 'The Argument from Nonexistent Pleasures'.

G. E. Moore devoted quite a lot of attention to hedonism in *Principia Ethica* and *Ethics*. The evidence suggests that he was genuinely hostile to hedonism. He used a lot of uncharacteristically loaded terminology in his discussion, and he presented some heated objections. One of these is the (already mentioned) objection from disgraceful pleasures. His argument based on "the Heap of Filth" turns on an essentially different point. In this case Moore was not trying to show that a human life full of pleasure could be bad; he was trying to show that a possible world without pleasure might nevertheless be good—especially if it were full of beauty. W. D. Ross attempted to show that a world in which pleasure is properly distributed to deserving people might be better than an otherwise similar world in which the same amount of pleasure is distributed to undeserving people. These arguments are discussed in sections 3.6 and 3.7.

One of the main themes of this book is that there is an important distinction between the forms of hedonism that emphasize *sensory* pleasure and those that emphasize *attitudinal* pleasure. Sensory pleasure is a feeling or sensation. You have it when you are experiencing "pleasurable sensations". Attitudinal pleasure is (as the name suggests) a propositional attitude. You have it when you are enjoying, or taking pleasure in, or delighting in, something. In Chapter 4

I introduce the distinction, and I formulate a kind of hedonism based on the idea that attitudinal pleasure is the Good. I also discuss the extent to which this kind of hedonism is affected by some of the objections discussed earlier. My aim in the book is to defend certain forms of attitudinal hedonism, not sensory hedonism.

Another main theme of the book is the plasticity of hedonism. Attitudinal hedonism is especially receptive to variations and modifications. In Chapter 4 I illustrate this plasticity by formulating a kind of attitudinal hedonism intended to replicate Mill's notorious "qualified hedonism". This gives me another opportunity to discuss a way in which a form of hedonism can evade some of the classic objections. In this case, the evaded objection is the objection from worthless pleasures.

There are two appendices to Chapter 4. In one of these I focus on the distinction between attitudinal and sensory pleasure. I discuss some applications of the distinction to some other problems about pleasure. In the other appendix I sketch some possible interpretations of the hedonism of Epicurus. Part of my aim here is straightforwardly historical: I try to explain what Epicurean hedonism might be. But another part of my aim is theoretical: I try to demonstrate again that hedonism can be constructed in a lot of different ways.

In Chapter 5 I continue chipping away at the objections. I try to deal with the objections from false pleasures as well as the objection from unconscious pleasures. Additionally, I present one of my favorite forms of hedonism—Desert-Adjusted Intrinsic Attitudinal Hedonism. I claim that this form of attitudinal hedonism generates results that should be attractive to those who want to give low ratings to lives filled with base, disgusting, and otherwise unworthy pleasures. My aim here is to drive home the important fact that not all forms of hedonism imply that the life of sensuality is the best life.

Chapter 6 contains a discussion of an objection that applies to many axiological theories, not just hedonistic ones. The objection concerns the distribution of goods within a life. Many philosophers have claimed that the value of a life for the person who lives it is not simply a matter of *total amounts* of good and evil in that life; the *pattern* in which those goods are distributed within the life also matters. This objection, were it sound, would refute any axiological theory that contained a purely additive principle for the evaluation of lives. The forms of hedonism that I discuss in the book are all fundamentally intended to contain such additive principles. I attempt to explain why the forms of attitudinal hedonism defended here are not refuted by the 'Shape of a Life' objection.

Hedonism's plasticity is a major theme of the book. In Chapter 7 I pursue this theme yet further by trying to show that it is possible to construct a form of hedonism that will generate life evaluations very similar to those generated by the non-hedonistic axiology defended by Moore in *Principia Ethica*. Appendix D contains a similar effort on an even more unlikely target: I try to show that it is possible to formulate a hedonism that is pretty nearly equivalent to Stephen Darwall's so-called Aristotelian Thesis. If this is right, we can see that hedonism can be extended to the point where it will generate results equivalent to those generated by a theory that emphasizes "virtuous activity" and "flourishing".

Curious readers might wonder whether some of these axiological theories have been stretched too far. Maybe they have been stretched so far that it is no longer appropriate to categorize them as forms of hedonism. This raises a deeper question: what in general makes it correct to categorize an axiological theory as a form of hedonism? In Chapter 8 I attempt to answer this question and to do so in such a way as to justify my classification of the alleged hedonisms in this book. This turns out to be a trickier problem than might at first be expected.

Chapter 9 contains my replies to the last remaining objections to hedonism—Moore's objection concerning the heap of filth and Ross's objection concerning worlds in which pleasure is enjoyed by the undeserving. I point out that, strictly speaking, these objections do not bear on the forms of hedonism already discussed in the book. I extend the theories so as to make the objections apply, and then I tweak the forms of hedonism so that they evade the objections.

Chapter 10 contains a review of the main themes of the book and a description of my vision of the Good Life. It also includes an admission of some of the puzzles I failed to address here.

A friend who read the book in manuscript accused it of suffering from *appendicitis*. 'Too many appendices,' he said. But I respectfully disagree. There are some topics here that fit together to make (I hope) a coherent line of thought. Roughly, it goes like this: first I show that typical formulations of hedonism are incoherent. Then I formulate it correctly. Then I present a collection of classic objections. Then I start presenting my replies to the objections. As a first step, I reformulate the theory so as to have a more defensible form of attitudinal hedonism at hand. Then I consider more objections and replies. Some of these involve adjustments for truth, altitude, or desert. Finally, I draw the distinction between life-evaluating forms of hedonism and world-evaluating forms and reply to the final set of objections. Since some of these theories are somewhat far removed from the hedonism of Aristippus, it is important to consider the question whether they are properly categorized as hedonisms at all. Of course, I claim (and try to show) that they are. That is the core of the book. That material is in the *chapters*.

But in addition I wanted to discuss some interesting, closely related, but perhaps slightly tangential matters. Among these are some other defective formulations of hedonism, some further reflections on the distinction between attitudinal and sensory pleasure, formulation and discussion of other forms of hedonism, including the hedonism of Epicurus, and formulation and discussion of the question whether some allegedly non-hedonistic axiologies might be equivalent to some form of adjusted attitudinal hedonism. Readers can choose to skip some of this material if it is irrelevant to their interests. It is in the book because I find it interesting, and it has something to do with hedonism. All of that is in the *appendices*.

There are some things that curious readers might expect to find in a book about hedonism that they will not find here. One of these is a critical discussion (or perhaps even a defense) of arguments in favor of hedonism. You might think, for example, that there would be a passage in which I say something like this: 'Every person by nature ultimately seeks only pleasure and ultimately shuns only pain; therefore, pleasure is the only intrinsic good and pain is the only intrinsic evil.' Epicurus, Bentham, Mill, and other hedonists have argued in this way. But there is no such argument in this book.

I choose not to present any such argument since I am convinced that it would be hopeless. The first premise ('Every person by nature ultimately seeks only pleasure') seems to me to fly in the face of obvious facts. A masochist might ultimately seek pain; a miser might seek money; a sufficiently moral person might seek ultimately to do the right thing; a benevolent person might ultimately seek the happiness of others. The second premise ('If every person by nature ultimately seeks only pleasure, then pleasure is intrinsically good') seems to me to be indefensible. Though I cannot say exactly what Hume meant when he warned against deriving "ought" from "is", I suspect that this might be the sort of thing he had in mind. Even if psychological hedonism were true (which I deny), I cannot see how ethical hedonism would follow.[1]

So instead of *arguing for* hedonism, I operate in another way: I formulate a version of hedonism; I then subject it to all the main

---

[1] I discuss this argument briefly in my article 'Hedonism', in *Encyclopedia of Ethics*, 2nd edn.

objections I can think of. When it seems necessary, I revise that version of hedonism so as to generate versions of the doctrine that yield evaluations consistent with the intuitions of the objectors. I repeat the process until I have found a version (or a couple of versions) of hedonism that seem to me to be acceptable. They are not refuted by the standard objections. Insofar as there is an argument here, this is the form it takes. Perhaps it would be acceptable to say that my procedure is to attempt to get myself (and my patient and sympathetic reader) into reflective equilibrium with some form of hedonism.

A second thing that will not be found here is a discussion of Bentham's hedonic calculus. This may seem a bit surprising, since I devote quite a lot of attention to puzzles concerning the calculation of the amount of pleasure (or value) in various stipulated lives. Since Bentham did it first, why is there no discussion of his way of doing it? I of course have tremendous admiration for Bentham. He is a giant among hedonists. However, I think his discussion of the hedonic calculus is hopelessly confused. I sketch his view and explain my misgivings elsewhere. I see no point in repeating them here.[2]

---

[2] I discuss Bentham's hedonic calculus in the article 'Hedonism'.

CHAPTER 1

━━━━━

The Quest for the Good Life

1.1. *Pleasure and the Good Life*

Since the earliest days of recorded philosophy, philosophers have been interested in a cluster of questions about the Good Life. This focus can easily be seen in the writings of Plato and Aristotle and in their remarks about Socrates. It can also be seen in descriptions of the various schools of philosophy that followed the Golden Age. It has even been suggested that some of these schools understood the point of philosophy in general in such a way as to forge an essential link between doing philosophy and living the Good Life. The Epicureans and Stoics, for example, seem to have advertised in this way, each claiming that students who enrolled in their programs of study would thereby be given a good shot—perhaps the best possible shot—at getting to live the Good Life. Subsequent philosophers have continued to be interested in this topic, though it seems to have lost its central position as the whole point of doing philosophy.

In this book I defend one of the oldest, simplest, and most intuitively plausible views on this question. I claim that the Good Life is the pleasant life. I claim that pleasure is the Good. Since I make these claims, I am a hedonist.

Since its earliest days, hedonism has been in bad repute. Critics have dismissed it with scorn. They have presented a barrage of classic objections. Advocates of the view often insisted that the hedonism they defended was not refuted by the objections of the critics. They frequently claimed that their view had been misunderstood or misrepresented. They often tried to explain more carefully what they had in mind when they said that the pleasant life is the Good Life. I join this line of defenders. I try to explain what I mean (and what I think some of my predecessors meant) by saying that pleasure is the Good, and I try to show that, when charitably interpreted, hedonism is not refuted by the classic objections that have been raised against it.

1.2. *Clarification of "the Good Life"*

The central intuition of hedonism is that the pleasant life is the Good Life. But this sentence—'The pleasant life is the Good Life'—is open to a number of interpretations. It can be misunderstood. In fact, I think it has been misunderstood and that the misunderstandings have in many cases led critics to dismiss hedonism prematurely.

Something like this often happens: a hedonistic philosopher proposes a theory about the Good Life. He says, 'Pleasure is the Good; possession of a lot of pleasure makes for a good life.' Another philosopher comes along and denies this, pointing out that it is possible for a person to be disgusting and disgraceful even though he has a lot of pleasure. Thus, the second philosopher concludes, having a lot of pleasure does not necessarily make you a good person or ensure that you lead a good life.

But, as I see it, the dispute might be at cross-purposes. Perhaps the first philosopher took the question about the Good Life in one way, and proposed a view about that question as he conceived it, and the second philosopher took it in another way, and rejected the view as an answer to the question as he conceived it. Such disputes would be pointless. If we are to have a meaningful debate, we must have a shared understanding of the question.

Thus it seems to me that we should attempt to make the question at least a little bit clearer before we begin. To clarify the question, let us distinguish among several different things that we might have in mind when we ask whether someone has a good life.

A. When we speak of a good life, we might mean a *morally good* life; or (to use an old-fashioned-sounding phrase) a life of virtue. So, for example, if certain popular views about the life of virtue are correct, we could say that Mother Teresa had a good life in this sense. If a Kantian view is correct, we might want to say that someone who steadily acted for the sake of duty would therefore have had a good life. If we think that the moral virtues are traits from some list (e.g., justice, wisdom, courage, temperance) then we might think that a person who exemplifies these traits (and few vices) would therefore have a good life in this sense.

B. When we speak of a good life, we might use 'good' in a sense in which it means 'good as a means' or 'causally good'. We use the word in this sense when we say, for example, 'although it was not good in itself, it was still a good thing that I had my teeth drilled'. Such things are good because of what they cause or prevent or lead to. A life might be like that. So when you say that Mother Teresa had a good life, you might mean that her life as a whole was *beneficial*. You might say this if you thought it was a good thing that she lived her life as she did—a good thing because of its effects, largely on other people who benefited from her good works.

C. Another sort of good life would be the beautiful life. We might want to know what makes a person's life *aesthetically* good. A certain person's life might make a fine subject for a moving and beautiful biography, or even for a novel or play. Yet at the same time, that life might have been pretty rotten in itself for the one who lived it. Tragic figures come to mind. If someone lived the life of King Lear, we might think he had an aesthetically outstanding life—a skilled playwright might be able to cook up a good play about it—but a life that was less than ideal for him. Only a man absurdly obsessed with being memorialized in drama could want such a life.

D. Someone might take the question about the Good Life to be equivalent to a question about what sort of life best exemplifies human life. He might be looking for lives that are good examples, or ideal specimens, of human life. Imagine that you are setting up a museum exhibit designed to illustrate some of the main species here on Earth. You might want to include a good sample of a blue whale, and a good example of a garter snake. Additionally, you might want to include a good example of a human being. An ideal candidate for that position would be someone who leads a 'good human life' in this "exemplar" sense.

E. Finally, we come to the sense of the phrase that is relevant here. Sometimes, when we speak of the Good Life, we have in mind the concept of a life that is good in itself for the one who lives it. Some philosophers speak here of 'personal welfare' or 'well-being'. A good life, in this sense, would be a life that is outstanding in terms of welfare, or well-being. Other philosophers seem to have the same idea in mind when they speak of 'a life well worth living'.

I think we may be able to get ourselves to focus on the relevant notion if we engage in a little thought experiment.[1] Imagine that you are filled with love as you look into the crib, checking on your newly arrived firstborn child. The infant is sleeping peacefully. You might think of various ways in which the baby's life could turn out. What schools will he attend? What career will he choose? What sort of personality and intellect will he have? Will he someday have children

---

[1] I first appealed to this thought experiment in 1988 in my 'On the Advantages of Cooperativeness'. Since that time I have come to see that it is problematic. Robert Adams appeals to the same test in his *Finite and Infinite Goods*. Stephen Darwall elevates it to the status of a metaethical analysis of the concept of welfare in his *Welfare and Rational Care*.

of his own? Your concern for the baby might express itself in the hope that, whatever he does, things will turn out well for him. You might hope that this baby gets a good life—a life good in itself for him. That hope—the hope for a life good in itself for the one who lives it—is a hope about the topic of this book.

It is not entirely clear that this thought experiment will always work. Suppose a religious fanatic looks into his child's crib. Suppose he wants the child to have a wonderful life. Suppose he thinks that the best imaginable life for the child is one in which the child becomes a martyr for God. This religious fanatic might be filled with love, and he might be thinking about the Good Life for his child. But it is not clear that he is expressing a hope about what we would normally think of as the child's *welfare*. Perhaps he is thinking about what he takes to be moral or religious virtue. Perhaps he is thinking about the most beneficial life the child could live. So the mere fact that he is a parent filled with love, and is looking into his child's crib, and is saying something about 'the Good Life', does not absolutely guarantee that he is thinking about the topic of this book.[2]

These five concepts of the goodness of lives are indeed five distinct concepts.[3] In the absence of actual views about what makes for a morally good life, or a useful life, or a beautiful life, or a good life in itself, or an exemplary life, it might be hard to prove conclusively that these are different ideas. But there are some considerations that may help to make the differences more apparent. Reflection on these differences may also help to clarify the concept that is of central importance here.

I am convinced that it is one thing to have a morally good life, and another to have a life good in itself for the one who lives it. Many would agree that Mother Teresa had a morally good life. Perhaps this is because she tried so hard to be helpful to others. Perhaps she always tried to do her duty for duty's sake. Maybe she never committed a sin. But it is consistent with this to suppose that things did not turn out well for her. Remarks in some of her personal letters indicate that she suffered from persistent depression, especially as she got older and her health began to fail. In some letters she said that she felt as if God had abandoned her, and that her life was meaningless. In addition to this, she suffered from a number of painful physical ailments. Some who advocate her beatification appeal to these facts in support of her

---

[2] I thank Chris Heathwood for helping me to see this point.

[3] Owen McLeod has reminded me that there are more than just five such concepts. There is the concept of the legally good life, perhaps the etiquettically good life, the religiously good life, etc. Even this list is not intended to be complete.

claims to sainthood. She endured considerable suffering as she tried to do her morally good works. In this case, it seems to me that we might want to say that Mother Teresa's own personal welfare was not outstandingly high. Though her life might have been one of the most impressive in terms of moral goodness (Scale A), that life was not outstandingly good in itself for her (Scale E). Her moral standing was high, but her welfare was low.[4]

We can make the case even more dramatic. Imagine Mother Teresa again. Imagine that there is some sort of malicious but powerful deity. Imagine that the deity watches Mother Teresa closely, even looks into her heart. When she is motivated by her goodwill to perform morally admirable actions, the deity gives her heartburn, or serious pain in the knee and elbow. The better she is from the moral point of view, the worse things go for her. Since she is such a good person, her life is a disaster for her. She suffers constantly. In this imagined situation, Mother Teresa's life is morally good but intrinsically bad for her. This strongly suggests that these two kinds of evaluation diverge. They evaluate lives from two different perspectives.

Similarly, there's a difference between the extrinsically good life (Scale B) and the life good in itself for the one who lives it. I assume that Mother Teresa did a lot of good in the world. She made things better for others. Her life as a whole was tremendously beneficial. So in one sense it was a good life. That is, it was extrinsically good, or good as a means. At the same time, we can easily imagine that doing all these good deeds took a toll on her. She sacrificed her own welfare in order to benefit others. As a result, her life went less well for her. She suffered; she took less pleasure in this life. We can imagine that she lived with constant frustration; she was not happy. This illustrates a way in which a person can have a life that is good for others (Scale B), but not so good for herself (Scale E).

I think it is interesting to note that this talk of the beneficial life presupposes the concept of the life good in itself for the one who lives it. Presumably, when Mother Teresa benefited others, she did this by making their lives better. But when we say that she made their lives better, we surely do not mean to say that she made their lives *better for others*. That would just induce a long chain of lives, each making the next better for others. Rather, what we mean is that Mother Teresa helped other people to live lives that were better in themselves for

[4] The information about Mother Teresa's suffering can be found in her letters, excerpts of which have been published in the *Journal of Theological Reflection*. The topic is discussed in 'Mother Teresa's Letters Reveal Doubts' by Satinder Bindra that appeared in the CNN/World website dated September 7, 2001.

those others. That is, as a result of Mother Teresa's efforts, each of those others got a life that was somewhat better in itself for that other person than the life that other person would have gotten had it not been for Mother Teresa's efforts. So if you fully understand the idea of the beneficial life, then you must also understand the idea of the life good in itself for the one who lives it.

It takes only the briefest reflection to see that there is a difference between the aesthetically good life (Scale C) and the life good in itself for the one who lives it. King Lear's life is widely taken to be an example of an aesthetically good life. I would not wish it for my beloved first-born child.

Suppose that it is typical, or normal, for human lives to be filled with suffering and misery. Then a good example of a human life would have to be one that illustrated this unfortunate fact about people. It would have to be a life of relatively low welfare. This shows that it is at least possible that a life could rank high on Scale D (which assesses lives for their value as exemplars) while ranking low on Scale E (which assesses them for their welfare-value). A life might be good as an example of a human life, while being not so good in itself for the unfortunate individual who has to live it.

My focus here is on a question about the life that is good in itself for the one who lives it. If such lives turn out (by some surprising chance) also to be good for others, or beautiful, or morally outstanding, or good examples of lives, then I will be delighted. But if in the end it turns out that there are no connections among these scales of evaluation, I will not be dismayed. I will still be interested in the Good Life (in the sense I have tried to identify). When I say that the pleasant life is the Good Life, what I mean is that the pleasant life is the life that is good in itself for the one who lives it; it is the life of high personal welfare.[5] Thus, I focus on goodness as evaluated by Scale E.

1.3. *What is the Question about the Good Life?*

There are several different questions we could ask about the Good Life. One is a fundamentally metaethical question: what do we mean when we say that a certain life is "good in itself for the one who lives

---

[5] I sometimes suspect that some writers—especially ancient writers—conceived of the Good Life as the life that was at once good on all five (or more) scales. To be truly excellent, on this conception, a life would have to be morally good, useful, beautiful, typical of humans, and good for the one who lives it. I certainly would not defend the claim that the pleasant life would have to be truly excellent in this five (or more)-fold way.

it"? To answer this question, we would have to engage in conceptual analysis, or at least semantical theorizing about ethical language. Perhaps we would have to consider various forms of naturalism, nonnaturalism, emotivism, prescriptivism, and other theories about the meanings of ethical terms.

A much more practical question concerns the steps one must take in order to have a good life. We might focus on some puzzles such as these: If you hope to have a good life, is it essential to complete high school? Are your chances of getting a good life better if you take a job working for a big company, or would you be better off going into business for yourself? What about investment strategies? And how about the details of your personal affairs? Is it a good idea to marry young, or would you be better off waiting until you reach a more settled period in your life?

Those are undoubtedly interesting questions, but they are not examples of the sort of question I mean to discuss here. Indeed, it seems to me that we cannot do a fully responsible job of answering these practical questions until we have a somewhat clearer answer to the question I do mean to ask.

I mean to be asking, not for an analysis of the meaning of the phrase 'the Good Life', and not for a lot of practical tips about how to get a good life. Rather, I mean to be searching for a suitably general statement of necessary and sufficient conditions for a life's being good in itself for the one who lives it. I want to know, in the abstract, what features make a life a good one for the one who lives it. Ideally, I would like to find a principle that would yield a ranking of lives—a principle that would tell us when one life is better in itself for the one who lives it than some other life would have been. I would like to find a theory that would locate the fundamental sources of value in lives. Ideally, I would like the theory to assign specific (perhaps numerical) values to those elements, and then to give a systematic way of aggregating those values so as to yield a value for the whole life.

As I proceed, it may very well appear that I have been making some large and controversial assumptions in metaethics. More exactly, it may appear that I have assumed some sort of Moorean or other objectivism about the meaning of 'the Good Life'. That is because I will frequently write about considerations that show that certain statements about the Good Life are "true" and will present and discuss various arguments for and against theories. In some cases, I will say that certain views are "closer to the truth" than others. All this suggests that I think that there is some objective truth about good and evil.

While I am inclined to accept some such view in metaethics, I think it plays no role in what follows. I am inclined to think that my arguments and claims are all firmly in a branch of substantive normative ethics—axiology. I think that my remarks can be understood (and perhaps interpreted) in accord with any plausible metaethical view. Perhaps I am describing an independent moral reality; perhaps I am describing the valuation scheme of some ideal observer; perhaps I am just emoting or issuing imperatives. I prefer to remain neutral on that issue.

1.4. *Why Should We Be Interested in this Question?*

My focus in this book is the attempt to develop a view about the sort of life that would be good in itself for the one who lives it. I am interested in this topic for a couple of reasons. For one thing, I am inclined to believe that philosophical discussions since ancient days have presupposed, roughly, that the central project of an important part of moral philosophy is the attempt to identify the Good Life in this sense. So there is ample historical precedent for undertaking the project.

I am also inclined to think that many familiar theories about rationality presuppose this notion. According to these theories, the concept of rationality is to be explained by appeal to the concept of individual welfare. What's rational for you to do is what will most enhance your welfare (usually weighted for probability). Your welfare, as I see it, is to be explained by appeal to the Good Life. Those who have high welfare are precisely those who live good lives. Some consequentialist views in the normative ethics of behavior are similarly linked to views about the Good Life. On these views, the morally right act is the one that most enhances the aggregate of welfare of all affected.

Another reason to pursue this topic is a bit more practical. Medical personnel are often called upon to give evaluations of "quality of life". For example, if a fetus is discovered to have some serious abnormality, parents might want to know about the quality of life the baby would enjoy (or suffer) if allowed to live. If the baby were destined to have a life of very low quality, they might think that it would be better to abort this fetus and try again. So they might ask the doctor to make some predictions about the baby's expected quality of life. But what is the doctor to think about? Should he reflect on likely income adjusted for inflation? Or net worth? Or the baby's chances of having a satisfying social life? As I see it, the real question in such cases presupposes an answer to our question: will the baby get a life good in itself for the baby? And if not, how bad in itself for the baby will it be? This provides yet another reason to be interested in the Good Life.

My own view is that the project needs no such justification. The question about the Good Life is intrinsically worthy of our attention. We are people. We are alive. It is reasonable for us to wonder about what would make our lives good ones.[6]

So I take the question about the Good Life to be a substantive axiological question about what sort of life is good in itself for the one who leads it. The answer (if one should be discovered) might have some connection to questions about the rationality or moral rightness of behavior; but then again it might not. It might have some connection to questions about virtue and vice and excellence of character; but then again it might not. I proceed on the assumption that it is an independent question in axiology.

In what follows I will try to be wary of arguments that presuppose some other interpretation of the question. So, for example, if someone were to say that a life filled with sensual pleasures is not a good one because it involves lots of disgraceful, immoral behavior, I will be cautious. Maybe the person who puts forth that argument is confusing evaluation of a life in terms of goodness for the one who lives it with evaluation of a life in terms of its moral excellence. The life of sensual pleasure might still rate high on one scale of evaluation, even if it is off the bottom of the other scale.

1.5. *What are the Main Sorts of Answer that have been Given?*

It seems to me that the most widely discussed answers to our question fall into a couple of main categories. They are as follows:

a. *Eudaimonism.* Aristotle seems to endorse this view in the *Nicomachean Ethics* when he says 'the general run of men and people of superior refinement say that [the highest of all goods] is happiness, and identify living well and doing well with being happy'.[7] A bit later he

---

[6] Near the end of the *Apology*, Socrates says that the unexamined life is not worth living. Although I am not entirely sure that I understand what he meant, I think the remark could naturally be taken to mean that if a person does not engage in philosophical reflection on the Good Life and the goodness of his own life (in other words, if he has not examined his life), then his life cannot be good in itself for him (his life is not worth living). The Socratic claim seems to be this: if you don't think about the Good Life, you can't be having one. So understood, the doctrine seems very implausible. Surely there are plenty of unreflective, philosophically unsophisticated people who have been happy, and whose lives have been morally good, beneficial to others, and good in themselves for those who lived them. To say otherwise, it seems to me, is to suggest that if you are not happy in the peculiar way preferred by some philosophers, then your life is not worth living. This seems to me to be an astonishing view (whether Socrates' or not).

[7] *Nicomachean Ethics*, I. 4.

says, 'Also, the view that a happy man lives well and fares well fits in with our definition: for we have all but defined happiness as a kind of good life and well-being.'[8] Of course, this is all very obscure since we have not said what happiness is.

At any rate, I use the term 'eudaimonism' to refer to the view that the Good Life is the happy life. We might state the core of a typical version of this view by saying that the value in itself of a life for the person who lives it is directly proportional to the net amount of happiness that the person enjoys throughout her life.

My reaction to eudaimonism is the same as Aristotle's: the theory is hardly more than a platitude.[9] Since the concept of happiness is so obscure, telling us that the Good Life is the happy life is just the *beginning* of the discussion. If we decide to start in this way, we are still left with the fundamental problem: we need to know what makes for happiness.

b. *Preferentists* maintain that what makes a life good is that desires of some sort are satisfied rather than frustrated within that life. The view comes in many forms. Localistic preferentists start with all the ordinary desires that fill your day: the desire for lunch, the desire for a cold beer, the desire for a raise. They think the value of your life is determined by the extent to which those "local" desires are satisfied. Other preferentists are "globalists". They say that the relevant desires are desires concerning your life as a whole (or at least desires concerning "global" features of your life). If you want to live a certain sort of life, and you do live that sort of life, then your life is so far good in itself for you.

There are other important distinctions among preferentists. Some *actualist* forms of preferentism claim that the value of a life is determined by the extent to which actual desires (local or global) are satisfied. *Hypothetical* versions claim that the value of a life is determined by the extent to which certain hypothetical (or would-be) desires are satisfied. In typical forms, the relevant would-be desires are the ones you would have if you were rational or well informed. These are sometimes called 'full-information theories'.[10]

I am inclined to reject all actualist forms of preferentism. The central problem with these theories is that it seems possible for people to have desires for things that would not enhance their lives, and for

---

[8] Nicomachean Ethics, I. 8.   [9] Ibid. I. 7.

[10] All the forms are nicely catalogued in the introductory essay in Christoph Fehige and Ulla Wessel's monumental book *Preferences*. Fehige lists thirteen different categories in sect. 1.2, the suggestion being that one could claim that the good life is the one containing lots of satisfied preferences from category N, for each of the thirteen categories.

them to fail to have desires for things that would enhance their lives. Masochistic people, people who hate themselves, people who feel themselves unworthy, and others are examples. All such people would be worse off if their actual desires were satisfied.[11] Indeed, in the extreme case there might even be a person who desired just one main thing: to have his life go worse in itself for him. An actualist preferentist would then have to say that if this person's desire were satisfied, his life would be going better (because a desire was satisfied) and at the same time worse (because that's what he desired, and his desire was satisfied). The theory seems paradoxical.

Hypothetical forms of preferentism have a different problem. Suppose a person in fact does not have the desires he would have if he were fully informed, or rational, or whatever. Suppose those hypothetical desires are satisfied. That is, suppose he gets the things he would want if he had been rational, or fully informed. Suppose that he finds these things worthless. He does not enjoy having them. They seem mere nuisances. It seems wrong to say that his possession of these things is making his life better in itself for him. The most we can say, it seems to me, is that the possession of these things would have helped to make his life better if he had wanted them, and were enjoying them.[12]

Furthermore, it seems that the hypothetical preferentist is guilty of a sort of paternalism.[13] He pretends to base his axiology on each person's desires. 'What's good for you is the satisfaction of your own desires—whatever they may be.' This seems very open-minded and liberal. But then when he learns that some people have "wrong" desires, he changes his tune. Now he says, 'What's good for you is the satisfaction of the desires I think you should have.' And he apparently is willing to insist that your life is going better for you when these hypothetical desires are satisfied *whether you enjoy these satisfactions or not*. In this case it seems that his theory in fact has little to do with preferences. There are certain things he thinks will make your life go better for you whether you want them or not. Why not just give us a list of those things? The theory then becomes a form of the Objective List Theory (see below).

---

[11] Extensive and effective criticism along these lines can be found in ch. 3 of Robert Adams's *Finite and Infinite Goods*, as well as in Richard Kraut's 'Desire and the Human Good'. The main objections are carefully summarized and discussed in ch. 3 of Tom Carson's *Value and the Good Life*.

[12] For a nice statement of this objection, see James Griffin, *Well-Being*, 11.

[13] For an impressive presentation of this line of criticism, see Adams, *Finite and Infinite Goods*, ch. 3.

c. *Perfectionism.* Suppose we think that there is a certain "ideal form" associated with each species. This ideal form represents the perfect specimen—the most perfect realization of that sort of creature. The ideal form would be seen as having certain distinctive features and behaviors. On this view, then, there is a set of characteristics that are typical of the ideal form. Suppose we subtract from that set all the characteristics that are also in the ideal forms of other species. Then what is left is a set of characteristics that are distinctive of the species and in this sense "peculiarly ideal". We might say that you have a good life to the extent that you have the features and behaviors in that set relative to your species (presumably the human species).

Some people attribute something like this view to Aristotle. They take note of a famous argument in the *Nicomachean Ethics* where Aristotle seems to argue that the good for man cannot be excellence in nutrition, or growth, or anything else that men have in common with beasts. Rather, it must be 'activity of soul in accordance with virtue', since this is a function distinctive of people.[14]

More recently a number of philosophers have resurrected this view.[15] In general, those who endorse this sort of view say that the Good Life for a person is the life manifesting to a high degree the excellences peculiar to persons; the value of a life for a person is the extent to which the person manifests those excellences, less the extent to which he or she manifests various deficiencies.

I think these theories are open to a variety of objections. Some of the most serious are fundamentally matters of metaphysics. Suppose a perfectionist thinks that what is distinctive of humans is our capacity for rational, goal-directed behavior. He therefore thinks that a human being lives a good life if he engages to an impressive extent in this sort of behavior. But if there should happen to be some nonhuman creatures on another planet who also have the capacity for rational, goal-directed behavior, then this capacity is not distinctive of us. We share it with another species. In that case, engaging in it cannot be our peculiar excellence. Surely it is odd to suppose that what is good for me depends upon whether there are rational beings on Mars![16]

---

[14] Aristotle, *Nicomachean Ethics*, I. 7.

[15] The view has been found in Hurka's *Perfectionism*. However, Hurka says (p. 17) that he does not intend his form of perfectionism to be a theory about individual welfare. 'Perfectionism should never be expressed in terms of well-being. . . . It [does not give an account] of what is "good for" a human being in the sense tied to well-being.' He presents it as a theory about another conception of goodness.

[16] Many critics have pressed this criticism. A good discussion can be found in Carson's *Value and the Good Life*, 141.

Furthermore, there is this nagging problem: suppose the peculiar function of some type of animal is to serve as prey for a predator slightly higher up the food chain. Then one of the prey animals is living the Good Life if it is killed and eaten by the predator. That seems utterly implausible. The theory seems to generate plausible results only in cases in which the peculiar function of some species involves doing something that is guaranteed to be enjoyable. Otherwise, doing "your thing" might make your life worse for you.

More generally, suppose that some creature has a peculiar function. Suppose that the fulfillment of that function is not enjoyable. The creature takes no pleasure in it, has no desire to do it, and finds no satisfaction in doing it. If he does it at all, he does it only because "it is his role in life". I cannot see why we should say that this creature's life is going well for him, or that his welfare is high. I acknowledge that the creature would be a good example of his type, and that he could serve as an "exemplar". Perhaps advocates of this view have confused two scales of evaluation. Perhaps they have mixed up considerations relevant to the evaluation in terms of 'goodness as an example of the type' with evaluation in terms of 'goodness in itself for the creature'.

d. *Objective List Theories*. Some philosophers maintain that there are several different things each of which helps to make a life better. Ross, for example, suggests that virtue, pleasure, knowledge, and justice are each a source of value in a life.[17] Perhaps his view is that each of them independently helps to make a life good in itself for the one who lives it, and the Good Life is the life adequately supplied with a suitable combination of all of them. Parfit has dubbed such theories 'Objective List Theories'.[18]

My problem with such Objective List Theories should be familiar by now. Suppose some pluralist tells me that knowledge and virtue will make my life better. Suppose I dutifully go about gaining knowledge and virtue. After a tedious and exhausting period of training, I become knowledgeable. I behave virtuously. I find the whole thing utterly unsatisfying. The pluralist now tells me that my life is going well for me. I dispute it. I think I might be better off *intellectually* and *morally*, but my welfare is, if anything, going downhill. Surely a man might have lots of knowledge and virtue and yet have a life that is not good in itself for him.[19]

---

[17] Ross, *The Right and the Good*, ch. 5.

[18] Parfit, *Reasons and Persons*, Appendix I, 'What Makes Someone's Life Go Best'.

[19] Parfit makes a suggestion along these lines in the final paragraph of Appendix I in *Reasons and Persons*.

I think similar problems would infect other forms of pluralism, too. That is, this problem would arise unless advocates could somehow guarantee that the items on the list would be things that would simply *have to be enjoyed by the one who had them*. I would be prepared to look more closely into a form of pluralism that had that feature.[20]

e. *Hedonism*. Finally we come to hedonism. Hedonism is roughly the idea that the Good Life is the pleasant life. Or somewhat more exactly, it is the view that a life is better in itself for the one who lives it as it contains a more favorable balance of pleasure over pain.

Hedonism comes in many forms. Before selecting the present title for this book, I thought I would call it 'Forms and Limits of Hedonism'.[21] That would not be such a bad title, since quite a lot of this book is devoted to a discussion of these different forms, and one of my aims is to show that the limits of hedonism are further out than they are often assumed to be. My discussion of hedonism will begin in Chapter 2.

---

[20] I think it is important to distinguish between (a) pluralist theories according to which there are several goods, and each is something that is necessarily enjoyed, and (b) hedonist theories according to which enjoyment is the Good, and enjoyment in certain things—the ones on some objective list, for example—is especially good. I discuss such forms of hedonism in chs. 4, 5, and 7. I explain the distinction in ch. 8.

[21] Alluding thereby to the title of David Lyons's wonderful book on utilitarianism.

CHAPTER 2

Hedonism: A Preliminary Formulation

2.1. *Problems Concerning the Formulation of Hedonism*

I want to defend a number of substantive views concerning hedonism. These include views about the forms it can take and the plausibility of the doctrine in many of its guises. However, before turning to my presentation and defense of these views concerning the truth or plausibility of hedonism, I think it is important to have a clear conception of the nature of the doctrine. Otherwise, you may not know what I am trying to defend.

In common parlance, 'hedonism' suggests something a bit vulgar and risqué. We may think of someone like the former publisher of a slightly scandalous girlie magazine. He apparently enjoyed hanging out with bevies of voluptuous young women, drinking and dining perhaps to excess, traveling to tropical resorts where the young women would reveal extensive amounts of tanned flesh, and reveling till dawn. In an earlier era the motto was 'wine, women, and song'. Nowadays, we are required to substitute the somewhat more P.C. 'sex, drugs, and rock 'n' roll'. No matter what the motto, the vision is misguided. It reveals a misconception of the views of most serious hedonists (though, perhaps, it gets one of them approximately right). In an apparent expression of exasperation, Epicurus lamented this sort of misunderstanding. He insisted: 'So when we say that pleasure is the goal we do not mean the pleasures of the profligate or the pleasures of consumption, as some believe, either from ignorance and disagreement or from deliberate misinterpretation, but rather the lack of pain in the body and disturbance in the soul.'[1] Mill was similarly troubled by attacks from critics who apparently thought he was defending a doctrine worthy only of swine. Like Epicurus, he struggled to explain that his conception of hedonism did not have the unsavory implications. Yet even today some

---

[1] 'Letter to Menoeceus,' in *The Epicurus Reader*, 30.

critics of hedonism seem unable to conceive or unwilling to concede that hedonism can be anything other than some sort of vulgar sensualism. It behooves us, therefore, to take a moment to formulate the view with a bit more care.

Immediately, however, a problem arises. The professional literature on hedonism is filled with defective formulations of the view. Critics and advocates alike seem to have real trouble saying just what hedonism is supposed to be. There is apparently a genuine puzzle about how to state the hedonistic idea. I have to admit that I am fascinated by this puzzle. However, I also have to admit that some readers might not share my enthusiasm. They might be bored silly by a long discussion of failed formulations of the view. Thus, some of what I have to say is relegated to an appendix at the end of this chapter. I beg the reader's forbearance as I discuss just one typical formulation before proceeding. This one is due to William Frankena.

In his *Ethics* (2nd edition), Frankena gives a brief account of the fundamental thesis of hedonism. He says this:

> to see just what a hedonist about the good is claiming we must use a series of statements. 1. Happiness = pleasure, or happiness = pleasantness. 2. All pleasures are intrinsically good, or whatever is pleasant is good in itself.... 3. Only pleasures are intrinsically good, or whatever is good in itself is pleasant in itself.... 4. Pleasantness is the criterion of intrinsic goodness. It is what makes things good as ends.[2]

Frankena's statement seems to me to illustrate at least six mistakes, some of which also appear in other attempted formulations of the view.

i. First we should note that in (1) Frankena says that hedonists identify happiness with pleasure. While some hedonists may have suggested such a view, it is by no means essential to hedonism as I understand it. Clearly a philosopher could be hedonist while simply refusing to commit himself to any view about the nature of happiness. As I see it, hedonism is a view about what makes a person's life *good in itself for the person*, not a view about happiness.

Furthermore, even if a hedonist were to maintain that there is an important connection between pleasure and happiness, he could deny that this connection is identity. He might say that pleasure is something that one can enjoy at a given moment. A person can experience pleasure briefly, and can experience it even if his life as a whole is pretty miserable. Happiness is not like this, he could say. We count

---

[2] Frankena, *Ethics*, 2nd edn., 84.

no man happy until we have accumulated evidence concerning a long period of his life—perhaps the whole of it. Such a hedonist might describe the connection between pleasure and happiness by saying that in general a person lived a happy life if and only if he experienced many moments of pleasure and relatively few moments of pain during his life. This view, obviously, is not equivalent to the view that happiness and pleasure are the same thing.

To drive home the difference between happiness and pleasure, note that a person might experience pleasure at a time when he is not happy (e.g., if he is also experiencing a lot of pain at the same time). Equally, a person might be happy throughout a period of time even though he experiences no pleasure at many of the moments during that time (e.g., if he is happy just to be alive, well fed, and not in pain).

A philosopher could recognize these facts about pleasure and happiness, and could go on to insist that it is pleasure alone that plays the crucial role in increasing the intrinsic value of a person's life. Such a philosopher would be a hedonist, but he would not claim that happiness is identical to pleasure. Thus, I think it is a mistake to say that hedonism essentially involves the idea that pleasure and happiness are the same thing.

ii. Frankena says in (2) that 'whatever is pleasant is good in itself'. I think this is a mistake, too. Indeed, I think that no careful hedonist would want to maintain that *pleasant things* are intrinsically good; they want to maintain that it is the pleasure we get from pleasant things that is intrinsically good. To see this clearly, consider a typical, uncontroversially pleasant thing: if I have been out shoveling snow on a cold winter's day, I may enjoy a warm, soapy shower when I come indoors. Consider the event that is my taking of that warm and soapy shower. That event is a pleasant thing. Yet the hedonist does not want to say that *the taking of the shower* itself is intrinsically good. The hedonist typically would want to say that taking the shower was extrinsically good because it produced so much pleasure for me.

This same mistake appears as well in (3) and (4).

iii. Another apparent error pervades Frankena's formulation. This is an error of omission: he fails to say anything about pain. It is impossible to give an adequate hedonistic evaluation of anything (a life, the consequence of an action, a possible world) without taking into account the adverse impact of the pains that occur within that thing. Thus, insofar as he fails to mention pain, Frankena's account is at least seriously incomplete.

iv. Frankena says in (3) that 'only pleasures are intrinsically good'. This is another common mistake. It appears as well in several other attempted formulations of hedonism.[3] If taken at face value, (3) would imply that no pleasure-containing complex thing (such as a life, or a possible world) could be intrinsically good. Clearly, no matter how much pleasure it contains, no possible world "is a pleasure" (whatever precisely that may mean). As Frankena suggests in (4), the hedonist certainly does want to allow for the possibility that such complex things can be intrinsically good. Generally, the hedonist wants to say that a complex thing is intrinsically good if and only if it contains a favorable balance of pleasures over pains. If he says this, he cannot also say that pleasures are the "only things that are intrinsically good".

v. Frankena does not say anything explicit about the evaluation of complex things such as lives. This is another respect in which Frankena's statement is incomplete.

vi. Finally, I note the puzzling remark in (4) about pleasantness "making things good as ends". Frankena's remark seems to imply that, according to hedonism, if a thing is pleasant, then it is good as an end. But as I have already mentioned above in (ii), the possession of the property of *being pleasant* does not make things good as ends according to hedonists. The taking of a hot, soapy shower might be very pleasant, but it is not good as an end according to hedonists. Rather, hedonists want to say that the property of *being a pleasure* makes things good as ends (if 'good as an end' is equivalent to 'intrinsically good'). Thus, hedonists would say that taking the shower is good as a means, since it leads to a lot of pleasure, and the pleasure is good as an end.

It is possible that in (4) Frankena is trying to say that things that are not themselves pleasures are made to be good as ends by their containment of pleasures. Perhaps this is what he means when he says that pleasantness is the criterion of intrinsic value. If this is right, then we see that (4) conflicts with (3), since (3) implies that nothing other than a pleasure can be intrinsically good.

Enough of this. It should be clear that there is a puzzle about the formulation of hedonism. (If it is not yet sufficiently clear to you, you are invited to take a look at Appendix A, where another typical formulation of hedonism is criticized.) I wish now to turn to the more 'positive' task of formulating a clear answer to the question 'What is

---

[3] I discussed this mistake at some length in my 'On the Intrinsic Value of Pleasures'. I also discuss it below in Appendix A.

hedonism?' My answer to this question begins with some brief (and preliminary) remarks about pleasure and pain.

2.2. *Default Hedonism*

In order to simplify later discussion, I think it will be useful to have a sort of default hedonism available. Then, with this in hand, we can attempt to construct a variant to represent the hedonism of Aristippus. Later, I will construct another variant to represent the hedonism of Epicurus. And later still, I will try to make use of this default hedonism as a starting point when constructing other forms of hedonism. So let us first formulate our default, maximally simple version of hedonism.

First we need to make some assumptions about pleasure and pain.

i. We assume that pleasures are certain feelings or sensations. (Later, we will have reason to reconsider this assumption.) When a person experiences a feeling of pleasure, there is an event, or "episode", that consists in that person's feeling pleasure at that time. Each such episode lasts through a period of time, and so it has a *duration*. The pleasure experienced in the episode is of a certain *intensity*—or "strength" or "vividness". Of course, in real-life cases the intensity of pleasure in an episode will vary through time. Perhaps at the outset of the episode, the pleasure is of low intensity. Then it rises to a crescendo and subsequently fades. When the intensity reaches zero, the episode ends. In order to accommodate this fact, we will stipulate that the intensity of an episode of pleasure is the *average* strength of the feeling of pleasure in that episode.

ii. We assume that each episode of pleasure contains a certain 'amount' of pleasure, and that this amount is in principle subject to measurement. (We need not assume that these amounts can in practice be precisely determined either by introspection or by any existing technology.) The amount of pleasure in an episode depends upon intensity and duration, with longer-lasting and more intense pleasures being said to contain more total pleasure. For purposes of exposition I will imagine that there is a standard unit of measurement for these amounts. I call one unit of pleasure a "hedon".

iii. We assume that pains are also feelings that come in episodes with intensity and duration. Each such episode contains a determinate amount of pain. I call one unit of pain a "dolor".

iv. We assume that pain is 'opposite' to pleasure, so we can speak of a balance of pleasure over pain. In other words, it makes sense to subtract the number of dolors of pain that a person feels during a stretch of time from the number of hedons of pleasure that he feels during that time. The resulting number indicates a sort of "hedono-doloric balance". This is often called "net pleasure", or "pleasure minus pain". The mathematical operation has a point only if one hedon of pleasure is (in some important but elusive sense) "equal in size but opposite in sign" to one dolor of pain.

v. We assume that it is possible in principle to compare the amount of net pleasure in some combination of pleasures and pains to the amount of net pleasure in some other combination of pleasures and pains. Thus, consider a person's whole life. It contains a lot of episodes of pleasure and pain. There must be a way of evaluating the life as a whole by appeal to facts about the pleasures and pains contained therein.

We need also to make some assumptions about the concept of intrinsic value. For present purposes it will be sufficient merely to say that a thing has intrinsic value when it has value "in itself". The intrinsic value of a thing is a component of its value that depends on the intrinsic features of the thing rather than on its relations. Thus, for example, the intrinsic value of an episode of pleasure must depend upon facts about that episode of pleasure itself (such as the strength of the feeling, or its duration, or some phenomenological feature such as the pleasure's "feel") and not upon extrinsic features (such as its cause, or its effects, or the attitude that someone takes toward it).

I will assume that we can represent intrinsic values with numbers in a typical way. Positive numbers represent amounts of intrinsic goodness, with higher numbers representing greater amounts of intrinsic goodness. Negative numbers represent amounts of intrinsic badness. The numbers are not to be taken too seriously. An amount of value that here is represented as '+10' might just as well have been represented as '+100' or '+1000'. The important facts are that positive numbers represent amounts of goodness; negative numbers represent amounts of badness; and relationships among these numbers represent relationships among the corresponding amounts of intrinsic value.

Since intrinsic values depend upon intrinsic features, it follows that if two things are intrinsically alike, they must have the same intrinsic value. This has implications for hedonism. If we say that episodes of pleasure are the fundamental bearers of positive intrinsic value, then we will have to say that if two episodes of pleasure are intrinsically alike, then they must have the same intrinsic value.

Later I will have much more to say about intrinsic value. In particular, I will have some things to say about some of the metaphysical features of the items that are the bearers of the most fundamental sort of intrinsic value. But for now I hope it will not be necessary to say much more.[4]

With these assumptions as background, we can formulate a simple kind of hedonism. It is not clear that any actual hedonist has ever endorsed precisely this view. But some critics of hedonism seem to understand hedonism in something like this way, since their criticisms are best interpreted as attacks on such a doctrine. So, here is Default Hedonism (DH):

i. Every episode of pleasure is intrinsically good; every episode of pain is intrinsically bad.

ii. The intrinsic value of an episode of pleasure is equal to the number of hedons of pleasure contained in that episode; the intrinsic value of an episode of pain is equal to − (the number of dolors of pain contained in that episode).

iii. The intrinsic value of a life is entirely determined by the intrinsic values of the episodes of pleasure and pain contained in that life, in such a way that one life is intrinsically better than another if and only if the net amount of pleasure in the one is greater than the net amount of pleasure in the other.

The first component of this formulation serves to indicate that DH is a form of "universalistic hedonism"—it says that every episode of pleasure is good in itself. Thus, it makes no provision for "worthless pleasures" or "overridden pleasures", or any other pleasures that fail to have positive intrinsic value. (It says a corresponding thing about the intrinsic badness of all pains.)

The second component of the doctrine serves to assign an amount of intrinsic value to each episode of pleasure and to each episode of pain. In the case of pleasures, the amount of intrinsic value in such an episode is always a positive number equal to the number of hedons it contains. As a result, "bigger" pleasures are said to be intrinsically better. This means that more intense pleasures are intrinsically better than less intense ones, durations being equal. Similarly, longer-lasting

---

[4] Note that I did not mention the Isolation Test. That was intentional. I do not understand the Isolation Test well enough to endorse it. Nor did I say that things have their intrinsic values of necessity. In the present context, where we are taking the bearers of intrinsic value to be "episodes", I am inclined to reject the necessity principle. Later, when we reconsider the metaphysics of the bearers of intrinsic value, I will reconsider the necessity principle.

pleasures are better than briefer ones, intensities being equal. In the case of comparisons between pleasures that differ in both intensity and duration, the one containing more hedons of pleasure is always the better.

The intrinsic value of any episode of pain is guaranteed to be a negative number by the minus sign in the second component of DH. Thus, every episode of pain has a negative intrinsic value determined by the number of dolors of pain it contains. In other words, every episode of pain is intrinsically bad. "Bigger" episodes of pain (ones that contain more dolors of pain) are therefore intrinsically worse than "smaller" ones.

The third component of DH ensures that DH is a form of "pure" hedonism. In effect, it says that nothing other than pleasures and pains has any direct effect on the intrinsic value of a person's life. As a result of (iii), we cannot say that knowledge, or virtue, or preference satisfaction has any direct impact on the intrinsic value of a life. Of course, if the possession of a bit of knowledge leads to pleasure, then the possession of that bit of knowledge has some positive *extrinsic* value. But in itself it must be worthless on DH.[5]

It would be natural to combine with DH the assumption that *extrinsic* values are somehow determined by the production or prevention or signification of pleasure and pain. This is hardly surprising, but it does have one implication that should be noted. An episode of pleasure certainly can have a negative extrinsic value. In other words, there can be (extrinsically) bad pleasures. An advocate of DH would say that if a pleasure leads to later pains, and the pains are sufficiently bad, then the pleasure itself is extrinsically bad. Of course, in light of (i) the pleasure continues to be intrinsically good. A corresponding thesis holds in the case of pains, some of which are extrinsically good.

DH does not have the defects I claimed to have detected in the formulation due to Frankena. Notice, first, that DH does not say

---

[5] Notice that in all this, I did not say that "the absence of pain" is good, or that "the absence of pleasure" is bad. In this I seem to have departed from some of the great hedonists of the past. For example, note that Bentham says: 'A thing is said to promote the interest, or to be for the interest, of an individual, when it tends to add to the sum total of his pleasures; or, what comes to the same thing, to diminish the sum total of his pains' (*Principles of Morals and Legislation*, 341). And notice that Mill says something quite like this, too: 'pleasure, and freedom from pain, are the only things desirable as ends' (*Utilitarianism*, 10). However, I think it is a big mistake to say that absence of pain is good in itself. The measurement problems would be enormous. How could we calculate amounts of absence of pain? I assume that 'absence of pain' refers to that state in which one feels no pain. In my view, and according to DH, the mere absence of pain has no intrinsic value. The question about the relation of "absence of pain" to pleasure is discussed below in connection with Epicurean Hedonism in Appendix C. Chisholm discusses this question in *Brentano and Intrinsic Value*, 61.

anything about happiness. It would be consistent with DH to say almost anything about happiness, though of course some hedonists might want to say that the amount of happiness in a life is also determined by the amounts of pleasure and pain contained therein. That would be possible. But DH itself does not *require* any views about happiness.

Notice, second, that DH does not imply that *pleasant things* are intrinsically good. DH does not mention pleasant things. It mentions episodes of pleasure and episodes of pain, and complex things containing them. If we assume that a pleasant thing is a thing that gives pleasure, such as a warm, soapy shower, then it would be consistent with DH to say that such things are extrinsically good.

Notice, next, that DH contains a number of claims about the intrinsic values of pains. According to (i), each of them is intrinsically bad. According to (ii), the intrinsic badness of one of them is determined by the number of dolors of pain it contains. And according to (iii), adding greater amounts of pain to a life serves to make that life worse in itself (assuming that it does not affect the amount of pleasure in the life). So DH does not forget to incorporate appropriate doctrines about "The Bad".

DH does not imply that pleasure is the only intrinsic good. Indeed, as (iii) makes clear, plenty of things other than episodes of pleasure can be intrinsically good according to DH. For example, any life containing a favorable balance of pleasure over pain is alleged by (iii) to be intrinsically good. But whenever such a thing is intrinsically good, its goodness derives entirely from the pleasures and pains contained therein.

So it should be clear that this proposed formulation of hedonism is different from the one stated by Frankena. I am inclined to think that DH is sufficiently clear for present purposes. It provides a basis for further discussion. Real-life forms of hedonism (I will claim) can be seen as variants, or modifications, of DH. Some discussion of hedonism can begin on the assumption that hedonism is adequately represented by DH. DH may be false, but it is not internally incoherent.

It should also be clear that DH does not imply that the Good Life has to be something like the life of the magazine publisher described at the outset. In fact, given a standard set of assumptions about the pains associated with hangovers, heart attacks, sexually transmitted diseases, and loneliness in old age, DH might imply that such a life is not very good at all. And given an uncontroversial set of assumptions about the pleasures of good health, the possession of a rewarding job, and a happy and secure family life, DH might imply that the Good Life is much less scandalous. Perhaps a person who wants to maximize his lifetime hedono-doloric balance should think more about finishing college, embarking on a rewarding career, and finding a loving and loyal spouse.

2.3. *The Hedonism of Aristippus*

One of the central themes that I want to urge in this book is a doctrine that I call 'the plasticity of hedonism'. This is just a fancy way of indicating that I think that hedonism comes in many forms. Hedonism is really a fairly large *family* of axiological theories, rather than a particular theory. As a first illustration of this alleged plasticity, I would like very briefly to discuss the hedonism of Aristippus.

Aristippus of Cyrene (c. 435–350 BC) is generally recognized as the founder of the so-called Cyrenaic school of hedonism. He apparently wrote quite a lot, but nothing survives beyond a few supposedly witty remarks.[6] The hedonism of Aristippus is alleged to be distinctive in several ways. For one thing, Aristippus is alleged (by Diogenes Laertius) to have maintained that physical, bodily pleasures are more valuable than mental, intellectual pleasures. It is not clear that this will require any alteration in the default hedonism, since the Aristippean view will be accommodated if we just assume that physical pleasures tend to be more intense than mental ones. Then the added intrinsic value of the physical over the mental will be guaranteed merely because we continue to say that more intense pleasures (*ceteris paribus*) are intrinsically better than less intense ones. So let us add a parenthetical remark in which we say this:

Physical pleasures are in general more intense than mental ones, and so episodes of physical pleasure generally contain more hedons than mental ones.

For a second thing, Aristippus is alleged to have said that we should go for near-term pleasures rather than long-term ones. This might be thought to be an integral component of his hedonism. Maybe he

---

[6] Diogenes Laertius provides many examples of his humor. I will repeat just one of these examples here. Aristippus worked in the court of Dionysius of Syracuse. According to the story, Dionysius spat upon Aristippus, but Aristippus didn't make a fuss. When asked about this, Aristippus replied by saying: 'If the fishermen let themselves be drenched with sea water in order to catch a gudgeon, ought I not to endure to be wetted with negus in order to take a blenny?' Diogenes claims, on the basis of remarks such as this, that in addition to his philosophical insight, Aristippus also had quite a remarkable sense of humor.

thought that the value of a pleasure decreases as it gets further out in time.[7] That would require some fairly extensive and subtle modifications of DH. But a more reasonable view would be this: though future pleasures are just as valuable in themselves as same-size present pleasures, the future ones are so uncertain that it would be more prudent to go for the near-term ones. If interpreted in this way, this is not a view in axiology at all. Rather, it is a view about prudence: it is more prudent to pursue near-term pleasures, since you cannot be sure about your chances of achieving the pleasures of the future. In this case, we have no reason to modify our default hedonism at all. In deference to Aristippus, I will just add a parenthetical remark about the uncertainty of the future:

Since we have no way of knowing what the future will bring, it might be prudent to aim for near-term pleasures rather than temporally distant ones (even if they in fact turn out to be of the same size).

For a third thing, it is said that Aristippus defended the notion that each person should pursue his own pleasure, perhaps because each person could never experience the pleasures of any other person. You can see hints of this sort of interpretation in the following passage from the *Internet Encyclopedia of Philosophy:*

When the Cyrenaics say that 'pleasure' is the highest good, they do not mean that pleasure in general is good, so that we should seek to maximize the overall amount of pleasure in the world, as utilitarians say. Instead, they mean that, for each of us, our *own* pleasure is what is valuable *to us,* because that is what each of us seeks. Also, each of us can only experience our own pleasures, and not the pleasures of other people. Thus, the Cyrenaic view is a form of egoistic hedonism.[8]

These remarks seem to me to be problematic. One problem is that there seems to be some confusion of hedonism as a view in axiology with hedonistic egoism as a view about what sort of actions we should perform. The latter would be a doctrine in the normative ethics of behavior. Hedonism (as I understand it) says nothing about what we should do, or what we should seek. It says something about what's intrinsically good. So the contrast between Aristippean hedonism and utilitarianism seems to be a case of apples and oranges.

---

[7] I would find this doctrine troublesome, since it implies that the intrinsic value of a given episode of pleasure could change as it becomes closer in time. That seems to me wrong, since I think that every episode of pleasure has its intrinsic value in virtue of its intrinsic features, and distance in time is apparently not intrinsic. It would suggest that while the episode itself remains intrinsically unchanged, its value steadily increases as it gets temporally closer.

[8] O'Keefe, 'Cyrenaics'.

Secondly, there seems to be a confusion in the remark about what is valuable *to us*. Insofar as hedonistic utilitarians have a view about what is valuable *to us*, they mainly seem to agree with Aristippus—each person values his or her own pleasure.[9] But hedonism is not a view about what is *valuable to us*. It is intended to be a view about what is intrinsically valuable. And Aristippus and Mill agree entirely about that—according to each of these views, every episode of pleasure is intrinsically good. From the fact that each person can experience only his own pleasures, nothing of any interest follows about the intrinsic value of pleasure. I am sure that Mill and Bentham and any other universalist hedonists would agree that each person experiences only his or her own pleasures. This has no bearing on what is of value.

I guess that if we wanted to incorporate something of this egoism, we could do it by adding another parenthetical remark. We could say that although all pleasures are intrinsically good, each person pursues (or should pursue, or has reason to pursue?) his own pleasures. Since the remark seems to me to have almost nothing to do with hedonism, I prefer to leave it out. I would prefer to let it appear in the statement of some egoistic theory about prudent, or morally right, behavior.

Relying on the remarks of Diogenes Laertius, we can formulate a variety of hedonism on behalf of Aristippus. It turns out, strangely enough, to be DH but with just a couple of parenthetical remarks added.

Aristippean Hedonism

i. Every episode of pleasure is intrinsically good; every episode of pain is intrinsically bad. (But physical pleasures tend to be much more intense, and hence tend to contain more hedons of pleasure, than mental pleasures. And since near-term pleasures are more certain than far-off ones, it is prudent to pursue them instead of their temporally distant cousins.)

ii. The intrinsic value of an episode of pleasure is equal to the number of hedons of pleasure contained in that episode; the intrinsic value of an episode of pain is equal to − (the number of dolors of pain contained in that episode).

iii. The intrinsic value of a life is entirely determined by the intrinsic values of the episodes of pleasure and pain contained in the life, in such a way that one life is intrinsically better than another if and only if the net amount of pleasure in the one is greater than the net amount of pleasure in the other.

---

[9] Mill notoriously seems to appeal to this very fact as a premise in his proof of utilitarianism in ch. 4 of *Utilitarianism*: 'Each person's happiness is a good to that person, and the general happiness, therefore, is a good to the aggregate of all persons.' (Note that Mill explicitly defines happiness as 'pleasure and the absence of pain'.)

Like DH, Aristippean Hedonism, or "AH", implies that every episode of pleasure is intrinsically good. We can therefore say that AH is also a form of universal sensory hedonism. AH also implies that the intrinsic value of a person's life is determined entirely by the intrinsic values of the pleasures and pains occurring therein. No other thing (e.g., knowledge, virtue, freedom, goodwill) plays a similarly direct role in the determination of intrinsic values of complex things. Therefore, we can say that AH, again like DH, is a form of pure hedonism.

AH differs from DH in only a couple of respects. For one thing, AH contains the added claim that physical pleasures are generally more intense than mental ones. If this is understood as an empirical claim about real-life episodes of pleasure, then I am inclined to think that it might be true. (I have not done enough research to verify it.) However, in light of the possibility that these extra-intense physical pleasures might be more likely to lead to later pains, and some of those pains might be pretty intense, a cautious hedonist would not endorse the Aristippean notion that we should "go for the physical". If someone is interested in piling up the largest possible lifetime supply of hedons, he might do well to bypass some very intense physical pleasures in favor of some rather milder mental ones. In the long run, this might be the pleasanter path to follow. Apparently, Aristippus advocated the riskier approach.

AH also differs from DH in its attitude toward time. According to AH, it is always (or perhaps only generally) more prudent to seek the near-term pleasure in preference to the more temporally distant one. DH says nothing about the temporal location of pleasures it would be prudent to pursue. This seems appropriate since, as I see it, axiological doctrines should stick to axiology and leave prudence to others.

On the face of it, however, the Aristippean claim seems unreasonable. Suppose you are given a choice of two pleasures. Suppose you are told on unimpeachable authority that the first pleasure would occur within the next five minutes, and would contain exactly 300 hedons. On the other hand, the second pleasure would occur tomorrow and would contain 10,000 hedons. Neither pleasure will lead to further pleasures or pains. Each is guaranteed. You cannot have both. AH, as I have formulated it, implies that you should pursue the much smaller near-term pleasure. This seems to me to be foolish. I am inclined to say, 'Grow up. Learn to defer gratification. You only make things less good for yourself in the long run by choosing the near-term pleasure in a case such as this.' In any case, the parenthetical remark about the alleged advantages of near-term pleasures is not an axiological doctrine. It is an inessential (and dubious) claim about prudence.

But my aim here is not to refute AH. Rather, it is merely to show that AH is little more than a trivial variant of DH. In fact, it is just DH with some added non-axiological claims. This illustrates the plasticity of hedonism. So far, we have seen that it can take two forms.

I would like to present and explain some of the classic objections to hedonism. However, before I turn to that project, I want to discuss (briefly) another inadequate formulation of the view. Readers with little patience for this sort of thing are encouraged to move directly to Chapter 3.

APPENDIX A
Another Defective Formulation

As I mentioned at the outset, when philosophers attempt to provide clear and accurate statements of the hedonistic doctrine, they often become entangled in a briar patch of confusion. I illustrated this in Chapter 2 by appeal to the formulation presented by William Frankena in his *Ethics*.

Another good example is provided by a passage from Richard Brandt. Brandt has made enormous contributions to our understanding of hedonism, and his work is often insightful and well informed. Yet even he seemed to stumble when he tried to say what hedonism is. Here is the passage from Brandt's *Encyclopedia of Philosophy* article 'Hedonism', in which he gives his summary statement of the essence of hedonism:

[Ethical hedonism] is the thesis that only pleasant states of mind are desirable in themselves; that only unpleasant states of mind are undesirable in themselves; and that one state of affairs is more desirable in itself than another state of affairs if and only if it contains more (in some sense) pleasant states of mind than the other (the quantity of value in a state of affairs being measured by the quantity of pleasure in it).[1]

As I see it, Brandt's formulation of the hedonistic thesis is defective in several important ways.

a. Brandt says that hedonism involves the view that "pleasant states of mind are desirable in themselves". This seems wrong. (I do not mean to say that the hedonism here is wrong. What I mean to say is that Brandt's remark fails to express the thought that hedonists want to affirm.) Suppose I am tired and cranky. I take a nap and wake up refreshed and with new energy for the job at hand. I find this new state of mind (the state of mind of being refreshed and energetic) to be a pleasant state of mind. Brandt's formulation suggests that hedonists then would want to say that this very state of mind is therefore desirable in itself. Yet no careful hedonist would want to say that. The careful hedonist might want to say that *the pleasure* I get from being in this state of mind is desirable in itself;[2] the state of being refreshed and energetic is at most extrinsically desirable in virtue of its connections to the associated pleasure.

b. Brandt says that hedonism involves (A) the view that *only* pleasant states of mind are desirable in themselves and (B) the view that a state of affairs is more desirable in itself than another if and only if it contains "more pleasant states of mind". In saying these two things, Brandt seems to have committed himself to a contradiction.

---

[1] Brandt, 'Hedonism', 432.
[2] Other hedonists might want to say that what makes this a pleasant state of mind is the fact that I take pleasure in it. In that case, it is not the pleasant state of mind that is good in itself; it is instead the pleasure that I take in this state of mind.

Imagine some fans at a ball game. Suppose the home team wins, and many fans experience pleasant states of mind. Assume that there are 100 such pleasant states of mind altogether. A smaller number of fans had been rooting for the visitors, and they experience some unpleasant states of mind. Assume that there are 50 such unpleasant states of mind altogether. Now consider the whole state of affairs that consists in the occurrence of 100 pleasant states of mind and 50 unpleasant states of mind. Call this whole state of affairs 'the Outcome'.

When Brandt says in (B) that a state of affairs is intrinsically better than another if and only if it contains more (in some sense) pleasant states of mind, he undoubtedly means to be speaking about complex states of affairs such as the Outcome. Brandt's remark (together with some uncontroversial assumptions) implies that the Outcome is intrinsically good—for it contains more pleasant states of mind than an intrinsically neutral state of affairs such as, for example, there being plastic.

But the Outcome is not "a pleasant state of mind". It is not any sort of state of mind. It is a complex state of affairs that includes quite a few states of mind, some pleasant and some unpleasant. Thus, what Brandt says in (B) is inconsistent with what he said in (A), for what he said in (B) implies that the Outcome is desirable in itself, whereas what he said in (A) implies that the Outcome is not desirable in itself.

This seems to me to be a deep problem with many popular formulations of hedonism. First it is asserted that only pleasures are intrinsically good, and then it is claimed that complex things such as lives or worlds or total consequences of action are also intrinsically good if they contain a suitable preponderance of pleasures over pains. You cannot have it both ways, since lives and worlds and total consequences are not pleasures.

c. The remarks about a state of affairs being better if it contains "more pleasant states of mind" is surely wrong, although I should note that Brandt says 'in some sense'. Maybe he does not mean what his words seem to say. On one natural interpretation, 'more pleasant states of mind' means 'a larger number of pleasant states of mind'. If that is how Brandt was using the term 'more', then his remark would mean that one state of affairs is better than another if the number of pleasant states of mind that the one contains is greater than the number of pleasant states of mind that the other contains. I suspect it is obvious that this cannot be right. Consider the following pair of states of affairs:

SofA 1: 100 pleasant states of mind *plus* 9 unpleasant states of mind.
SofA 2: 101 pleasant states of mind *plus* 1,000,000 unpleasant states of mind.

Here SofA 2 contains a larger number of pleasant states of mind than SofA 1 (101 is more than 100), but it surely might not be intrinsically better than SofA 1. Clearly, the presence of almost 1,000,000 more unpleasant states of mind in SofA 2 must help to decrease the value of SofA 2. If all of the unpleasant states of mind in these states of affairs are of the same absolute size as the pleasant states of affairs in them, then SofA 2 is much worse than SofA 1.

Brandt could not have meant this. He could not have thought that the *sheer number* of pleasant states of mind is the relevant factor. Brandt's words are open to another interpretation. 'More pleasant states of mind' might mean 'states of mind that are more pleasant—pleasant to a greater degree'. So understood, Brandt's remark would mean this: one state of affairs is intrinsically better than another if and only if it contains states of mind that are *more pleasant* than those contained in the other. But a moment's reflection will make it obvious that this would be just as unsuitable—though for different reasons. Suppose the first state of affairs contains a very small number of pretty large pleasant states of mind. Suppose the second state of affairs contains a huge number of pleasant states of mind, each just a tiny bit smaller than the ones in the first state of affairs. Then the states of mind in the first state of affairs are "more pleasant" in the current sense than those in the second, but the first state of affairs is not intrinsically better.

d. Yet another interpretation is still possible. Brandt might have meant to say that one state of affairs is more desirable in itself, or intrinsically better than another, if it contains a more favorable balance of pleasurable over unpleasurable states of mind than the other. Yet even this would be wrong, since a state of affairs might contain a greater balance of pleasant over unpleasant states of mind, but not be intrinsically better. Suppose the outcome of a certain ball game contains ten very tiny pleasant states of mind and no pains, but the outcome of a second ball game contains five absolutely huge pleasant states of mind and no pains. Then the outcome of the second game might be better than the outcome of the first, though it contains a smaller balance of pleasant states of mind over unpleasant (10/0 in the first state of affairs, and only 5/0 in the second).

Although I shall not attempt to establish this point here, in fact mistakes similar to the ones Brandt made in the quoted passage are surprisingly common.[3] It appears that even the most persnickety philosophers often encounter difficulties when they try to formulate hedonism. So here we have yet another illustration of one of my main themes—that there is a puzzle about the correct formulation of hedonism.

[3] I pursued this line of criticism in my 'On the Intrinsic Value of Pleasures'.

CHAPTER 3

Classic Objections to Hedonism

Let us now turn to a consideration of some classic objections to hedonism. It is not clear that the philosophers who presented these objections intended to be attacking a view precisely like our default hedonism, DH. But I will take the liberty of interpreting these objections as objections to the view I have sketched. Perhaps this will help to make the real import of the view clearer. It will also eventually lead me to introduce some alternatives to the theory.

3.1. *The Argument from Worthless Pleasures*

Starting with the earliest discussions of the topic, anti-hedonistic philosophers have claimed that certain kinds of pleasure are not good, and do not serve to enhance the value of any life. They have appealed to such pleasures in their attacks on hedonism.

Aristotle hints at this in the *Nicomachean Ethics* where he speaks of 'disgraceful' and 'base' pleasures.[1] Broad makes the case quite persuasively in *Five Types of Ethical Theory*. He more or less defines malice in such a way that a person enjoys malicious pleasure if he takes pleasure in some other person's suffering.[2] Brandt makes a similar point in his argument against hedonism in *Ethical Theory*. He describes some women who attended beheadings in evening dress in Germany.[3] He suggests that if they enjoyed the occasion, their enjoyment was not intrinsically desirable. Brentano makes a similar claim, although his discussion is open to various interpretations. Let us consider the passage in Brentano.

---

[1] *Nicomachean Ethics*, X. 3.
[2] Broad, *Five Types of Ethical Theory*, in the excerpt included in Brandt's *Value and Obligation*, 53–4.   [3] Brandt, *Ethical Theory*, 316.

In 'Two Unique Cases of Preferability', Brentano says:

> What of pleasure in the bad? Is it itself something that is good? Aristotle says that it is not.... The hedonists expressed the contrary view ... But their view is to be rejected.... Pleasure in the bad is, as pleasure, something that is good, but at the same time, as an incorrect emotion, it is something that is bad.[4]

All of these philosophers, and others as well, have hinted at an argument against hedonism based on the fact that some pleasures are base, or disgraceful. I will attempt to formulate the argument clearly, so that useful discussion may ensue. And as I formulate it, I will try to construe the argument in such a way as to make it directly relevant to our default hedonism, DH.

Suppose some terrorist really hates children. Suppose he sets off a bomb at a playground, and then watches the news on TV. When he sees the suffering children choking and gasping and bleeding, and learns of the many injuries and deaths, this terrorist feels a thrill of pleasure. His pleasure is caused by the misery of his victims.

Suppose the terrorist does this many times over, and each time is delighted by the fruits of his labor. Suppose at the same time that his life is not filled with counterbalancing pains. If DH were true, the life of this terrorist would be good in itself for him. We would have to agree that things turned out well for him, and the quality of his life was high. Many of us, I suspect, would be inclined to reject this evaluation, and with it DH. The problem here is that while the life of the terrorist was filled with large doses of pleasure, these pleasures were the pleasures of cruelty. Pleasures such as these might seem to make a life worse, rather than better.

When we consider a case such as this, it is essential that we keep in mind the fact that we are talking about evaluation of the life in itself, *for the one who lives it*. We are not asking whether the terrorist led a morally good life, or whether he led a life that was good for others. Nor are we asking whether his pleasures were admirable. We are asking whether he led a life that was good in itself for him. Though his pleasures were caused by wholly inappropriate objects, one could still insist that if he experienced a lot of pleasure and no pain, his life was good *for him*. If we focus clearly on the relevant scale of evaluation, we should see that it is not entirely obvious that the objection is decisive. Perhaps the life of the terrorist, though disgraceful and morally indefensible, was not so terribly bad in itself for him. Many anti-hedonists prefer not to say this.

---

[4] Brentano *Origin of our Knowledge of Right and Wrong*, 90.

Other philosophers have reminded us of other worthless pleasures. In a memorable passage, Moore says: 'It is commonly held that certain of what would be called the lowest forms of sexual enjoyment [might be] the most pleasant states we ever experience.'[5] In this context he speaks of 'a perpetual indulgence in bestiality'. He says that if hedonism were true, then this perpetual indulgence in bestiality would be 'heaven indeed, and all human endeavors should be devoted to its realisation. I venture to think that this view is as false as it is paradoxical.'

Let us try to visualize the life to which Moore here alludes, adjusted so as to be directly relevant to DH. Imagine a person—we can call him 'Porky'—who spends all his time in the pigsty, engaging in the most obscene sexual activities imaginable. I stipulate that Porky derives great pleasure from these activities and the feelings they stimulate. Let us imagine that Porky happily carries on like this for many years. Imagine also that Porky has no human friends, has no other sources of pleasure, and has no interesting knowledge. Let us also imagine that Porky somehow avoids pains—he is never injured by the pigs, he does not come down with any barnyard diseases, he does not suffer from loneliness or boredom.

Moore's point (as modified to apply here) is that DH implies that Porky's life is one of the best we can imagine—'heaven indeed'. Yet, as Moore indicates, that implication is a bit hard to swallow.

Objectors claim that Porky's life is not very good in itself for him in spite of the stipulated fact that it contains a lot of intense and long-lasting pleasures. This example is thought to illustrate a way in which pleasure can be worthless. As Aristotle said, base pleasures do not enhance the value of a life.[6]

I present a possible hedonistic reply to this objection in section 4.4. That reply is intended to show that certain forms of hedonism (though not DH) yield the result that Porky's life is not so good. I give only lukewarm endorsement of the version of hedonism there discussed. Later, in section 5.3 I present a reply that seems to me to be somewhat more plausible.

[5] Moore, *Principia Ethica*, ch. III, sect. 56.

[6] In *Ethics*, 146–7, Moore presents a closely related argument against hedonism. He discusses the idea that 'one whole will be intrinsically better than another, whenever and only when it contains more pleasure, no matter what they may be like in other respects'. He goes on to say that this view (intended to be a form of hedonism) 'involves our saying that…the state of mind of a drunkard, when he is intensely pleased with breaking crockery, is just as valuable, in itself—just as well worth having, as that of a man who is fully realizing all that is exquisite in the tragedy of King Lear, provided only the mere quantity of pleasure in both cases is the same'. He acknowledges that there is no way of proving that this implication is false; but he thinks it self-evident that anyone who accepts this implication is making a mistake.

3.2. *The Argument from False Pleasures*

Shelly Kagan discusses one of the most common and forceful objections to hedonism in his 'Me and My Life'.[7] According to Kagan, hedonism implies that what determines the quality of a person's life is something completely internal to the person—in this case a certain mental state. Kagan thus says that hedonism is a form of "mental statism". Hedonism, like all forms of mental statism, implies that if two lives are alike with respect to mental states, they must also be alike with respect to value. In particular, hedonism implies that if two lives are alike with respect to pleasures and pains, then those lives are of equal value. This remains true even if one of the individuals takes his pleasures from correctly perceived interactions with real human beings, and the other individual is a mere brain in a vat, utterly unconnected with other people but taking himself to be living a life like the first person's. Kagan thinks that this is a source of trouble for hedonism.

Rather than letting the issue turn on farfetched cases involving brains in vats, Kagan, following Tom Nagel, considers the fairly realistic case of a happy businessman. The businessman is happy because, as he thinks, his career is going well, he is respected in his community, and he has a loving family. In the example, all of his assumptions are false. The businessman is in fact held in utter contempt by his colleagues, deeply deceived by his adulterous wife, and hated by his children. Each has his or her reasons for engaging in the deception, but the result is the same: the businessman's happiness is completely dependent upon his widespread misapprehension of his circumstances. If he knew the truth about his colleagues, his wife, and his children, he would be miserable. Kagan concludes the discussion of this example by saying, 'In thinking about this man's life, it is difficult to believe that it is all a life could be, that this life has gone about as well as a life could go. Yet this seems to be the very conclusion mental state theories must reach.... So mental state theories must be wrong.'[8]

Since we are considering objections to our default hedonism, let us be sure to understand the case appropriately for present purposes. Let us stipulate that the businessman experiences many episodes of

---

[7] Kagan repeats these arguments in his *Normative Ethics*, 34–6. Similar objections to hedonism can be found in many places. Adams, e.g., makes essentially the same point in his *Finite and Infinite Goods*, 84.   [8] Kagan, *Normative Ethics*, 35.

pleasure, in each case as a result of some experience he takes to be "veridical". For example, he thinks he has the respect and affection of his wife and children. When they speak to him, he enjoys episodes of pleasure based, in part, on his conviction that their remarks express their real attitudes. In fact, however, they are misrepresenting their feelings. They feel nothing but contempt for him. All his pleasures are like this. In each case the pleasure arises from some deception or misrepresentation. They are all in this respect "false pleasures". If this businessman knew the truth, he would not enjoy any episodes of pleasure. He would feel pain instead.

The objection should be clear. DH implies that the businessman's life is a good one, yet none of us would want such a life; none of us would wish such a life for our loved ones; such a life is not easily thought to be ideal.

Variants of this objection have been presented by a number of anti-hedonists, and some of them may seem pretty persuasive.[9] Nevertheless, the hedonist need not be utterly crushed. Some such hedonists might reply by saying that the life of the deceived business-man is not so bad after all. Perhaps we can explain away our sense that something is amiss in the businessman's life by pointing out that we would not like to be deceived, and we would be pained to learn that our colleagues and family have been holding us in contempt for all these years. This helps to explain the fact that none of us would voluntarily choose to swap lives with the deceived businessman. We know things about his life that he does not know. Since we know these things, we would not enjoy the experiences he enjoys. Hence, his life seems unattractive to us. But since he does not know these things, and is feeling all these pleasures, maybe his life is not such a wreck after all.

Furthermore, if any of his deceivers should slip up, the business-man might discover his real situation. Then he would be miserable. We would not like to have a life constantly on the brink of misery. This may provide another reason to avoid swapping lives with the businessman. However, in the case as described, it is stipulated that he does not discover his real situation, and is not miserable. If we were to ask him how his life is going, he would surely insist that he is living a fine life. Some would say that since the businessman does not know about the deception, it does not hurt him. He is not aware of the fact that he is living on the brink of misery. Hence, it is not entirely clear

---

[9] Robert Nozick's example of the 'experience machine' comes to mind here. See his *Anarchy, State and Utopia*, 42–5.

that hedonism's implications are indefensible. Perhaps considerations such as these help to explain away our intuitive sense that his life is not all a life could be.

I will have more to say about this objection from false pleasures in Chapter 5.

3.3. *The Argument from Unconscious Pleasures*

In the *Philebus* (21a), Socrates and Protarchus are discussing a question about the Good Life. I think it is the same question we are discussing here. They have introduced two competing views. According to one of them, pleasure is the Good. According to the other, knowledge is the Good. Socrates gets Protarchus to agree to a procedure according to which they will consider first a life full of pleasure but without knowledge, and then a life full of knowledge but without pleasure. That seems a fair way to assess the relative merits of the two views.

They proceed to discuss a life full of pleasure but devoid of *nous*. That is, the person living this life does not have any knowledge, memory, consciousness, forethought, etc. The discussion proceeds as follows:

SOC. Would you choose, Protarchus, to live all your life long in the enjoy-
    ment of the greatest pleasures?
PRO. Certainly I should.
SOC. Would you consider that there was anything wanting to you if you had
    perfect pleasure?
PRO. Certainly not.
SOC. Reflect: would you not want wisdom and intelligence and forethought,
    and similar qualities? Would you not at any rate want sight?
PRO. Why should I? Having pleasure I would have all things.
                                    . . .
SOC. But if you had neither mind, nor memory, nor knowledge, nor true
    opinion, you would in the first place be utterly ignorant of whether you
    were pleased or not, because you would be entirely devoid of intelligence.
PRO. Certainly.
SOC. And similarly, if you had no memory you would not recollect that you
    had ever been pleased, nor would the slightest recollection of the pleasure
    which you feel at any moment remain with you; and if you had no true
    opinion you would not think that you were pleased when you were; and
    if you had no power of calculation you would not be able to calculate on
    future pleasure, and your life would be the life, not of a man, but of an
    oyster, or 'pulmo marinus'. Could it be otherwise?

PRO. No.

SOC. But is such a life eligible [to be considered among the best possible]?

PRO. I cannot answer you; the argument has taken away from me the power of speech.[10]

Moore interprets the argument as being primarily about the importance of consciousness.[11] He takes the point of the argument to be that hedonism implies that pleasures of which we are not conscious are just as valuable as ones of which we are conscious. He says, 'If we are really going to maintain that pleasure alone is good as an end, we must maintain that it is good, whether we are conscious of it or not.'

This seems to me to be a somewhat dubious interpretation of the text. I do not see any passage in which Socrates clearly mentions "pleasures of which we are not conscious". I am puzzled by the notion. It is not clear to me that it is possible for a person to experience pleasure at a time without being conscious of it. Thus, I prefer a different interpretation of the argument.

As I see it, Socrates has invited us to imagine two possible lives. One of these is the life of an ordinary human being, whom we can call 'H'. The other is the life of some oyster-like creature, 'O'. The lives are exactly alike with respect to pleasures and pains. We stipulate that for every episode of pleasure in the life of H, there is an exactly similar episode of pleasure in the life of O. Similarly for episodes of pain. So the lives are hedon-for-hedon, dolor-for-dolor duplicates. The lives differ with respect to knowledge, memory, forethought, etc., with H getting lots of these things, and O getting as little as possible (consistent with the stipulation that he is feeling these pleasures and pains). We stipulate that O has very little knowledge, and no memory or forethought. Some of the knowledge, etc. bears directly on the pleasure. H remembers that he has experienced pleasure, anticipates that he will get pleasure, and knows (or truly believes) that he has pleasure on all those occasions when he indeed does have pleasure. O experiences the same amounts of pleasure as H, but O immediately forgets his pleasures, never anticipates them, and does not recognize them as pleasures when they occur. The point of the argument, as I understand it, is that in spite of their hedono-doloric indiscernibility, the life of H is better in itself for H than the life of O is for O.

If we cast this as an argument against DH, it looks like this:

1. If DH were true, then the life of O would be just as good in itself for O as the life of H is for H.

---

[10] Plato, 'Philebus', in *The Dialogues of Plato*, ii. 353.   [11] Moore, *Principia Ethica*, 89.

2. But the life of O is not just as good in itself for O as the life of H is for H.
3. Therefore, DH is not true.

It seems to me that there is nothing self-contradictory in the idea that there could be a life like the one attributed to O. I think it could happen. In *The Man who Mistook his Wife for a Hat*, Oliver Sacks describes actual human beings whose memories are severely limited.[12] They cannot remember anything for more than a few seconds. I suppose that such a person would be somewhat similar to O in at least this respect: he would not recall his pleasures for more than a few seconds. Surely there could be a person whose intellectual limitations are even more severe than that. It seems consistent with this to suppose that such a person might experience episodes of pleasure. So the comment I made concerning Moore's interpretation of the argument does not apply to this interpretation.

I return to this argument in section 5.2.

3.4. *Brentano's Cigar*

In an amusing but obscure passage in *The Origin of Our Knowledge of Right and Wrong*, Brentano mentions that 'There are some who hold...that pleasure is the only thing good in itself, that pleasure is the good'.[13] Clearly, he is talking about hedonists. He goes on to say:

But only a moment's reflection is needed to shatter such illusory hopes....A foot is divisible into twelve inches; but an intense joy is not divisible in the same sense into twelve less intensive joys. Consider how ridiculous it would be if someone said that the amount of pleasure he has in smoking a good cigar is such that, if it were multiplied by 127, or say by 1,077, it would be precisely equal to the amount of pleasure he has in listening to a symphony of Beethoven or in viewing one of Raphael's madonnas. This is enough, I think, to suggest the further difficulties involved in trying to compare the intensity of pleasure with that of pain.

In *A Theory of Justice* John Rawls says some things that seem to embody a similar line of argument. (Though I should emphasize that he explicitly says he is talking about rationality, not moral obligation. By the end of the section, however, he seems to be talking about moral obligation. It is a puzzling passage. I discuss it because it is so suggestive.)

---

[12] Oliver Sacks, *The Man who Mistook His Wife for a Hat*, 23–42.
[13] Brentano, *Origin of Our Knowledge of Right and Wrong*, 30–1.

In section 84, Rawls says: 'It seems obvious that hedonism fails to define a reasonable dominant end.' He says a few things about how it is unbalanced and inhuman to take just pleasure as the sole dominant end—he suggests that it is as bad as being miserly, or obsessed with power, or in any other way monomaniacal. I see no argument against hedonism in these remarks. Then comes a passage that suggests an argument. He says:

And then too there is the fact that there are different sorts of agreeable feelings themselves incomparable, as well as the quantitative dimensions of pleasure, intensity and duration. How are we to choose a brief but intense pleasant experience of one kind of feeling over a less intense pleasant experience of another?[14]

The general drift of the passages is fairly clear, but the details of the argument remain obscure. Therefore what I will offer is really just a suggestion. One possibility is this: it is in many cases very hard to determine the relative amounts of pleasure associated with certain pleasant experiences. Brentano ridicules the notion, by asking us whether the olfactory experiences of smoking a cigar are 127 times less pleasant than the auditory experiences of hearing a symphony; Rawls is more abstract, merely mentioning 'different sorts of agreeable feelings'. Perhaps the point is that because we cannot determine these amounts, we cannot be under any obligation to determine the amounts. That's just an application of the principle that 'ought' implies 'can'. It might be thought that this casts doubt on hedonism:

Cigar Argument (Interpretation A)

1. Sometimes we cannot determine the relative pleasantness of two experiences.
2. If sometimes we cannot determine the relative pleasantness of two experiences, then sometimes we have no obligation to determine the relative pleasantness of two experiences.
3. If sometimes we have no obligation to determine the relative pleasantness of two experiences, then DH is false.
4. Therefore, DH is false.

I see no reason to accept (3). It embodies a misunderstanding of hedonism. Hedonism is a theory in axiology. It purports to tell us what makes a life good in itself for the one who lives it. The theory does not

---

[14] Rawls, *A Theory of Justice*, 557.

imply that we have any obligation to determine the value of anything. Therefore, the fact (if it is a fact) that we cannot calculate accurately the number of hedons in any episode of pleasure is no objection to DH.

There are other ways to interpret the passages. One of these is suggested by Rawls's remark about "different sorts of agreeable feelings themselves incomparable". Maybe Brentano and Rawls are focusing on widely different pleasant experiences such as, for example, the pleasant experience of smoking a cigar and the pleasant experience of hearing a symphony. They might admit that one of these experiences is more intense than the other, and they might admit that one of these experiences lasts longer than the other. But they might be raising a doubt about the notion that one of these experiences is 'more pleasant' than the other. They point out that these are dramatically different sorts of experience. How could anyone possibly think that there are two determinate numbers, m and n, such that the experience of smoking the cigar contains exactly m units of pleasure, and the experience of hearing the symphony contains exactly n units? These experiences are so different that it makes no sense to say that one contains 127 times more pleasure than the other. There is no such fact. If this is the point, then the argument goes this way:

Cigar Argument (Interpretation B)

1. Some pairs of pleasant experiences are so different that it makes no sense to say that there is some number, n, such that one experience is exactly n times more pleasant than the other.
2. If (1), then DH is false.
3. Therefore, DH is false.

I am not entirely sure that either Rawls or Brentano meant to present just this argument. But it is an interesting argument, and some might find it persuasive. Thus, it deserves some attention.

It seems to me that the Cigar Argument, under Interpretation B, presupposes a misunderstanding of sensory hedonism. It clearly presupposes a misunderstanding of DH. For the argument focuses on pleasant experiences such as the experience of smoking a cigar and the experience of hearing a symphony, and it raises doubts about the notion that there is some precise amount by which the pleasantness of one of these experiences exceeds the pleasantness of the other. The doubt is based on the obvious phenomenological differences between the two experiences. This is supposed to reveal a problem for hedonism.

The misunderstanding is this: the advocate of DH assumes that there is such a thing as "the feeling of pleasure itself". He assumes that when a person gets pleasure from smoking a cigar, the relevant item is not the experience of smoking a cigar. That has at best *extrinsic* value according to DH. The relevant item is the episode of sensory pleasure caused by smoking the cigar. Similarly, the relevant item in the symphony case is not the experience of hearing a symphony. Like the smoking of a cigar, that has only extrinsic value. The thing of intrinsic value here (if there is one) would be the episode of pleasure itself caused by hearing the symphony.

Thus the advocate of DH can readily acknowledge that the experience of smoking a cigar is utterly unlike the experience of hearing a symphony, and that these are in turn utterly unlike the experience of viewing one of Raphael's madonnas. DH does not presuppose that these experiences are in any way phenomenologically alike. Rather, the advocate of DH assumes that there is a distinct feeling of pleasure, and that each of these experiences is extrinsically valuable precisely because it causes an experience of pleasure. It is open to the advocate of DH then to insist that these experiences of pleasure are relevantly alike—they are experiences of one and the same phenomenologically given quality. Nothing in the remarks of Brentano and Rawls suggests a reason to think that these episodes of pleasure are incomparable in intensity. So the advocate of DH can reject premise (1) of the argument, under Interpretation B.

A third interpretation is still possible. This raises an even deeper question about the measurement of pleasure (and pain). Assuming that there is some distinct feeling of pleasure, perhaps Brentano and Rawls were trying to raise doubts about the very notion that episodes of this feeling come in precise amounts. Maybe the amount of pleasure in an episode of pleasure is indeterminate; maybe pairs of episodes of pleasure are simply incomparable, so that there is no number, n, such that it would be right to say that one episode contains exactly n times as much pleasure as another.

If this is the point, then the argument might be better put this way:

Cigar Argument (Interpretation C)

1. Some pairs of episodes of pleasure are incomparable in size: there is no number, n, such that one episode is exactly n times bigger than the other.
2. If (1), then DH is false.
3. Therefore, DH is false.

While I agree that there is a certain amount of arbitrariness in the system of hedons (and dolors) that I introduced in section 2.2, I think this is an inconclusive argument. Let me attempt to explain why.

I think we all agree that people have feet of different sizes. The lengths and widths of feet vary from person to person. As a result, shoe manufacturers have come up with systems for measuring shoe sizes. The systems used in different countries assign different numbers to different sizes. Every system of measuring shoe sizes is in some respect arbitrary. What's called a 10C in the United States could just as well have been called a 500XYZ. Nevertheless, there is an important respect in which the system of measurement is not at all arbitrary. We need a system of measurement that will enable us to match shoes to feet. Bigger feet need bigger shoes. Any system that does this is so far "accurate". If in addition it makes suitable discriminations— neither too fine nor too coarse—and it is easy to use and remember, it is a useful system for measuring. The arbitrariness of the system of measurement does not suggest that at some deeper level feet and shoes really do not have sizes. Of course they do.

I believe the same might very well be true of episodes of pleasure and pain. Perhaps, like feet, episodes have "size". And perhaps, like feet, those episodes are in principle measurable. I believe that a number of psychologists have attempted to construct systems of measurement for pleasure and pain.[15] Some of these systems are relevantly like the imaginary system of hedons and dolors that I introduced above. I of course acknowledge that the measurement of pleasures and pains is much more difficult than the measurement of feet and shoes. Feet are in principle available to observation by others, including shoe salesmen. You can easily place a foot on a measuring instrument. Pleasures and pains are (so far) not like that. But hedonism does not require that pleasures and pains be available for matter-of-fact measurement. It requires only that every episode of pleasure or pain have some size. Nothing said so far suggests that this is not the case.[16]

3.5. *The Argument from Nonexistent Pleasures*

The objections to hedonism based on false, worthless, and unconscious pleasures are fundamentally attacks on the notion that all pleasures

---

[15] A number of such systems are described in publications of the International Association for the Study of Pain. Their website can be found at: <www.iasp-pain.org>.

[16] I discuss these issues further in sect. B.3 of Appendix B.

are intrinsically good. In each case, the objector tries to show that there are some pleasures that are not intrinsically good. A life full of such pleasures would, contrary to DH, not be a good life.

Another sort of objection to hedonism should be mentioned. This sort of objection takes the opposite tack. The idea here is that some lives could be good ones (as evaluated on the relevant scale) even though they do not contain any pleasures. If there is such a life, then DH is false. Let us consider an example of this sort. I call it 'the life of Stoicus'. I describe this as 'The Argument from Nonexistent Pleasures' not because it claims that pleasures that do not exist might be good. Rather, the point is that a life might be good even though no pleasures exist in that life.

According to the story, Stoicus just wants peace and quiet. He wants to live an unruffled life. We must be clear about Stoicus's desires: it is not that he wants peace and quiet because he thinks that these will give him sensory pleasure. He wants peace and quiet as ends in themselves. In fact, he prefers not to experience any episodes of pleasure. He prefers not to have such pleasures in part because he fears that if he had some, they would ruffle his life. He feels the same way about sensory pain: he does not want it.

Suppose Stoicus gets exactly what he wants—peace, quiet, no episodes of sensory pleasure, and no episodes of sensory pain. Suppose that as he receives his daily dose of peace and quiet, Stoicus is content. He is satisfied with this life. Indeed, we can even suppose he enjoys the peace and quiet (provided that we don't slip into imagining that he gets pleasure as a result). Suppose he is completely satisfied with various facts about his life, including the fact that he is not experiencing any episodes of sensory pleasure. Suppose Stoicus eventually dies a happy man. He lived ninety years of somewhat boring but on the whole quite enjoyable peace and quiet. Stoicus thinks (right before he dies) that his has been an outstandingly good life.

DH implies that Stoicus did not have a good life. This follows, according to DH, from the fact that the life of Stoicus did not contain any episodes of sensory pleasure. But if Stoicus was happy with his life, and enjoyed the experiences that came his way, and got precisely what he wanted at every moment, it seems strange to say that his life was completely worthless for him. Surely it would be odd to say that whole schools of apparently rational philosophers have advocated a life-style that is guaranteed to yield worthless lives! Although the life of Stoicus is not the sort of life I would like to lead (given my tastes and preferences), I must confess that it seems a satisfactory life for someone with Stoicus's tastes. Dull perhaps, but at the same time pleasant enough (in its nonsensory way).[17]

In any case, the example of Stoicus provides the basis for another objection to DH. If the life of Stoicus was good in itself for Stoicus— even just *slightly* good—then DH is false. For DH implies that the value of the life of Stoicus must be zero.

I return to the objection based on this example involving Stoicus near the end of section 4.3. I try to show that though it might refute DH, it does not refute *hedonism*.

3.6. *Moore's Heap of Filth*

In *The Methods of Ethics*, Sidgwick patiently considers the question whether the mere, unobserved existence of beautiful objects might be good in itself. After careful consideration, he concludes that the existence of beautiful things is good only in relation to human minds, as possible objects of contemplation: '[B]eautiful things cannot be thought worth producing except as possible objects of contemplation.'[18] His point is that such objects have only extrinsic value, and would be worthless if no one took pleasure in them. The value is in the enjoying contemplation of these objects, not in their mere existence. Moore disagrees. In a memorable passage in *Principia Ethica* he presents an argument against Sidgwick's view. He asks us to consider a pair of possible worlds:

Let us imagine one world exceedingly beautiful. Imagine it as beautiful as you can; put into it whatever on this earth you most admire—mountains, rivers, the sea; trees, and sunsets, stars and moon. Imagine all these combined in the most exquisite proportions, so that no one thing jars against another, but each contributes to increase the beauty of the whole. And then imagine the ugliest world you can possibly conceive. Imagine it simply one heap of filth, containing everything that is most disgusting to us, for whatever reason, as far as may be, without one redeeming feature.... The only thing

---

[17] I think the life of Stoicus may be similar in important ways to the sort of life that the hedonist Epicurus extolled. He notoriously defended the view that 'pleasure is the absence of pain'—clearly a view not to be taken too literally. Perhaps he meant to say that the most pleasant sort of life is one not troubled by pain or sensory pleasure. In his 'Letter to Menoeceus' he says: 'When we maintain that pleasure is the end, we do not mean the pleasures of profligates and those that consist in sensuality, as is supposed by some who are either ignorant or disagree with us or do not understand, but freedom from pain in the body and from trouble in the mind.' I discuss the views of Epicurus at much greater length in Appendix C.

[18] Sidgwick, *The Methods of Ethics*, 114.

we are not entitled to imagine is that any human being ever has or ever, by any possibility, *can*, live in either, can ever see and enjoy the beauty of the one or hate the foulness of the other.[19]

Moore goes on a bit in the same vein. He says that he thinks it would be rational to hold that the beautiful world is better than the ugly one. This, he claims, shows that there are some intrinsic goods "beyond the limits of human existence". I think it is clear that Moore took this argument to refute any form of hedonism. In any case, I will interpret the argument in that way.

Let W_b be the beautiful world Moore described; let W_u be the world that consists entirely of one huge heap of filth. Let us understand the argument revised so as to apply to our default hedonism (though Moore himself formulated hedonism in another way). On the proposed interpretation, the argument goes like this: if DH were true, then W_b would be no better in itself than W_u. But W_b is better in itself than W_u. So DH is not true.

3.7. Ross's "Two Worlds" Objection

In *The Right and the Good*, W. D. Ross presents another argument against hedonism. The argument is like Moore's Heap of Filth in one respect: it essentially involves a comparison of two possible worlds that are alike with respect to pleasure and pain. But Ross's example does not involve differences in beauty and ugliness. Rather, the worlds in Ross's example differ with respect to *justice and injustice*.

Ross says:

If we compare two imaginary states of the universe, alike in the total amounts of virtue and vice and of pleasure and pain present in the two, but in one of which the virtuous were all happy and the vicious miserable, while in the other the virtuous were miserable and the vicious happy, very few people would hesitate to say that the first was a much better state of the universe than the second. It would seem then that, besides virtue and pleasure, we must recognize, as a third independent good, the apportionment of pleasure and pain to the virtuous and the vicious respectively.[20]

Ross wants us to imagine two possible worlds. The worlds are supposed to be exactly alike with respect to several important features—amounts of virtue and vice, amounts of pleasure and pain. So let us stipulate that each world contains a million virtuous people and a

---

[19] Moore, *Principia Ethica*, 84.   [20] Ross, *The Right and the Good*, 138.

million vicious people, and let us stipulate that each world contains a million people who enjoy lives filled with pleasure of various sorts, and each world also contains a million people who live lives filled with pain. Let the relevant amounts be equal. So the worlds are very similar. The central difference concerns who gets what. In W_j, the virtuous people get to live the lives filled with pleasure, and the vicious people get to live the lives filled with pain. So we can say that in W_j "good things happen to good people, and bad things happen to bad people". It is the reverse in W_k. There, "bad things happen to good people and good things happen to bad people". As Ross says, the difference concerns "apportionment".

I want to be clear about what goes on in W_j and W_k. First, something about the pleasures themselves. Imagine lives filled with pleasures that would be counted as good on any plausible form of hedonism. For example, it can be imagined that the pleasure-lovers in these worlds take deep pleasure in such things as genuinely beautiful works of art and the innocent frolicking of healthy, happy children. The objects of pleasure are the same in the two worlds.

Now, something about the people who enjoy these pleasures. The crucial difference between W_j and W_k is that these delightful pleasures are enjoyed by decent, virtuous, deserving people in W_j, but by horrible, vicious, undeserving people in W_k. Thus, to make the thought experiment more concrete, we may imagine that the pleasures in W_j are enjoyed by generous philanthropists and sweet-tempered saints. They serve as volunteers at Children's Hospital; they donate the artworks to the Children's Museum there. That is where they enjoy the beauty of the art and the frolicking of the children. These aesthetically sensitive volunteers in W_j fully deserve to be enjoying their pleasures. On the other hand, the pleasures in W_k are enjoyed by thieves who have stolen the art from those to whom it rightly belongs, and they are also kidnappers who have kidnapped the frolicking children. So while the *objects* deserve to be enjoyed, *these thieves and kidnappers* do not deserve to be enjoying them.

A corresponding thing happens with respect to pains. In W_j the pains are suffered by horrible, vicious criminals who have been found guilty (and who *are* guilty) of terrible crimes. In W_k the pains are suffered by innocent, sweet-tempered children who do not deserve any suffering at all.

The crucial thing to note about these worlds is that they are exactly alike with respect to total amounts of pleasure and pain. We can adapt Ross's point to present purposes by reinterpreting it in this way. The objection then is this: DH implies that these worlds are equally valuable in themselves. Yet the just world, W_j, is much better in itself than the equally pleasant but unjust world, W_k. Therefore, DH is false.

If we wanted to follow our pattern for constructing names of arguments, we could call this 'The Argument from Undeserved Pleasures'. Part of the point of the argument seems to be this: hedonism implies that a deserved pleasure is just as valuable as an undeserved one; that a life full of deserved pleasures is just as good as a life full of similar but undeserved pleasures. And, furthermore, that a deserved pain is just as bad as an undeserved one; that a life full of deserved pain is just as bad as a life full of undeserved pain. All of these implications seem hard to swallow. And so Ross is inclined to reject hedonism.

I present my evaluations of these arguments from Moore and Ross in Chapter 9.

Although there are other important and interesting objections to hedonism, this collection should be sufficient for now. I want to begin, in the next chapter, to formulate some kinds of hedonism that seem to me to evade these objections. Later (mainly in Chapters 6 and 9) I will consider more objections, and yet other forms of hedonism.

CHAPTER 4

―――

Attitudinal Hedonism

I am going to defend a form of hedonism. Thus, I am going to say that *pleasure* is the feature that makes a person's life better in itself for him, and that *pain* is the feature that makes it worse. But I am not going to defend Default Hedonism, and I am certainly not going to defend Aristippean Hedonism. Instead, I am going to defend a version of the theory according to which it is *attitudinal* pleasure, not *sensory* pleasure, that serves to make a life better. Before I state the theory, I need to say a few things about attitudinal pleasure and pain.[1]

4.1. *Attitudinal Pleasure*

Although I did not make much a fuss over this point when I introduced DH, that theory (like Aristippean Hedonism) is a form of *sensory* hedonism. It takes the fundamental bearers of positive intrinsic value to be episodes in which a person feels a pleasurable sensation. 'Pleasure' in this context is assumed to indicate some sort of feeling, or sensation. But Attitudinal Hedonism understands pleasure to be something different—an attitude.

The distinction between sensory pleasure and attitudinal pleasure is ancient, though often overlooked or misunderstood. I suspect that Epicurus might have been sensitive to it.[2] A person experiences *sensory pleasure* at a time if he feels pleasurable sensations then. If you like the tastes of champagne and caviar, you might experience sensory pleasure as you sip a cool glass of your favorite and nibble on caviar. I more often

---

[1] In fact, I will say the things about pleasure, and I will not mention pain. My assumption throughout is that corresponding things are true of pain.

[2] In the passage where he says, that 'when we maintain that pleasure is the end, we do not mean the pleasures of profligates and those that consist in sensuality, as is supposed by some who are either ignorant or disagree with us or do not understand'.

get my sensory pleasures from cold beer and salty peanuts. The point here, however, is that sensory pleasures are *'feelings'*— things relevantly like feelings of heat and cold; feelings of pressure, tickles, and itches; the feeling you get in your back when getting a massage.

Attitudinal pleasures are different. A person takes attitudinal pleasure in some state of affairs if he enjoys it, is pleased about it, is glad that it is happening, is delighted by it. So, for example, suppose that you are a peace-loving person. Suppose you take note of the fact that there are no wars going on. The world is at peace. Suppose you are pleased about this. You are glad that the world is at peace. Then you have taken attitudinal pleasure in a certain fact—the fact that the world is at peace. Attitudinal pleasures are always directed onto objects, just as beliefs and hopes and fears are directed onto objects. This is one respect in which they are different from sensory pleasures. Another difference is that attitudinal pleasures need not have any "feel". We know we have them not by sensation, but in the same way (whatever it may be) that we know when we believe something, or hope for it, or fear that it might happen.[3]

Sensory pleasures are often intertwined with attitudinal pleasures, so that when people are pleased about something, they often also simultaneously feel sensory pleasure. As you sip your champagne, you get some pleasurable tastes (sensory pleasures), and you may also take pleasure in the fact that you are drinking the champagne (an attitudinal pleasure). Regardless of the frequency of this intertwining, the phenomena are distinct and can come apart. Here is an example that shows that you can have attitudinal pleasure without sensory pleasure. Suppose you are in intense sensory pain and feeling no sensory pleasure at all. Suppose you notice that the pain is becoming less intense. You might be pleased that the pain is becoming less intense. I would describe your situation by saying that you take attitudinal pleasure in the fact that your sensory pain is becoming less intense. In this situation you might still feel no sensory pleasure at all, even though you are taking attitudinal pleasure in a certain fact. All you strictly "feel" is diminished pain. This shows that attitudinal pleasure is distinct from sensory pleasure. You can take pleasure in something at a time when you don't *feel* any pleasure.

The case of the injured motorcyclist demonstrates the same point. Suppose a motorcyclist has been severely injured in a crash. The doctors

---

[3] For an interesting, insightful discussion of the distinction between sensory and attitudinal pleasure, see Irving Thalberg's 'False Pleasures'.

have given him a powerful anaesthetic that makes it impossible for him to feel the pain. The anaesthetic also makes it impossible for him to feel any sensory pleasures. He is numb all over. He still might take attitudinal pleasure in the fact that he was not killed, or in the fact that his motorcycle was not damaged in the accident. This shows again that you can experience attitudinal pleasure while not experiencing any sensory pleasure. They are distinct phenomena.

The examples I have described suggest that it is possible to take attitudinal pleasure in some fact at a time when you do not feel any sensory pleasure. The phenomena are thus distinct, though I do not think they are entirely separable. As I see it, it is not possible for someone to experience sensory pleasure at a time without also then experiencing attitudinal pleasure. That is because I think we can define sensory pleasures as feelings in which the feeler takes intrinsic attitudinal pleasure. In other words, what makes a feeling be a sensory pleasure, in my view, is the fact that the person who feels it takes intrinsic attitudinal pleasure in the fact that he himself is then feeling it.[4]

The forms of hedonism I mean to defend involve the claim that attitudinal pleasure is the chief good for man. I am like Epicurus. I do not want to defend a form of hedonism that extols the wonders of sensory pleasures—'the pleasures of the profligate or the pleasures of consumption, as some believe, either from ignorance and disagreement or from deliberate misinterpretation'.[5] I have no interest in defending the idea that sensory pleasure is the chief good for man.[6]

When a person takes attitudinal pleasure in some state of affairs, he may take this pleasure in the state of affairs because he thinks it is related to some other state of affairs, and he takes pleasure in that other state of affairs. The most familiar instance of this sort of thing is

---

[4] For further discussion, see Appendix B, in which I discuss the distinction between attitudinal and sensory pleasure. I give a more detailed account of this view, according to which sensory pleasures are precisely those sensations in which we take intrinsic attitudinal pleasure. In addition, I discuss a number of other respects in which careful recognition of the distinction can be useful.

[5] Epicurus, 'Letter to Menoeceus', 30–1.

[6] But to be fair, I should point out a consequence of the view that whenever a person feels sensory pleasure, she is taking intrinsic attitudinal pleasure in the way she feels. This view implies, on many forms of attitudinal hedonism, that whenever someone feels sensory pleasure, something of intrinsic value is going on. It is important to keep in mind, though, that one might take small pleasure in the fact that one is feeling big sensations. There is no guaranteed equivalence between magnitude of pleasurable sensation and magnitude of attitudinal pleasure taken in sensation. Furthermore, some forms of attitudinal hedonism may discount the value of an attitudinal pleasure taken in some sensory feeling if that feeling is sufficiently disgraceful. A number of variants of this approach are discussed in this chapter and the next.

the instrumental case. I take pleasure in the fact that the waiter is heading for our table. Why? Because I think he is bringing beer and peanuts, and I take pleasure in the fact that I soon will be enjoying them. Another sort of case is "compositional". I take pleasure in the fact that I am tasting beer and peanuts. Why? It might be because I take pleasure in the fact that I am tasting beer and I take pleasure in the fact that I am tasting peanuts.[7] In cases like this, the person takes attitudinal pleasure in one state of affairs in virtue of the fact that he takes pleasure in others. In such cases, I say that the person is taking 'extrinsic attitudinal pleasure'.

But in some cases a person takes attitudinal pleasure in some state of affairs, p, and there is no other state of affairs, q, such that he takes pleasure in p in virtue of the fact that he takes pleasure in q. In such cases, I say that the person takes *intrinsic attitudinal pleasure* in p. The ultimate object of his enjoyment is p itself.[8]

I should make a few further points about intrinsic attitudinal pleasure[9] before proceeding.

a. *The awareness of pleasure.* A person can be pleased about something without being fully aware of the fact that he is pleased about it. For example, if you are completely wrapped up in a woodworking project, you may get into "the zone". You may focus so intently on the project at hand that you forget about everything apart from the wood and the tools. You may take no note of the passage of time. You may not be thinking about yourself, or your current state of mind. Yet, if later someone were to ask you, it might be immediately apparent to you that you enjoyed working on that project. Thus, you might take intrinsic attitudinal pleasure during a certain time in the fact that you are, for example, cutting these tenons, even though you are not then fully conscious of the fact that you are taking pleasure in the cutting of the tenons.

I am almost inclined to say that at least this much must be true: if you are taking pleasure in something, then if someone were to ask you, you would immediately recognize that you are taking pleasure in it. But, of course, the subjunctive conditional is too crude. You

---

[7] It might be, however, that I take pleasure in the interesting combination of tastes. In that case, I take pleasure in the combination but *not* in virtue of the fact that I take pleasure in each of the tastes.

[8] Of course there will be mixed cases in which someone takes both intrinsic and extrinsic pleasure in some state of affairs. In such cases I would be interested in the intrinsic component of his attitudinal pleasure.

[9] All of these remarks are intended to apply to *intrinsic attitudinal pleasure*. For each claim I make, it should be understood that I would make a corresponding claim about *intrinsic attitudinal pain*.

might be taking pleasure in something, but if someone were to ask, you would be so annoyed by the intrusion that you would lose your temper, put down your chisel and mallet, and storm out of the room. You might never recall that you had been enjoying yourself.

In this respect, pleasure is like belief. After the fact, if someone were to ask you if you earlier believed a certain tool to be a chisel, you might say that you had done so. You could say this truly, even if you had not consciously thought, 'this is a chisel', while you were working on the tenons.

b. *Pleasure and belief.* This point about pleasure and belief naturally leads to another. If you take pleasure in a certain state of affairs, you must believe it to be true. Thus, if I am pleased to be cutting these tenons, then I must think I am cutting these tenons. I might be pleased about it without its being at the forefront of my consciousness. But then I will believe it in approximately the same way. My belief that I am cutting tenons will not be at the forefront of my consciousness.

It might appear that there could be cases in which a person takes pleasure in some state of affairs without believing it to be true. For example, a person certainly could take pleasure at the things he observes in a movie, or in a novel, or in a play, without believing that those things are actually taking place.

I think that this sort of case (pleasures in fiction) does not cast doubt on the claim that attitudinal pleasure implies belief. We can see this if we reflect more carefully on the objects of our pleasure in fiction. Suppose you are enjoying yourself at the movies. You especially enjoy a scene in which Forrest Gump meets President Kennedy. Does my thesis about belief imply, in this case, that you believe that Forrest Gump actually did meet President Kennedy? The answer, of course, is 'No'. That is because (in anything like the ordinary case) you would not be prepared to say, 'I am pleased that Forrest Gump met President Kennedy' unless you thought he did. Rather, if you are just enjoying a movie while suspending disbelief, you would more likely say something like this: 'I am delighted by the way in which they make it seem that Forrest Gump could have met President Kennedy,' or 'I am amused and pleased to have this chance to see what it might have been like if Forrest Gump had met President Kennedy.' Thus, there are plenty of things that you do believe that can serve as the objects of your pleasure. You need not be taking pleasure in anything you fail to believe.[10]

---

[10] Michael DePaul raised the objection at the Chisholm Memorial Conference at Brown University in 2000. His commentary appears as 'A Half Dozen Puzzles Regarding Intrinsic Attitudinal Hedonism'.

c. *The transparency of pleasure*. Must a person correctly identify the object of his pleasure? Could a person be taking pleasure in some state of affairs, recognize that he is taking pleasure in something, but be confused or mistaken about the state of affairs in which he is taking pleasure? My answer is a tentative 'Yes'. I think that a person could be taking pleasure in a certain state of affairs, realize that he is taking pleasure in something, and still misidentify the object of his pleasure. For example, you might think you are taking pleasure in the taste of the wine, when in fact you are taking pleasure in the fact that you are being seen drinking wine from a bottle with a prestigious label. Perhaps it would take some real soul-searching (maybe with your shrink) before you could recognize the object of your pleasure.[11]

d. *Pleasure and truth*. Can we enjoy, or take pleasure in, a state of affairs that does not occur? Our ordinary ways of talking about enjoyment might suggest that this is impossible, but further reflection suggests that things are more complicated. Chisholm has provided a good example.[12] Suppose a candidate for office mistakenly thinks he won the election. Chisholm suggests that this candidate could be pleased about winning the election even though in fact he did not win it. Here is another case that might seem even more convincing. Suppose I mistakenly think that I will be meeting G. E. Moore soon. Suppose I am delighted about this. Clearly, I am pleased about *something*. It seems wrong to say that what I am pleased about is the fact that *I think I will meet Moore*. It seems better to say that I am pleased that *I am going to meet him* (even though I am not going to meet him). In what follows I will not assume that attitudinal pleasure is always directed toward truths. Perhaps the most we can say is that if you take pleasure in some state of affairs, then you must at least think that it is true.

e. *The plurality of pleasures*. I see no reason to doubt that a person could take intrinsic attitudinal pleasure in several different states of affairs at once. For example, a person might be pleased to be at a certain place, pleased to be thinking about hedonism, pleased to be talking with such charming and witty conversationalists, and pleased that he had such a good lunch. So a person can enjoy multiple, temporally overlapping pleasures.

---

[11] It should be obvious that a person could easily be mistaken about the *cause* of his pleasure. I might think that I am pleased because you are so witty and charming. In fact, I might be pleased because you put something funny in my drink.

[12] Chisholm, *Brentano and Intrinsic Value*, 28–9.

This point can be extended. A person could simultaneously be pleased about several things and pained about several other things. Right now, for example, while I am indeed pleased about a number of things like the ones I mentioned in the previous paragraph, I am also pained about the recent atrocity at the World Trade Center. I am also pained about the possibility that there will be a catastrophic war.

f. *The temporal orientation of pleasure.* There is a certain attractiveness to the idea that the objects of attitudinal pleasure must be simultaneous with the pleasure, while the objects of desire must be future relative to the desire. This temporal distinction between attitudinal pleasure and desire might help to sharpen the distinction between these phenomena, and thereby help to bring attitudinal pleasure into clearer focus.

Wayne Sumner seemed to be expressing a thought like this when he said,

Desires form one species of pro-attitude, identified by their intentionality and future-directedness. These features distinguish them from another species that includes such attitudes as enjoying something, finding it pleasant or agreeable... and so on. In contrast with desires, these attitudes can be directed only on contemporaneous states: I can enjoy only what I already have (or what is already happening).[13]

Sumner here seems to endorse two doctrines about desire and pleasure. If we allow ourselves some unexplained technical terminology, we can state them as follows:

DF: If at t, S desires that p be the case, then p is future relative to t.
PP: If at t, S takes pleasure in p, then p is present relative to t.

It seems to me, however, that attitudinal pleasure does not have the feature alleged by PP. A person can take pleasure in facts about the past, present, or future. Surely no one would be perplexed if a traveler, upon her return from an enjoyable journey, were to say, 'I am (now) very pleased that I had the chance to see the Parthenon'. That would seem to be pleasure in a past object. Nor would we be perplexed if the traveler, as she stands before the Parthenon, were to say, 'I am now very pleased to be seeing the Parthenon'. That apparently would be pleasure in a present object (the only temporal orientation Sumner seems to recognize). But it seems clear to me that that no one would be surprised if she were to say, prior to her journey, but at a time when

---

[13] Sumner, 'Something in Between', 13. See also Sumner, *Welfare, Happiness, and Ethics*, 128–30.

the itinerary was fixed, 'I am (now) very pleased that I will have a chance to see the Parthenon'. This seems to show that pleasure can be taken in seeing the Parthenon not only while seeing it and after seeing it, but before seeing it.[14]

I'm inclined also to reject DF. This doctrine implies that one cannot desire a state of affairs unless it is "future" relative to the time of the desire. This seems implausible. It often happens (at least to me) that after I have made a decision, I have a desire that my (already made) decision was the correct one. There's nothing even slightly odd about saying, 'I hope I made the right choice yesterday'. I could just as easily say that I now desire that my choice of yesterday was right. Perhaps it will be thought that what I really desire in such a case is that the *future effects* of yesterday's choice turn out to be acceptable. If so, consider the case of a person reflecting on the final days of a loved one. He might say, 'I now want it to be the case that she was free of pain during those last days before she died.' The object of desire here seems firmly embedded in the past. The desirer might know full well that her status during those final days will have no further effects. They are over and done with. Still, he desires that they had certain features.[15]

There are even deeper problems with Sumner's proposal. In some cases it is doubtful that the object of a desire has the relevant sort of temporal location. It is not merely that the object fails to be "future". Rather, the point is that it seems to make little sense to say that it is either future, or present, or past. Consider a case in which a person is concerned about a certain airplane. It was scheduled to land in San Diego at about this time. It might have landed early; it might be landing just now; it might land in a few minutes. Suppose the person wants it to be the case that either the plane did land safely, or that it is landing safely, or that it soon does land safely. He does not care which of these is the case. Sumner says that desires are 'future-directed'. But in this case it seems that the object

---

[14] It is interesting to note that although Sumner sets out to defend the idea that *pleasure* must be directed toward present objects, he uses a different term in his comment. He says, 'I can *enjoy* only what I already have.' The claim about present-directedness is much more plausible if restricted to enjoyment. There is nothing funny about saying that the traveler right now takes pleasure in, or is pleased about, having seen the Parthenon. But it would be a bit odd to say that she is right now *enjoying* the fact that she saw the Parthenon last week.

[15] Chris Heathwood pointed out that one could simply *define* desire in such a way that its object would have to be in the future. With the term defined in such a way, we would have to find a new term to express past-directed "desires". Perhaps we would use the word 'hope' in those cases. Or 'desire(past)'. Such maneuvers are possible, but pointless. The attitude seems the same whether the object is past or future. The introduction of a new term would violate Occam's razor.

of desire is a three-part disjunction, with disjuncts about past, present, and future. I see no principled way to decide upon any temporal orientation for a state of affairs like that, though it seems pretty clear that someone could want it to be true.[16]

Thus, though I am confident that there are important differences between pleasure and desire, I do not think we can distinguish them by appeal to their temporal features in the manner suggested by DF and PP.

4.2. *Measuring Attitudinal Pleasures and Pains*

Earlier I introduced the concepts of the hedon and the dolor as imaginary units of measurement for episodes of sensory pleasure and pain. I suggested that the number of hedons in an episode of sensory pleasure might be taken to be determined by the intensity of the feeling of pleasure in the episode (perhaps averaged over time) and the duration of the episode. It should be clear that the concepts of the hedon and the dolor will not simply carry over from our discussion of sensory pleasure and pain to our discussion of attitudinal pleasure and pain. That is because these latter things are *attitudes*, not *feelings*. As a result, we need to introduce some new system of measurement.

I think it makes sense to speak about "amounts" of attitudinal pleasure. Suppose some of my students have been working hard and have produced good term papers. I might be pleased about the quality of Keith's term paper, and I might also be pleased about the quality of Kate's term paper. I might be slightly more pleased about Keith's work, since it marks such a striking improvement over his earlier efforts. In such a case, it seems reasonable to say that there are some amounts, m and n, such that m is greater than n, and I take m units of intrinsic attitudinal pleasure in *Keith's paper being so good* and I take n units of intrinsic attitudinal pleasure in *Kate's paper being so good*. If in fact I am twice as pleased about Keith's work, then I would want m to be equal to $2n$. If I am *very pleased* about Keith's work, then I would want m to be a fairly large number.

At the outset, let us assume that the amount of attitudinal pleasure that someone takes in some state of affairs is determined by two

---

[16] This point applies just as well to pleasure. Suppose on Monday you receive a telegram from a loved one who is sight-seeing in Greece. She says, 'Parthenon on Monday.' You are pleased about this. You think it's wonderful that she did see, or is seeing, or soon will see, the Parthenon. I see no way to identify the temporal orientation of the object of your pleasure. Are you pleased about something *present*, or something *future*, or something *past*?

main factors—intensity and duration. Later we will consider several ways of introducing other factors and so measuring amounts in other ways.

The intensity of the pleasure in an episode of attitudinal pleasure is a matter of "strength". This is *not* to be confused with the strength, or "vividness", of any feeling or sensation. It is purely a matter of strength of attitude. The notion of strength of attitude is not novel. Surely there is nothing surprising about talk of strength of such attitudes as belief, or fear, or hope. Thus, there should be no serious obstacle to the introduction of talk about the strength of someone's attitudinal pleasure. Such talk means nothing more than this: sometimes we are pleased *to some degree* about something. Sometimes we are more pleased about one thing than we are about another.

The fact that intensity of attitudinal pleasure is distinct from the intensity of any sensation can be brought out by appeal to an example. Suppose again that I have been out shoveling snow on a cold day. I have come in to warm up. I'm taking a hot shower. Suppose I am fiddling with the temperature controls, trying to get the water to be just hot enough. The temperature gradually rises. My pleasurable sensation of heat gradually increases in intensity. As I feel more heat, I enjoy it more. For a while, I am increasingly pleased to be feeling increasing amounts of heat. But then I overdo it. The water is starting to get too hot. Now, as the intensity of my pleasurable sensation of heat increases still further, I begin to be less pleased to be feeling the heat. If I don't do something about it soon, the increase in the intensity of the feeling will become so great that I will stop enjoying it altogether. This should make clear that the intensity of the attitude of pleasure that I take in the feeling of heat is distinct from the intensity of the feeling of heat itself. The latter is the object of the former. When the latter (the feeling) goes too high, the former (the attitude) may start to decline.[17]

A thought experiment may be useful. Suppose a neuroscientist has been working for many years trying to discover a drug that would temporarily make it impossible for a person to experience sensory pleasures and pains. At last he has a promising formula. He decides to try it on himself. It seems to work. Smells, tastes, bodily feelings, all become hedono-dolorically flat. He cannot feel sensory pleasure or pain. He is at first thrilled. This suggests that his research has finally

---

[17] This case raises a number of interesting questions. I discuss it again in Appendix B.

been successful. *He takes great attitudinal pleasure in the fact that he is feeling neither sensory pleasure nor sensory pain.* Some time passes. The effect of the drug seems not to be wearing off. He begins to worry. Maybe this drug has caused a permanent change to his nervous system. That would be terrible. Now his attitude toward his own mental state begins to change. *He takes much less attitudinal pleasure in the fact that he is feeling neither sensory pleasure nor sensory pain.* If this goes on much longer, he will start taking pain in the fact that he has destroyed an important part of his own nervous system.

The example suggests, first, that attitudinal pleasure is distinct from sensory pleasure. It suggests in addition that intensity of attitudinal pleasure can vary without any concomitant variation in intensity of sensory pleasure. It suggests finally that one can have attitudinal pleasure (or pain) at a time when one does not have any sensory pleasure (or pain) at all.

Episodes of attitudinal pleasure have *durations*, too. It seems to make sense to say that person was pleased about something throughout some period of time. It also makes sense to say that after a certain date he was no longer pleased about it. In the movie *Fatal Attraction* the Michael Douglas character at first takes great pleasure in the fact that he is having an affair with the Glenn Close character. As time goes by, he begins to take much less pleasure in that fact. By the end of the movie it gives him nothing but pain.

I grant of course that it would be very difficult in practice to locate precise dates for the beginning and end of an episode of attitudinal pleasure. Perhaps the person himself would be unable to pinpoint the exact moment when he stopped being pleased by some fact. Perhaps it just gradually fades away. But the practical difficulty does not entail that there is no fact of the matter. Just as in the case of sensory pleasures, attitudinal pleasures may begin, rise to crescendos, and then fade away. I assume that this in fact happens.

Let us say that the amount of attitudinal pleasure in an episode is determined (as before) by the intensity and duration of that pleasure. So if a person starts taking pleasure in some fact at some time, and continues taking pleasure in it for a while, and then ceases taking pleasure in it, there is a certain episode of attitudinal pleasure. That episode has the person as its subject; it has the state of affairs as its object; its duration is the amount of time that it lasts; and its intensity is the average strength of the pleasure that the person takes in the state of affairs during the episode. I will use the term 'amount of attitudinal pleasure' to indicate the product of average intensity and duration.

I assume that a similar procedure would yield an amount of attitudinal pain in each episode of attitudinal pain.[18]

4.3. *Formulating Attitudinal Hedonism*

My formulation of Intrinsic Attitudinal Hedonism (IAH) is intended to follow the pattern already introduced in connection with DH and AH. The difference is that on this view the fundamental bearers of intrinsic value are episodes in which someone takes intrinsic *attitudinal* pleasure or pain in something, rather than episodes in which someone feels *sensory* pleasure or pain. Here it is.

Intrinsic Attitudinal Hedonism

i. Every episode of intrinsic attitudinal pleasure is intrinsically good; every episode of intrinsic attitudinal pain is intrinsically bad.

ii. The intrinsic value of an episode of intrinsic attitudinal pleasure is equal to the amount of pleasure contained in that episode; the intrinsic value of an episode of intrinsic attitudinal pain is equal to −*(the amount of pain contained in that episode).*

iii. The intrinsic value of a life is entirely determined by the intrinsic values of the episodes of intrinsic attitudinal pleasure and pain contained in the life, in such a way that one life is intrinsically better than another if and only if the net amount of intrinsic attitudinal pleasure in the one is greater than the net amount of that sort of pleasure in the other.

When formulated in this way, attitudinal hedonism is a form of *universal* attitudinal hedonism. That is, it is a theory according to which every episode of intrinsic attitudinal pleasure is good in itself. As in DH and AH, there are no worthless pleasures, or defeated pleasures, or transvaluated pleasures. Every attitudinal pleasure is alleged to be intrinsically good. (Similarly, every attitudinal pain is alleged to be intrinsically bad on this theory.) Of course, when I say that IAH implies that every pleasure is intrinsically good, I mean to be talking about *attitudinal* pleasures, not *sensory* pleasures.

IAH is also a form of *pure* attitudinal hedonism, since it implies that attitudinal pleasures and pains are the only things that contribute in the most fundamental way to the value of a life. This can be seen if we consider a case in which a person never takes any intrinsic attitudinal pleasure in anything. Then, no matter what else happens in his

---

[18] Later, in sect. 8.4, I will refine the concept of an episode of intrinsic attitudinal pleasure. In effect, it will be replaced by the concept of a basic intrinsic value state. For the time being, however, the simpler notion should be adequate.

life, the value of his life for him according to IAH cannot rise above zero. No matter how much knowledge, virtue, honor, wealth, health, longevity, loving relationships, etc. he may have, if he takes pleasure in nothing, there is no basis for attributing positive intrinsic value to his life according to IAH. Corresponding claims may be made about pains and evil. We can summarize this point by saying that, if IAH is true, a life without attitudinal pleasure or pain is a life without value.

I think we can say that IAH (like DH and AH) is a form of "mental statism". The value of a life depends, according to this theory, on facts about the mental states of the person who lives that life. This follows naturally from the plausible assumption that episodes of intrinsic attitudinal pleasure and pain are mental states.

An implication of this is that if two lives are alike with respect to mental states, then they are alike with respect to the relevant sort of value. In other words, if two people are indiscernible with respect to mental states, then the value in itself for him of the first person's life is equal to the value in itself for her of the second person's life. The principle does not have to be so broad. We can narrow it: if two people are indiscernible with respect to intrinsic attitudinal pleasures and pains, then their lives are of equal intrinsic value for them. It may appear that this feature of the theory makes it vulnerable to criticism. The Argument from False Pleasures seems to be an instance of this sort of objection. I discuss this issue further in Chapter 5.

IAH and DH generate similar results in a wide range of cases. The most striking overlap occurs in cases in which attitudinal pleasures and pains coincide with sensory pleasures and pains. Suppose there is a person who always takes intrinsic attitudinal pleasure in his sensory pleasures. Suppose also that the amount of attitudinal pleasure he takes in his sensory pleasure is always proportional to the number of hedons in the pleasure: if he feels ten hedons of sensory pleasure, he takes ten units of intrinsic attitudinal pleasure in that fact. Suppose also that he is similarly attitudinally pained by his sensory pains, and that he never takes any intrinsic attitudinal pleasure or pain in any other sort of fact.[19] In this case, the evaluation of his life according to IAH is exactly the same as the evaluation of his life according to DH.

One theory—IAH—would explain the evaluation of his life by appeal to facts about his hedonic and doloric *attitudes*; the other—DH—would

---

[19] I have committed myself to a conception of sensory pleasure and pain that makes these remarks redundant. On my view, a sensory pleasure is defined as a sensation in which the sensor takes intrinsic attitudinal pleasure. I introduce these remarks here primarily because I suspect that some readers may not want to endorse my view about sensory pleasure and pain.

explain it by appeal to facts about his hedonic and doloric *sensations*. But since in this unusual case the attitudes march in lockstep with the sensations, the outcomes would be the same. I doubt that this sort of coincidence happens often in real life. Most of us are pleased about things other than our sensory pleasures. If a person were intrinsically pleased about more things than just his pleasurable sensations, IAH would give his life a higher rating than DH would give it.

IAH and DH give dramatically different evaluations in cases in which there is a significant discrepancy between attitudinal pleasures and sensory ones. If a person took a considerable amount of intrinsic attitudinal pleasure in things other than his sensory pleasures (and there were no counterbalancing pains), IAH might judge that he had a very good life, while DH might assign it a much lower value.

This might be the ideal moment for us to reconsider one of the classic anti-hedonistic arguments discussed in Chapter 3—the objection based on the possibility of a good life without pleasure. Recall the objection based on the life of Stoicus. He was a man of simple tastes. He wanted peace and quiet. He wanted the opportunity to engage in tranquil meditation. He thought that sensory pleasures (and pains) would disrupt the tranquillity of the life he desired. I stipulated that Stoicus got what he wanted. He lived a long and happy life devoid of sensory pleasure and pain. On his deathbed he declared that his life had been a good one. But DH implies that Stoicus had a life that was worthless in itself for him. That is because the life did not contain any episodes of sensory pleasure or pain. The evaluation seems to me to be wrong.

IAH evaluates the life of Stoicus differently. According to IAH, Stoicus had quite a good life. The evaluation of the life is predicated on the fact that there were many occasions on which Stoicus took intrinsic attitudinal pleasure in various facts—that he was living in peace, that it was quiet, that he was suffering no bodily pains, that he was "suffering" no bodily pleasures, that he was engaging in meditation. If we assume that these episodes of intrinsic attitudinal pleasure were long-lasting and fairly strong, and if we assume that Stoicus did not suffer any major pains, IAH yields the result that his life was very good in itself for him.

The reader might be dubious about this evaluation. Perhaps he will think to himself, 'It is not clear to me that Stoicus had such a good life. I am sure I would not want to swap lives with Stoicus. His life seems to me to be a boring and unsatisfactory life. So if IAH implies that it is a good life, then so much the worse for IAH.'

This reaction is based on a misunderstanding of IAH. IAH rates the life of Stoicus as a good one. Its evaluation is based squarely on the stipulated fact that Stoicus enjoyed lots of things that happened to him. IAH does not imply that if things just like those things happened to another person, then that other person would have a life as good as the life of Stoicus *whether he enjoyed those things or not.* On the contrary, IAH implies that if the other person did not enjoy those things, then his life would be worthless. That's because the source of value, according to IAH, is located precisely in the enjoyment of the things, not the things enjoyed. Where the enjoyment is missing, there is no value.

Therefore, in order to make the imaginative swap relevant to the issue, the reader must try to imagine having the life of Stoicus *complete with all the tastes and preferences of Stoicus; complete with all the stipulated enjoyments of Stoicus.* When the experiment is performed properly, the reader is required to agree that if he were to live the life of Stoicus, he would enjoy the peace and quiet, he would enjoy the meditation, he would be pleased to be feeling no sensory pleasure—just as Stoicus was. If he were living the life of Stoicus, he would not be bored by all this tranquillity. In this case, I think the appropriate conclusion for the reader to draw is this: 'If I were to live the life of Stoicus, I would enjoy the things that he is stipulated to enjoy. As a result, I would be happy and content. I guess that it would be a pretty good life—though very different from the sort of life I am enjoying here in the actual world.'

Cases relevantly like the case of Stoicus are sometimes brought up in order to provide support for preferentism. Indeed, I have described the case in such a way as to make it seem that what makes the life of Stoicus good for him is that he gets what he wants. It is important to see that the satisfaction of desire is irrelevant to the case. According to IAH, what makes the life of Stoicus good is that he enjoys what he gets, not that he gets what he wants.

Let us take a moment to reflect on desire (which is not relevant to IAH) and enjoyment (which is). Enjoyment and desire are alike in several respects. For one thing, each of them is a psychological attitude. For another, each of them happens at a time. For yet another, each comes in various intensities, and these can be represented with numbers. Finally, we can somewhat clumsily represent every desire as the desire for a state of affairs. As a result, every desire can be expressed in canonical form in something like this way: 'At 8.00 p.m., Stoicus desires that he be permitted to live in peace.'

In many typical cases people desire things they will later enjoy if they get them. If their desires are satisfied, they will enjoy getting what they formerly desired to get. Perhaps as a result of this sort of connection, it is tempting to conflate these things. But let's not do that.

Simply as a matter of empirical psychology, desire is distinct from enjoyment. A person may enjoy something he never desired, and a person may desire a thing he never enjoys. Think of a person who never had champagne—indeed has no concept of champagne. All he wants is beer. Yet if we switch drinks on him, and give him an unexpected glass of champagne, he might enjoy it. Even as he drinks, it might be wrong to say that he desires to be drinking champagne, or to be drinking "this stuff". He might be savoring the taste, and enjoying the drink so much, that he doesn't even think about the further question whether he wants to be drinking this tasty drink.

Equally, a person might have lost the capacity to enjoy certain things. Perhaps someone has taken a drug that makes it impossible for her to enjoy beer. When she drinks beer, it tastes like a urine sample. But the old desires may linger. She may still want a beer. When she gets it, she does not enjoy it. Enjoyment is distinct from desire. Attitudinal hedonism is different from preferentism.

I claimed that the favorable evaluation of the life of Stoicus does not depend upon the fact that he got what he wanted. This may seem strange. Could a person take pleasure in many things throughout his life *even though his desires are not being satisfied*? I think this is possible. Let us try to imagine a case that illustrates the point. We can imagine someone in many ways like Stoicus. Perhaps he is a "brother" in the same ancient school. As a result of some long period of rigorous mental training, the brother has managed to extinguish all his desires. He is now content to accept whatever life may provide. Imagine that what he in fact gets is precisely what Stoicus gets—peace and quiet, no sensory pleasure or pain, and a chance to meditate in tranquil surroundings. Suppose that this brother is steadily delighted to receive these things. 'Ah,' he says, 'How nice. More tranquillity. Although I did not desire it, and would not have been disappointed if it had not turned up, I am pleased to have it. I shall savor it while it lasts, but will not be frustrated if it ends.'

Imagine that this Stoic brother gets the same amounts of peace and quiet that Stoicus got. Imagine that he enjoys these things just as much as Stoicus did. Then IAH implies that his life is just as good in itself for him as the life of Stoicus was for Stoicus, *even though this brother did not get what he wanted*. We cannot appeal to the satisfaction of desires to explain the favorable evaluation of the brother's life since we have stipulated that he has extinguished his desires. His life is good for him because it is filled with enjoyment, not because it is filled with satisfaction of desires.

4.4. *The Objects of Enjoyment; Mill's Hedonism*

Attitudinal pleasures, unlike sensory pleasures, have objects. Attitudinal pleasure is always pleasure taken in some state of affairs. This feature of attitudinal pleasures makes it possible for IAH to take many forms, depending upon restrictions that we may place on the sorts of objects in which attitudinal pleasure is taken. I would like to discuss one relatively simple sort of restriction here. Further variations will be presented and explored in Chapter 7, and in Appendix D and elsewhere.

In a famous passage Mill says:

It is quite compatible with the principle of utility to recognize the fact, that some kinds of pleasure are more desirable and more valuable than others. It would be absurd that while, in estimating all other things, quality is considered as well as quantity, the estimation of pleasures should be supposed to depend on quantity alone.[20]

In the following paragraphs, Mill alludes to a distinction between "higher" and "lower" pleasures. The higher pleasures are evidently ones that involve our "higher faculties"—presumably these are the pleasures of the intellect. Such things as the pleasures you get from reading great literature, enjoying excellent music, or studying philosophy. The lower pleasures are evidently ones that involve our "lower" faculties—presumably these are the pleasures of the body. He calls these 'sensual indulgences', 'bodily pleasures'.[21] It is pretty clear that these are the pleasures associated with such bodily functions as eating, drinking, getting a massage, and doing what you need to do in order to reproduce.

Mill's point in the passage is clear. He wants to say that higher pleasures are more valuable than lower pleasures even in cases in which the pleasures are equal in intensity and duration. This will enable him to say that, according to his own form of hedonism, the life of unbridled sensual pleasure is not nearly as good as a life filled with intellectual, aesthetic, and moral pleasures, even if those pleasures are not very intense.

---

[20] Mill, *Utilitarianism*, 12.   [21] Ibid. 14.

Mill tries to justify his claim that the mental pleasures are more valuable than the bodily. He appeals to the preferences of experienced judges in suitable choice situations. Suppose there are two pleasures— for example, Porky's pleasure in the pigsty and the elevated pleasure that an art lover gets from seeing a beautiful painting. Mill claims that such an experienced judge, who is equally capable of experiencing both pleasures, putting aside all extraneous reasons to prefer one to the other, would prefer to have the aesthetic pleasure. That, allegedly, shows that it is the higher pleasure. 'On a question which is the best worth having of two pleasures...the judgment of these who are qualified by knowledge of both...must be admitted as final.'[22] He apparently thinks that such experienced judges would overwhelmingly choose mental pleasures over bodily ones when in suitable choice situations.

Mill's theory, with its emphasis on higher and lower pleasures, has come in for a tremendous amount of criticism. Moore and others have attacked virtually every element of the theory. Defenders have claimed that, when properly understood, at least some of the core elements of the theory are defensible.[23] However, my aim here is not to give an account of Mill's theory or to defend it. In fact, I think quite a lot of what he says about higher and lower pleasures is just about indefensible. Rather, my aim is to show that we can develop a form of attitudinal hedonism that has many of the features that Mill was apparently trying to incorporate into his own hedonism.

One of the most troubling aspects of Mill's theory is that he seems to be thinking that the pleasures associated with the "higher faculties" are feelings or sensations that are somehow intrinsically different from the pleasures associated with the "lower faculties". This would seem to be an essential feature of the view if he is going to say that higher pleasures have more intrinsic value than lower ones even when they are equal in sheer amount. Since it is widely assumed that intrinsic values cannot be affected by extrinsic features such as causes or effects, it is hard to see how the pleasures could differ in intrinsic value unless they were different in some intrinsic feature, such as "how they feel".

---

[22] Mill, *Utilitarianism*, 15.

[23] In 'Mill, Moore, and the Consistency of Qualified Hedonism', I tried to defend Mill at least this far: I tried to show that his theory of qualified hedonism could be formulated in such a way as to be consistent. Some of Moore's criticisms, I claimed, were based on needlessly uncharitable interpretations of the theory.

Moore and others have been especially vigorous in their attacks on this aspect of Mill's theory. '[I]f you say "pleasure," you must mean "pleasure": you must mean some one thing common to all different "pleasures," some one thing, which may exist in different degrees, but which cannot differ in *kind*.'[24] The implication is clear: if the difference between a higher pleasure and a lower pleasure is simply a matter of *source* or *cause*, then this cannot ground a difference in intrinsic value. Intrinsic values cannot be affected in this way by extrinsic features.

But we can avoid all this controversy if we simply drop all talk of sensory pleasure and imagine instead an axiology based on attitudinal pleasure. We can say that higher pleasures are not pleasures that feel a special way, or that have been caused in a special way, but rather are episodes of attitudinal pleasure in which pleasure is taken in suitably "higher" objects. Thus, following Mill, we can say that when a person takes intrinsic attitudinal pleasure in some moral, intellectual, or aesthetic matter, his episode of pleasure as a whole is "higher", and thus more valuable in itself. When he takes intrinsic attitudinal pleasure in some mere bodily feeling, as for example the feeling he gets when engaging in sex or mud-wrestling, then his pleasure is lower, and thus less valuable in itself. If we allow ourselves a certain amount of conceptual leeway, we can construct the theory in such a way that the objects of attitudinal pleasures are intrinsic elements in the episodes of pleasure. Thus, we can avoid conflict with the principle that intrinsic values depend upon intrinsic features. The objects will actually be intrinsic features of the episodes. This can be made somewhat more precise.

Every state of affairs is a potential object of someone's pleasure. That is, for any state of affairs, p, someone might take pleasure in p. We can say, following up on some of Mill's ideas, that some of these objects are better suited to be objects of pleasure than others. The fact that some painting is beautiful, the fact that some line of research is enlightening, the fact that some argument is valid, the fact that some pattern of behavior is morally admirable—all of these are excellent objects for someone to be pleased about. On the other hand, the fact that my body feels like *this* (experienced while mud-wrestling), the fact that I am feeling such-and-such tingles in my private parts, etc.— all of these are less well suited to be objects of attitudinal pleasure.

Let us assume that every potential object of intrinsic attitudinal pleasure can be ranked on a scale according to its suitability to serve as

---

[24] Moore, *Principia Ethica*, 80.

an object of such pleasure. We can say that the scale positions such objects according to their "altitude". Mental, moral, and aesthetic objects have high altitude. Physical, bodily objects have low altitude. Perhaps Mill would say that the altitude of an object can be determined by offering suitable choices to large numbers of experienced judges. When such judges prefer to be pleased about one object rather than another, that fact shows that the one object has greater altitude than the other. I prefer not to say anything along those lines. I let altitude simply be an (alleged) objective fact about each potential object of intrinsic attitudinal pleasure.

We can assume that every altitude is represented by a positive number between zero and one, with higher numbers representing higher altitudes. On this scheme there are infinitely many possible altitudes, since there are infinitely many fractions between zero and one.[25]

Now, again following Mill (but keeping at some considerable distance from his very words), we can say that every episode of intrinsic attitudinal pleasure is good in itself; but we can add that the intrinsic value of such a pleasure is not simply a matter of quantity of pleasure taken. Rather, to find the intrinsic value of an episode of pleasure, we multiply the amount of pleasure in that episode by the altitude of the object of the pleasure. The resulting number is the "altitude-adjusted" amount of pleasure in the episode. The axiological thesis then is that the intrinsic value of an episode of pleasure is equal to the altitude-adjusted amount of pleasure it contains.

The result of this procedure should be obvious. If a person takes a certain amount of intrinsic attitudinal pleasure in a high-altitude object, his episode of pleasure has considerable intrinsic value. If another person takes the same amount of intrinsic attitudinal pleasure but in a low-altitude object, then his episode of pleasure has much lower value. I will stipulate that no object has an altitude of zero. As a result, there is no instance in which the multiplication of raw amount times altitude yields a product of zero. Every episode of intrinsic attitudinal pleasure is intrinsically good.

---

[25] On this interpretation, there are infinitely many different altitudes. Altitude functions in the manner of intensity or duration, making for greater value when other things are held equal. Trade-offs between altitude and intensity are permitted, so that a more intense low-altitude pleasure might be more valuable than a less intense high-altitude pleasure. On another interpretation there would be just two altitudes—"high" and "low". That view might go on to say that no amount of low-altitude pleasure is as good as even the tiniest amount of high-altitude pleasure. It is not clear to me that Mill's text requires one interpretation or the other. For a good discussion of the "two altitudes" approach, see Noah Lemos, 'Higher Goods and the Myth of Tithonus'.

With this as background, we can state another form of intrinsic attitudinal hedonism. It goes like this:

Altitude-Adjusted Intrinsic Attitudinal Hedonism

i. Every episode of intrinsic attitudinal pleasure is intrinsically good; every episode of intrinsic attitudinal pain is intrinsically bad.

ii. The intrinsic value of an episode of intrinsic attitudinal pleasure is equal to the altitude-adjusted amount of pleasure contained in that episode; the intrinsic value of an episode of intrinsic attitudinal pain is equal to − (the amount of the pain contained in that episode).

iii. The intrinsic value of a life is entirely determined by the intrinsic values of the episodes of intrinsic attitudinal pleasure and pain contained in the life, in such a way that one life is intrinsically better than another if and only if the net amount of altitude-adjusted intrinsic attitudinal pleasure in the one is greater than the net amount of that sort of pleasure in the other.

AAIAH is a form of universal attitudinal hedonism. It implies that every episode of intrinsic attitudinal pleasure is intrinsically good. If we were to allow objects with altitudes of zero, the theory would lose its universality. We would have to say in that case that it is *nearly universal*. It would then imply that every episode of intrinsic attitudinal pleasure is intrinsically good—except for episodes in which pleasure is taken in the very lowest of objects. Those episodes have intrinsic value of zero.

AAIAH is also a form of pure attitudinal hedonism. It implies that nothing other than an episode of pleasure can directly enhance the intrinsic value of a life. Knowledge, virtue, honor, wealth, etc. are all intrinsically worthless on this scheme. The sole ultimate source of intrinsic value in a life is pleasure—though of course pleasure taken in higher-altitude objects is said to be better. A life without intrinsic attitudinal pleasure could not have a positive intrinsic value according to this theory.

Recall Porky from Chapter 3. He took pleasure in wallowing in the mud with the sows. His pleasures were intense and long-lasting. We stipulated that he did not feel much pain. DH and AH implied that he had a good life. Given natural assumptions about Porky's attitudinal pleasures, IAH has the same implication. But AAIAH has different implications for this case.

AAIAH does not focus on the intensity of any sensations. On this theory sensory pleasures are irrelevant. What matters here is the amount of intrinsic attitudinal pleasure that Porky enjoys, adjusted for altitude. Let us assume that he takes quite a lot of intrinsic attitudinal pleasure in various facts—that he feels like *this* (where *this* is intended to indicate some sensory "feel" that Porky is enjoying); that he is doing *that*, that the pigpen smells like *this*. We can imagine that things like these are the objects of his intrinsic attitudinal pleasure. If we assume (as any Millian would) that these objects have very low altitudes, like 0.004, then no matter how intense and long-lasting the episodes of attitudinal pleasure are, their intrinsic value as judged by AAIAH will be very small. It would take a huge amount of such pleasures to make Porky's life as good as yours or mine.[26]

Suppose Mill takes intrinsic attitudinal pleasure in certain intellectual, moral, and aesthetic objects. For example, he takes pleasure in the fact that a certain form of argument is valid, or in the fact that certain formerly oppressed groups are now enjoying more freedom. If we assume that these objects have high altitudes, like, for example, 0.97, then even if such pleasures are brief and mild, they could still have high intrinsic values. AAIAH would evaluate a life full of very "mental" pleasures—presumably a life like Mill's—as being quite good. This is probably the way Mill wanted it to be.

It may be useful to say a few words about the specific feature of AAIAH that makes it consistent with the principle that intrinsic values depend upon intrinsic natures. According to AAIAH, the fundamental bearers of intrinsic value are episodes in which someone takes intrinsic attitudinal pleasure in some propositional object. An example of such an episode might be this:

E1: Porky taking intrinsic attitudinal pleasure of intensity +7 and duration +9 around noon on Monday, January 14, 2002, in the fact that *Porky is wallowing in the mud with the sows* while *Porky is wallowing in the mud with the sows* has an altitude of 0.004.

The theory then says that the altitude-adjusted amount of pleasure in E1 is determined by several factors: the intensity of Porky's attitudinal pleasure in E1 (which is +7), the duration of Porky's pleasure in E1 (which is +9), and finally the altitude of the object of Porky's pleasure in E1 (which is 0.004). The product of these numbers is 0.252—a very small number. Clause (ii) of AAIAH then says that the intrinsic value of the episode is equal to the altitude-adjusted amount of pleasure it contains. So the episode is not very good. The important point here is that the intrinsic value of the episode is now entirely determined by intrinsic facts about the episode—its intensity, its

---

[26] If we allow for altitudes of zero, we might even say that such objects are so low that they have zero altitude. Then the altitude-adjusted amount of pleasure in the episodes would be zero. Then AAIAH would imply that Porky's life is worthless.

duration, and the altitude of its object. The fact that it has precisely that object is an intrinsic feature of the episode. If Porky had taken pleasure in something else, there would have been a different episode of pleasure.

I have devoted considerable space to this discussion of AAIAH because I have been trying to accomplish a couple of tasks. For one thing, I am interested in demonstrating the plasticity of attitudinal hedonism. In this case, merely by introducing the idea of an adjustment for altitude, we generate a new form of intrinsic attitudinal hedonism. This theory yields results different from those yielded by DH, AH, and other forms of hedonism. Although I did not attempt to establish it, I think it is easy to see that AAIAH is distinct from IAH. So long as objects differ from one another in altitude, evaluations produced by AAIAH can differ from those produced by IAH.

I have another reason for introducing AAIAH. It concerns the interpretation of Mill. Many philosophers have insisted that Mill's axiological remarks are simply incoherent. Moore, for example, described Mill's view as 'simply fallacious', a 'naked and glaring contradiction', 'contemptible nonsense'.[27] So I wanted to take a few pages to formulate a theory that is clearly in the spirit of Mill's, but which is not confused or absurd. This is not to say that I think the proposed theory is true or utterly unproblematic. The point is simpler: the theory is coherent and relevantly like Mill's. How much ink could have been saved if only he had made better use of the concept of intrinsic attitudinal pleasure!

Finally, I have been interested in discussing AAIAH because it constitutes a possible reply to the Argument from Worthless Pleasures (discussed above in Chapter 3). Since we can always insist that worthless pleasures are pleasures taken in low-altitude objects, we can say that there is a form of hedonism that implies that a life is not made much better by the presence in it of such pleasures. We have already seen that Porky's life gets a lower evaluation on this theory. If we were to admit objects with an altitude of zero (and the objects of Porky's pleasures might be good candidates for such a ranking), the theory would be consistent with the idea that a life could be full of pleasure, yet worthless. That demonstrates that hedonism does not have to be a doctrine worthy only of swine.

The drawback of the theory is the reliance on the barely explained concept of altitude. What justification is there for saying that mental

---

[27] Moore, *Principia Ethica*, 67, 71, 72.

objects have higher altitude than physical ones? And what justification is there for saying that pleasure taken in higher-altitude objects is always better in itself? Perhaps it is nothing more than this: if we make these assumptions, the theory will generate the numbers we (or some of us, anyway) want it to generate. One might hope for something a bit deeper.

Appendix B
Reflections on the Attitudinal/Sensory Distinction

In Chapter 4 I drew a distinction between sensory pleasures and attitudinal pleasures. I claimed that this distinction provides the basis for a similar distinction between two families of hedonism. I suggested that I would be more interested in defending forms of attitudinal hedonism.

I think the distinction between the two conceptions of pleasure is important in the context of formulating an adequate hedonistic axiology. However, I think the distinction is independently worthy of attention. It has a number of other applications. In this appendix, I discuss the application of the distinction to four puzzles about pleasure.

B.1. The Nature of Sensory Pleasures

Reflection on sensory pleasures quickly reveals an enormous phenomenological heterogeneity. Perhaps this can be expressed more simply: sensory pleasures are all "feelings", but they do not "feel alike". Consider the warm, dry, slightly drowsy feeling of pleasure that you get while sunbathing on a quiet beach. By way of contrast, consider the cool, wet, invigorating feeling of pleasure that you get when drinking some cold, refreshing beer on a hot day. Each of these experiences involves a feeling of pleasure—a sensory pleasure, in my terminology—yet they do not feel at all alike. After many years of careful research on this question, I have come to the conclusion that they have just about nothing in common phenomenologically. Yet they are both pleasures. Why?

Many answers have been suggested. Some have said, for example, that what makes all of these sensations pleasures is the fact that each of them is causally related to some other sensation that is a feeling of "pleasure itself". Others have said that there is no such feeling as the alleged feeling of "pleasure itself". Some have claimed that what makes these feelings pleasures is something about desire or motivation: the one who feels the sensations wants to be feeling them when he is feeling them, or he is motivated to have them begin or continue once started. Others have proposed yet other views about the unifying feature of this heterogeneous collection of sensations. Elsewhere, I have tried to show that none of these proposed solutions to this "heterogeneity puzzle" works. I will not review the arguments here.[1]

Appeal to the attitudinal/sensory distinction provides what we need to solve the problem. I believe that what makes a feeling count as a sensory pleasure is the fact that the person who experiences that feeling takes intrinsic attitudinal

---

[1] You can find the discussion in my 'Two Questions about Pleasure'.

pleasure in the fact that he himself is then feeling it.[2] This explains how the heterogeneity of sensory pleasure comes about. The answer is simple: we take intrinsic attitudinal pleasure in sensations of many different sorts. When a happy sunbather enjoys the feelings of warmth on the beach, those warm, dry, drowsy feelings are sensory pleasures. When a jolly tippler enjoys the cool, wet, invigorating sensations caused by a cold one going down the hatch, those feelings are sensory pleasures. The explanation is the same in both cases: the sensations are sensory pleasures because the person who has them takes intrinsic attitudinal pleasure in the fact that he or she has them.

The proposed view about sensory pleasure has some implications that some may find surprising. For one, the view implies that *being a pleasure* is not an intrinsic property of any sensation that in fact is a pleasure. Consider the cool, wet, tingly sensation you get when sipping a cold beer. Suppose it is a sensory pleasure. On the view I have proposed, that very sensation is a pleasure in virtue of the fact that you take pleasure in it. If you had not taken pleasure in it, it would not have been a pleasure. Its being a pleasure depends upon the fact that it stands in a certain relation to you—the relation of being something in which you take intrinsic attitudinal pleasure. Thus, what makes it a sensory pleasure is a relational fact about that sensation. It is not an intrinsic feature. An intrinsic duplicate of that sensation might fail to be a sensory pleasure. It all depends upon whether the person who experiences it takes pleasure in it.

Similarly, the proposed view implies that no sensory pleasure is essentially a pleasure. Consider again the cool, wet, tingly sensation of the cold beer. It is a sensory pleasure. But it is a sensory pleasure only in virtue of the fact that you took attitudinal pleasure in it. If you had not taken pleasure in it, it would not have been a sensory pleasure. I see no reason to suppose that you *had to* take pleasure in it. Your tastes could have been different; your recent experiences could have been different; the condition of your brain and nervous system could have been different; you might have reacted differently to the taste sensations as a result of taking some drugs. Thus, you might have had that very same sensation without enjoying it. In any of these cases, on my proposed account of sensory pleasure, that very sensation which was a sensory pleasure would not have been a sensory pleasure. So it is not essentially a pleasure. It is a pleasure in virtue of a contingent fact about it: you liked it.

The corresponding view about sensory pain yields the same conclusion: sensory pains are not intrinsically or essentially pains. Each of them has the property of *being a sensory pain* in virtue of the fact that it stands in a contingent relation to the one who experiences it. The relation is *being such that x takes intrinsic attitudinal pain in the fact that he himself is then feeling it.*

The proposed view suggests that there might be two different ways in which we could manage pain. According to the view, a person is experiencing

---

[2] There is a corresponding puzzle about the heterogeneous collection of sensations called 'pains'. I would offer a corresponding solution: each of them is a sensory pain because the one who feels it takes intrinsic attitudinal pain in the fact that he is then feeling it.

sensory pain when (a) he has some sensation and (b) he takes intrinsic attitudinal pain in the fact that he has that sensation. It would seem, therefore, that sensory pain could be eliminated either (a) by making the sensation stop, or (b) by making the person stop taking attitudinal pain in it. The first approach is illustrated by certain pain-reducing drugs that function primarily by "deadening" the offending sensations. If you make a person numb, his pain will cease—perhaps along with other sensations. If successful, the patient might say, 'I can't feel it any more.' The second approach is illustrated by other techniques, including certain kinds of brain surgery, hypnotism, counseling, and the use of drugs that alter the patient's reaction to pain. These drugs, for example, allow the person to continue feeling the previously painful sensation, but they alter his reaction to them. If successful, the drugs would not eliminate the sensations; they would just make the person cease being pained by them. A typical report of the successful application of the drug would be: 'It still feels pretty much the same, but it doesn't bother me any more.'

A corresponding phenomenon occurs in connection with pleasure. We can distinguish between two types of anhedonia. In one type, the unfortunate victim cannot feel pleasurable sensations. Perhaps there has been some nerve damage. He just does not feel sensations relevantly like the ones most of us enjoy. In the second type, the victim does feel those sensations, but he does not enjoy them. Some descriptions of anhedonia associated with depression make it seem that depressed people suffer from this second sort of interference with pleasure. A typical report of a person suffering this second sort of anhedonia is: 'I still get the same sensations, but I don't enjoy them any more. They mean nothing to me.'

B.2. The Delightfulness of Pleasure, the Awfulness of Pain

Careful application of the attitudinal/sensory distinction may enable us to gain some insight into the old puzzles about the delightfulness of pleasure and the awfulness of pain. Since the literature focuses mainly on examples involving pain, I will discuss the issue from the doloric perspective, though my remarks are intended to apply to the case of pleasure as well.

The issue arises in a couple of different forms. In one form, it goes like this: *awfulness* seems to be an essential component of our concept of pain. The doctrine that pains are unpleasant seems to be almost analytic. We are inclined to say, 'If it doesn't hurt, it isn't a pain.'[3] Yet, at the same time, we have been told of strange individuals who feel pains but apparently do not mind. Their pains, we are told, do not hurt them. Examples of such individuals are people who have taken certain mind-altering drugs, Indian fakirs who sit peacefully on beds of nails, masochists, and individuals who have

[3] In his 'A Defense of Pain', Earl Conee cites a number of philosophers who accept this doctrine. Daniel Dennett is quoted as saying, 'Pain is perfect misery, the worst of evils', in *Brainstorms*. Much of what I say here is influenced by Conee's remarks in the cited paper and in his dissertation 'Pleasure and Intrinsic Value'.

been subjected to certain types of brain surgery. But if pains are *essentially* painful, this should be impossible.

If we make use of the distinction between attitudinal and sensory pain (and the proposed account of sensory pain), the solution to the puzzle is simple. I have proposed that we define sensory pain by saying that a sensation is a sensory pain if and only if the person who feels it takes intrinsic attitudinal pain in the fact that he himself is then feeling that sensation. In other words, I take sensory pains to be sensations (of heat, or cold, or pressure, or the pricklings of many nails, or *anything*) in which the experiencer takes intrinsic attitudinal pain.

Given this account of sensory pain, it becomes a necessary truth that all pains are "disliked" or "awful". But we must be careful about the scope of the modal operator. More exactly, what turns out to be true is this:

NP: Necessarily, if a certain sensation, S, is a sensory pain for a person, P, at a time, t, then P takes intrinsic attitudinal pain in the fact that he himself is experiencing S at t.

NP is intended to do justice to our sense that "if it is a pain, it must hurt".

Nevertheless, if we focus our attention on any particular sensation that happens to be a sensory pain, we will see that it is only a *contingent* fact that the person who experienced that sensation happened to take pain in it. He might have been neutral about it; he might even have enjoyed it. It all depends upon such contingent facts as whether he has recently taken certain mind-altering drugs, or whether he has undergone brain surgery. If his circumstances had been different in some of these ways, he would not have been pained by the sensation. And his circumstances could have been different in the relevant respects. In that case, given my account of sensory pain, it would not have been a pain.

As a result of this, we can see that if we focus on any particular sensory pain, we are focusing on a thing that might not have been a pain. *Being a pain* is not an essential property of any sensory pain. Thus, this is not true:

*PN: If a certain sensation, S, is a sensory pain for a person, P, at a time, t, then necessarily, P takes intrinsic attitudinal pain in the fact that he himself is experiencing S at t.

What shall we say about the fakirs, masochists, hypnosis victims, and others who experience pain but do not mind? Do such cases cast doubt on NP? It seems to me that the existence of such individuals is consistent with NP. We just have to be careful about how we describe their experience. As I see it, what happens in such cases is that the individual experiences a sensation that any normal person would find painful—perhaps the individual himself formerly found similar experiences painful, or would find them painful were it not for the drugs or hypnosis or whatever is affecting him. Thus, there is some justification for calling the sensations 'pains'. More carefully, they are sensations that would be pains if experienced under ordinary circumstances. But because of the unusual circumstances, the person does not take intrinsic attitudinal pain in his feelings. Thus, the feelings (as felt by him on that occasion) are not strictly *pains*. They are sensations that are intrinsically just like pains, sensations that would be pains if experienced by any normal person, sensations intrinsically like sensations that were pains when experienced by this individual in the past. So we call them 'pains', but on the proposed analysis they are not.

So we can introduce two concepts of sensory pain. On the one hand, there is the strict and official concept of sensory pain. This applies to sensations of just about any phenomenological type—feelings of heat or cold, pressure or motion, burnings, or pricklings of nails. What makes such a sensation a sensory pain is a contingent relational fact about it: the person who experiences it takes intrinsic attitudinal pain in the fact that he is then feeling it. Given this account of sensory pain, it follows that it is necessary *de dicto* that if something is a strict sensory pain, then the person who experiences it takes intrinsic attitudinal pain in the fact that he feels it. However, given the contingency of its status as a pain, it would not be correct to say of each such pain, *de re*, that it is necessarily such that the one who experiences it takes intrinsic attitudinal pain in it.

Thus, if the question is: 'Are pains necessarily painful?', the answer is 'Yes and no. It depends upon precisely what you mean.' If you are talking about sensations that are in fact sensory pains for the one who has them, then yes, it is necessary that if they are pains, they are painful. The one who has such a pain must be pained by it. But if you are talking about sensations that are intrinsically like things that would normally be pains, then no, they do not have to be painful. A fakir, or masochist, or person on drugs can have such a sensation without being pained by it. He might even enjoy it.

B.3. Painful Pleasures, Pleasant Pains

Here is a closely related puzzle about pleasures and pains: suppose a snow-shoveler has been out shoveling snow on a cold day.[4] He's chilled to the bone. He comes indoors and steps into a warm shower. The sensations caused by the splashing of the warm water are pleasurable. He turns the hot water handle a bit further. The sensations change; it now feels hotter. He likes it more. Again, he makes the water warmer, and his pleasure increases. But then he turns the handle a bit too far, and the water starts being too hot. Now, as the intensity of his sensation is increasing, his pleasure is not increasing. He makes the water still hotter. Now it starts to be really uncomfortable. His pleasure turns into pain. He steps back from the water and readjusts the handles until the water becomes more temperate.

The case might seem paradoxical. A certain sensation was declared to be a pleasure. As it got more intense, it became a greater pleasure. But then when the very same sensation became even more intense, it started becoming less

---

[4] I mentioned this example earlier, at the beginning of Ch. 2.

of a pleasure. Eventually, the same sensation became so intense that it started being a pain. How can one sensation first be a pleasure, then, as it becomes more intense, become less of a pleasure, and then a pain? How can something that is a pleasure become a pain? Are there "painful pleasures"?

This case has relevance not only for the phenomenology of pain and pleasure, but also for axiology. What is a sensory hedonist to say about such a case? Earlier, when I formulated DH, I said that the number of hedons in an episode of sensory pleasure is determined by the intensity and duration of the pleasure in that episode. And according to DH, the intrinsic value of an episode of pleasure is supposed to be equal to the number of hedons it contains. But now it may appear that if intensities of pleasure become too great, the episodes start containing *fewer* hedons—or at any rate, that the episodes start being *less valuable*. How is this possible?

This sort of case might appear puzzling, but once we have the attitudinal/sensory distinction at our disposal, it is easy to see our way clear. We should be careful to respect certain distinctions as we describe the case of the snow-shoveler. More precisely, we should be careful to distinguish between (a) *sensations of heat* that he feels and (b) *attitudes of intrinsic attitudinal pleasure and pain* that he takes in those sensations. First let me describe the situation more carefully, taking note of the sensory and attitudinal elements.

At first, when he steps into the shower, he feels a certain sensation of heat. He takes attitudinal pleasure in that sensation, so it is a sensory pleasure. There are two distinct intensities here. One is the intensity of the sensation of heat; the other is the intensity of the attitudinal pleasure that he takes in the fact that he feels the heat. At the outset, both intensities are moderately high. The water feels pretty hot; he likes it pretty much. Then as he raises the temperature of the water a bit too high, the intensity of the sensation of heat increases. He feels "more heat", perhaps "too much heat". As this happens, the intensity of his attitude of pleasure begins to decrease. He takes less intrinsic attitudinal pleasure in his sensation of heat. Then, when the water becomes definitely too hot, his sensation of heat becomes too intense. When this happens, his attitude of intrinsic pleasure fades to zero and is replaced by intrinsic attitudinal pain. In other words, he starts taking attitudinal pain in the fact that he is feeling this sensation of sensory heat. As a result, the sensation of heat, which formerly was a sensory pleasure, starts being a sensory pain.

The case might pose a problem for a defender of DH or other forms of sensory hedonism. For, as so far formulated, DH is based on the idea that the amount of pleasure in an episode is a function of intensity and duration. Intensity has been understood to mean *intensity of sensation*. That approach yields incorrect results in cases such as the one described. But a slight refinement of the concept of intensity may avoid the trouble. The sensory hedonist can reconceptualize intensity by saying that the intensity of an episode of sensory pleasure is not the strength of the pleasant feeling, but rather the strength of the attitude of pleasure that the experiencer takes in that feeling.[5] Since, in the case described, the attitude of pleasure decreases when the intensity of the sensation of heat increases, it will then be open to the sensory hedonist to say that as the sensation of heat increases, the amount of pleasure in that sensation decreases.

But I have little interest in defending DH. I'm more concerned to see if the case poses a problem for a defender of IAH. I think it does not. Recall that according to IAH, the intrinsic value of an episode of intrinsic attitudinal pleasure is determined by the amount of such pleasure in the episode. The amount of pleasure in the episode is determined in part by the intensity *of the intrinsic attitudinal pleasure* that the person takes in that episode, not by the intensity of any sensation. So even if it is pleasure in a sensation, and the sensation is becoming more intense, the value of the pleasure will decrease if the intensity of the attitude of pleasure is decreasing.

Furthermore, if the attitude of pleasure is replaced by an attitude of pain, then, even if the object remains the same, the episode of pleasure terminates and is replaced by a subsequent episode of pain. That is what happened in the example of the snow-shoveler in the shower. Thus, the case may be interesting, and may call for some adjustments in some forms of sensory hedonism, but it is handled smoothly by Intrinsic Attitudinal Hedonism.

B.4. Masochism

I have defined sensory pleasures as precisely those feelings we intrinsically enjoy having, and sensory pains as those we intrinsically "disenjoy" having. As a result, I am committed to a very strong version of the view that there is an analytic link between sensory hedonic and doloric phenomena and pro and con attitudes.

Some have suggested that there is no such link between sensory pleasures and pains, on the one hand, and pro and con attitudes on the other. They appeal to a number of psychological facts to illustrate the lack of linkage. More particularly, it is sometimes claimed that the phenomenon of masochism shows that there is no such linkage, since the masochist has definite pro attitudes toward sensory pains; he seems to take pleasure in his pains.[6] If this is right, my accounts of sensory pleasure and sensory pain may be wrong. For I have defined sensory pleasures (pains) as feelings such that

---

[5] Another approach is possible. The defender of DH could say that when he spoke of sensory pleasures, he never meant to be talking about feelings of heat and cold, tingles and throbs. Actually, he might say, none of these is a sensory pleasure. A genuine sensory pleasure is a feeling of a different sensation—the sensation of "pleasure itself". He could say that sensory hedonism is the view that episodes of this distinctive feeling are the fundamental intrinsic goods; more of this feeling is always better; a life filled with it is the Good Life. It is the intensity of this distinctive feeling of pleasure that bears on amounts of value. Variations in the intensity of a feeling of pleasure need not be linked to variations in the intensity of feelings that cause it. Well, a sensory hedonist could say these things. Personally, I doubt that there is any such feeling. I have never felt it.

[6] The phenomenon also casts doubt on a variety of other attitudinal accounts of sensory pleasure and pain. For example, it would cast doubt on the idea that pleasures can be defined as

the experiencer takes intrinsic attitudinal pleasure (pain) in the fact that he is feeling them.

David Seligman seems to think that the phenomenon of masochism proves that any such analysis is wrong. He says:

cases of masochism do indeed exemplify pleasant pains and hence ... no analysis of pain which attempts to define it in terms of unpleasantness can be satisfactory.... Pleasantness and unpleasantness are not intrinsic properties of sensations. Pains are *ordinarily*, though not *necessarily*, disliked.[7]

It seems to me that the phenomenon of masochism does not cast any doubt on my version of the thesis that sensory pleasures (pains) are precisely those feelings in which we take intrinsic attitudinal pleasure (pain). Thus, I think Seligman's view is mistaken.[8] Furthermore, I think that careful attention to the distinctions (a) between sensory and attitudinal pain and (b) between intrinsic and non-intrinsic attitudinal pain will make this evident. But in order to evaluate his argument, we need to reflect a bit more carefully on what masochism is supposed to be.

What is distinctive and unusual about the masochist's attitude toward pleasure and pain?

In his discussion of masochism in 'Three Contributions to the Theory of Sex', Sigmund Freud attempts to give a clear, concise account of the sexual aberration he calls masochism.[9] In one particularly striking passage, Freud tries to link masochism with sadism. He says that each may be seen as an exaggeration of the aggressive element in sexuality. In sadism this may seem fairly obvious. The extra oddity in masochism is that the aggression is directed against oneself. The perversions are linked also, according to Freud, in that the active form (sadism) is often encountered together with the passive form (masochism) in the same person. As Freud says, 'He who experiences pleasure by causing pain to others in sexual relations is also capable of experiencing pain in sexual relations as pleasure. A sadist is simultaneously a masochist.'[10]

This Freudian account of masochism is perplexing. In this translation, Freud says that a masochist "experiences pain as pleasure". What does this mean? How is it possible?

We might understand the view to be this: there are certain feelings that are in fact painful. They are sensory pains. When the masochist experiences these painful feelings, however, he experiences them "as pleasure". In other words, they feel pleasant to him. In his case, instead of hurting, they feel good. That's what makes him a masochist.

'feelings that we desire to have and to prolong'. This account apparently implies that masochists do not want pains. Like all the rest of us, the feelings they want are pleasures—after all, the feelings in question are feelings that the masochist desires to have and to prolong.

[7] Seligman, 'Masochism', 74–5.

[8] Although I agree with him when he says that pains are not *intrinsically* painful.

[9] Sigmund Freud, 'Three Contributions to the Theory of Sex', 569–71.   [10] Ibid. 570.

It should be clear that on this interpretation, the Freudian remark will not do. For in the first place it is very hard to understand what could be meant by saying that the feelings are in fact sensory pains but that they don't hurt at all; they feel like pleasures. Isn't it obvious that painful feelings have to hurt? And furthermore, if the masochist "experiences these feelings as pleasures", it would seem that these feelings must be pleasures. If he so experiences them, then that's what they are. And if the masochist enjoys that sort of thing, then he's not really very different from the rest of us. We all enjoy pleasure.

This account of the Freudian remark makes masochism almost unintelligible. For it implies that certain pains are pleasures. It also seems to leave out an essential feature of masochism. For this account seems to imply that someone could go in for serious masochism over a period of time *and yet never feel anything that was genuinely painful*. For if all of his "pains" were experienced by him as pleasures, when does he suffer any pain?

Perhaps the Freudian remark should be interpreted in another way. Perhaps he means to call attention to certain feelings. Since most people, or healthy people, or normal people would experience these feelings as pains, Freud calls them 'pains'. The remarkable thing about masochists is that when they have these feelings, they don't hurt. Rather, masochists experience these feelings as pleasures. So perhaps the point is that masochists experience as sensory pleasures certain feelings that normal people would experience as sensory pains.

It should be clear that this account fails also. It suggests that masochists differ from normal people merely in this: they get their pleasure from feelings that most people find unpleasant. On this account, the masochist does not enjoy anything that is genuinely painful for him. The feelings he enjoys would be painful to ordinary people, but they do not hurt him. To him, they feel good. In this case, it is hard to see why we would think that masochism is some sort of *perversion*. In fact, on this account it would be about as perverse as a sort of persistent misperception of colors or tastes. Suppose someone regularly saw green where ordinary people saw blue, or suppose he regularly tasted bitterness when ordinary people tasted sweetness. His perception would be unusual, but he would not be said to be suffering from some sort of perversion.

If masochism were nothing more than a regular tendency to feel pleasurable sensations where ordinary people would feel painful ones, then it would not be a psychological perversion. It would be strange, but not "sick" or "weird". We would have to look closely at the victim's nerve fibers. It would appear that there must be short circuit somewhere.

Yet another interpretation is possible. Perhaps the masochist really does feel certain pains. These feelings really hurt him. Perhaps what is remarkable about the masochist is that he experiences these pains as pleasures *in addition to* experiencing them as pains. That is, the very same feelings that hurt him also please him. No ordinary person would take pleasure in these feelings; they would simply be painful.

Again, this interpretation seems wrong. First, it seems a bit strange to say that the very same feeling is both a pain and a pleasure. Is that possible? Second, it raises a question about why the masochist would go out of his way to engage in these perverted activities. For suppose he feels some stinging, burning, whipping, or other feeling. Suppose he thereby suffers five dolors of sensory pain. Suppose he also thereby enjoys five hedons of sensory pleasure. His experience as a whole seems intrinsically worthless. Why doesn't he just stay home and watch a boring show on TV?

In Irwin Goldstein's paper on this topic, he says that masochists want to suffer pain; they want this because they feel that they deserve it.[11] We might try to capture this idea in a general principle about masochistic pain:

MG1: F is a masochistic pain for S at t iff
    i. F is a sensory pain for S at t
    ii. S wants to experience F at t because S thinks he's unworthy and deserves to suffer pain.

I think this is wrong in several ways. For one thing, it is not clear to me that all masochists have low self-esteem, or think they deserve to suffer. I guess some might. But a person who is really turned on sexually by pain might not be like that at all. In the current DSM-IV it says of paraphilias in general, 'Many individuals with these disorders assert that the behavior causes them no distress and that their only problem is social dysfunction as a result of the reaction of others to their behavior.'[12] So it appears that (ii) is false, if taken as a conceptual component of masochism. We should drop the reference to the claim about the belief in desert of suffering.

Consider this:

MG2: F is a masochistic pain for S at t iff
    i. F is a sensory pain for S at t
    ii. S wants to experience F at t.

Obviously, this is wrong. An utterly non-masochistic person might want to experience a painful feeling for any number of reasons: (a) he might be convinced that he is a sinner, and that his only chance of getting to heaven is through suffering; (b) he might believe in the maxim 'No pain, no gain', and he might want to gain. In cases (a) and (b), the person is not at all masochistic or otherwise unusual. Like any healthy and rational person, he might want to achieve some worthwhile goal, and he might recognize that in order to achieve it, he needs to suffer some pain. Sometimes that is a price one has to pay. There are still further possibilities. (c) He might be curious. (d) He might not realize that F will be painful.

DSM-IV describes sexual masochism as a 'paraphilia'. Thus, it is classed among disorders that have this common feature: 'intense sexually arousing

[11] Goldstein, 'Pain and Masochism'.
[12] *Diagnostic and Statistical Manual Mental Disorders*, 4th edn., 524.

fantasies, sexual urges, or behaviors generally involving 1) nonhuman objects, 2) the suffering or humiliation of oneself or one's partner, or 3) children or other nonconsenting persons'.[13] This suggests another way in which Goldstein's approach is wrong. He seems to think that masochists just want to be miserable—as if they go in for pain with no thought of benefit. He thus fails to mention that the masochist might be sexually turned on by pain.

Here is another suggestion:

MG3: F is a masochistic pain for S at t iff
  i. F is a sensory pain for S at t
  ii. S wants to experience F at t because S thinks that he will feel intense sexual pleasure if and only if he experiences F, and he wants to experience that intense sexual pleasure.

This is still not right. Imagine that a chivalrous knight would like to enjoy intimacies with a certain lady. A fire-breathing dragon blocks his way. He realizes that if he fights the dragon, and suffers some painful second-degree burns on the hands, he will then be able to experience some intense sexual pleasure with the lady. If not, not. Since he is keen on the sexual pleasure, he willingly fights the dragon. The knight is no masochist.

MG3 is wrong in another way, too. It makes a desire for sexual pleasure an essential element of masochism. This seems too narrow. Surely there are some masochists whose interest in pain has nothing (at least on the surface) to do with sexual pleasure.

I think the distinctive features of masochism are these: (i) the person actually does feel a sensory pain. Something really *hurts* the masochist. I have suggested that sensory pains are to be understood as bodily feelings in which the subject takes intrinsic attitudinal pain. Thus, this first element comes to this: there is some feeling that the masochist experiences; this feeling really hurts. He takes intrinsic attitudinal pain in the fact that he has that feeling. However, (ii) the masochist (unlike the rest of us) takes pleasure in the fact that these sensations hurt. This pleasure is *intrinsic attitudinal pleasure*, not some mere extrinsic pleasure that even an athlete in training might enjoy. The masochist really enjoys being in pain. That is what makes him seem so weird. Normal people do not take intrinsic pleasure in the fact that they are in pain. So my account of masochistic pain is this:

M4: F is a masochistic pain for S at t iff
  i. F is a sensory pain for S at t
  ii. S takes intrinsic attitudinal pleasure in the fact that he himself is taking pain in the fact that he himself is feeling F at t.

Given my analysis of sensory pain, clause (i) above means that S takes intrinsic pain in F. From this it does not follow that S prefers all things considered not to have F; nor does it follow that S finds it overall unpleasant

---

[13] Ibid.

to have F. All that follows is that S takes intrinsic pain in that feeling. It hurts him. The more pain he takes in the feeling, the greater a pain it is.

But the perverse fact about S is that he is glad to be suffering. He takes intrinsic pleasure in the fact that he is in pain. This is to be distinguished from the completely non-perverse case in which someone takes *extrinsic* pleasure in the fact that he is in pain. I might also point out that this account does not imply that there is a feeling that is simultaneously a pleasure and a pain. For I did not say that S takes pleasure in the fact that he is feeling F; I said that he takes pleasure in the fact that *F hurts*. So the proposed account of masochism does not confront that particular puzzle.

Let us now return to the point at issue. I proposed that we can define sensory pain in terms of attitudinal pain, sensory pleasure in terms of attitudinal pleasure. My proposals, somewhat abbreviated and combined, are these:

SP: A feeling, F, is a sensory pain (pleasure) for S at t if and only if S takes intrinsic attitudinal pain (pleasure) in the fact that he himself is feeling F at t.

Seligman claimed that the phenomenon of masochism involves "pleasant pains". He said that it follows from this that 'no analysis of pain which attempts to define it in terms of unpleasantness can be satisfactory'. Clearly, his remark is intended to imply that any account like SP must be false. Now that I have given my account of masochism, we can reconsider Seligman's claim: Does the phenomenon of masochism conflict with SP?

The short answer is, 'No. There is no conflict.' We can see this more clearly if we reflect on my proposed account of masochistic pain, M4. That account implies that masochistic pains are indeed sensory pains. That means (on my account) that the one who feels them *is intrinsically pained by them*. The pains of masochists are therefore "painful pains", and not pleasant pains. M4 also implies that the person who suffers these sensory pains has an odd attitude toward the fact that he is suffering them: he enjoys it. More exactly, he takes intrinsic attitudinal pleasure in the fact that he is pained by those feelings. This does *not* imply that the pains are pleasures, or that they are "pleasant pains". M4 does not imply that the masochist takes intrinsic attitudinal pleasure in the fact that he has the feelings. He might take extrinsic pleasure in that fact, since the fact that he is feeling those feelings makes it possible for him to take pain in them, and that makes it possible for him to take pleasure in the fact that he is in pain. None of this casts doubt on the analysis proposed in SP.

APPENDIX C
The Hedonism of Epicurus

Epicurus is widely recognized as one of the most influential of all hedonists. He took pains to explain that his form of hedonism was not to be confused with the hedonism of Aristippus or other sensory hedonists. He clearly did not advocate a life of debauchery or indulgence. I am inclined to think that he meant to advocate a view according to which a distinctive sort of attitudinal pleasure is the highest good, and a life of tranquil reflection is the Good Life. I consider him a creative and insightful predecessor—a man in whose shadow I am honored to walk. Unfortunately, his views have often been misunderstood—especially by hostile critics. It behooves us, therefore, to take some time to reflect on the hedonism of Epicurus, insofar as that is still possible.

C.1. The Evidence concerning Epicurean Hedonism

The extant evidence concerning the views of Epicurus is scanty and open to doubt. It consists of a few alleged quotations and some critical commentary written long after his death. There is no way to confirm the accuracy of the quotations. There is no way to determine how the quotations, even if perfectly accurate, are intended to fit into the larger picture of Epicureanism. There is no way to determine whether his ancient expositors got his views right. Furthermore, even if the quotations are perfectly authentic, and the expository remarks accurate, it is still possible that Epicurus held different views at different times. Maybe the quotations are not expressions of parts of the same theory; maybe the expositions are expositions of different and incompatible theories. In light of these facts about the evidence, we can at best hope to formulate a view *suggested by* the snippets of evidence still available to us.

What are the main sources of information about Epicureanism? First of all, there is the fairly long discussion of Epicurus in Book X of *The Lives of the Eminent Philosophers* by Diogenes Laertius. This contains some biographical information and a fairly extensive account of the views of Epicurus on various topics, including metaphysics, philosophy of mind, the evil of death, and hedonism. The final few pages are devoted to his views on ethics. The article by Diogenes includes some extensive quotations of works by Epicurus. For our purposes the most important of these are the 'Letter to Menoeceus' (LM) and the '*Principal Doctrines*' (PD). Most of the currently available direct information concerning Epicurean hedonism is contained in these documents.

Diogenes Laertius never knew Epicurus. Epicurus died in about 270 BC. Diogenes apparently wrote his book around the beginning of the third century AD. Diogenes knew Epicureanism largely from secondary sources.

He was a compiler of fragments, gossip from textbooks and encyclopedias, and hearsay. So while we cannot ignore what Diogenes says, we have to be cautious about his assertions.

The second main source of information about Epicurus is *On the Nature of Things* by Lucretius. Lucretius was a follower of Epicureanism, but he did not learn his Epicureanism from the founder. He got it from later sources, too. He was not born until 99 BC.

The third main source of information about Epicurus is Cicero's *De Finibus Bonorum et Malorum*. In this work, one of the characters is portrayed as a defender of Epicureanism. He presents a summary of Epicurean hedonism. Then another character states objections. The first character gives his replies. They engage in a fairly extensive and wide-ranging dialogue. Their discussion of the concept of static pleasure is especially interesting. Again, however, Cicero's work was written more than a century after the death of Epicurus.

When we look at the 'Letter to Menoeceus', we find several remarks concerning hedonism and the Good Life. In some of these remarks Epicurus seems to be saying that pleasure is the Good. He seems to want to say that every sort of pleasure is good in itself. Associated with this are remarks about the evil of pain. So, for example, we have these remarks:[1]

LM1: 'we say that pleasure is the starting point and goal of living blessedly. For we recognized [pleasure] as our first innate good, and this is our starting point for every choice and avoidance and we come to this by judging every good by the criterion of feeling' (p. 30).

LM2: 'this [pleasure] is the first innate good' (p. 30).

LM3: 'every pleasure is a good thing, since it has a nature congenial [to us]… every pain too is a bad thing' (p. 30).

LM4: 'pleasure is the goal' (p. 30).

Another collection of passages contain remarks about a distinctive sort of pleasure that Epicurus wants to hold out for special praise. This is "static pleasure". Static pleasure is officially defined (in LM6) as 'lack of pain in the body and disturbance in the soul'. Epicurus seems to advocate the view that this sort of static pleasure is far more valuable than the 'active' pleasures praised by the likes of Aristippus. Among the most important remarks about static pleasure are these:

LM5: 'simple flavours provide a pleasure equal to that of an extravagant lifestyle when all pain from want is removed and barley cakes and water provide the highest pleasure when someone in want takes them' (p. 30).

LM6: 'So when we say that pleasure is the goal we do not mean the pleasure of the profligate or the pleasures of consumption, as some believe, either

---

[1] All quotations are from *The Epicurus Reader: Selected Writings and Testimonia*, transl. and ed., with notes by Brad Inwood and L. P. Gerson (Indianapolis: Hackett Publishing Co., 1994). Parenthetical page references in this appendix are to this work.

from ignorance and disagreement or from deliberate misinterpretation, but rather the lack of pain in the body and disturbance in the soul. For it is not drinking bouts and continuous partying and enjoying boys and women, or consuming fish and the other dainties of an extravagant table, which produce the pleasant life, but sober calculation which searches of the reasons for every choice and avoidance and drives out the opinions which are the source of the greatest turmoil for men's souls' (pp. 30–1).

PD33: 'The cry of the flesh: not to be hungry, not to be thirsty, not to be cold. For if someone has these things and is confident of having them in the future, he might contend even with <Zeus> for happiness' (p. 38).

Epicurus apparently thought that pleasure and pain are associated in some important way with the satisfaction and frustration of desire. He drew distinctions among categories of desire in an effort to provide a sort of practical guide for the maximization of welfare construed hedonically. Among these remarks about desire is this typical passage:

LM7: We must reckon that of desires some are natural, some groundless; and of the natural desires some are necessary and some merely natural; and of the necessary, some are necessary for happiness and some for the freeing the body from troubles and some for life itself. The unwavering contemplation of these enables one to refer every choice and avoidance to the health of the body and the freedom of the soul from disturbance, since this is the goal of a blessed life. For we do everything for the sake of being neither in pain nor in terror. As soon as we achieve this state every storm in the soul is dispelled, since the animal is not in a position to go after nor to seek something else to complete the good of the body and the soul. For we are in need of pleasure only when we are in pain because of the absence of pleasure, and when we are not in pain, then we no longer need pleasure' (pp. 29–30).

Epicurus maintained a number of somewhat puzzling views about time. He seems in some passages to be saying that the duration of a pleasure is axiologically irrelevant. He appears to think that longer pleasures are no better in themselves than shorter ones (other things being equal). That would be an odd view, and certainly different from anything to be found in Default Hedonism, but it seems to be expressed in passages such as these, which I have taken from his 'Principal Doctrines':

PD18: 'As soon as the feeling of pain produced by want is removed, pleasure in the flesh will not increase but is only varied. But the limit of mental pleasures is produced by a reasoning out of these very pleasures [of the flesh] and of the things related to these, which used to cause the greatest fears in the intellect' (p. 33).

PD19: 'Unlimited time and limited time contain equal [amounts of pleasure], if one measures its limits by reasoning' (p. 33).

PD20: 'The flesh took the limits of pleasure to be unlimited, and [only] an unlimited time would have provided it. But the intellect, reasoning out the goal and limit of the flesh and dissolving the fears of eternity, provided us with the perfect way of life and had no further need of unlimited time. But it [the intellect] did not flee pleasure, and even when circumstances caused an exit from life it did not die as though it were lacking any aspect of the best life' (pp. 33–34).

PD21: 'He who has learned the limits of life knows that it is easy to provide that which removes the feeling of pain owing to want and make one's whole life perfect. So there is no need for things which involve struggle' (p. 34).

Epicurus evidently tried to convince his students that death—even early, untimely death—is not to be feared. This may help to explain why he claimed that duration of pleasure is irrelevant. Perhaps he wanted to ensure that his students would not fear early death out of a mistaken belief that early death would prevent them from cramming more value into their lives. Apparently in connection with this doctrine of the harmlessness of death, he seems to want to say that shorter lives are not necessarily less good. It appears that his view was that two lives could be equally pleasant, and therefore equally good for the ones who lived them, even though one was much longer than the other, and (loosely speaking) contained a greater gross amount of pleasure.

In addition to these relatively abstract views about pleasure and pain, Epicurus also endorsed a variety of more practical views. Some of these are expressed in aphoristic suggestions about how we ought to behave if we want to achieve the pleasant (and therefore good) life. Thus, for example, he encourages us to avoid spicy food and drink, and to retreat from the world. He thinks a life of quiet contemplation among like-minded friends will probably be the most pleasant. He is very sensitive to the dangers involved in choosing intense and immediate pleasures. He warns that these often prove to be more painful in the long run. His view of the pleasant life is therefore utterly different from that of Aristippus.

In a passage typical of this sort of thing, Epicurus says:

LM8: 'we do not choose every pleasure; but sometimes we pass up many pleasures when we get a larger amount of what is uncongenial from them. And we believe many pains to be better than pleasures when a greater pleasure follows for a long while if we endure the pains. So every pleasure is a good thing, since it has a nature congenial [to us] but not every one is to be chosen. Just as every pain too is a bad thing, but not every one is such as to be always avoided. It is, however, appropriate to make all these decisions by comparative measurement and an examination of the advantages and disadvantages. For at some times we treat the good thing as bad and, conversely, the bad thing as good' (p. 30).

Although there are other remarks that are relevant, these are typical of the main bits of allegedly direct evidence concerning Epicurean hedonism. These bits of evidence strongly suggest that Epicurean hedonism had certain distinctive features. It would be a good idea to keep these things in mind as we try to develop our formulation of Epicurean hedonism.

1. Our Epicurean hedonism will have to be a genuine form of *hedonism*. It will have to incorporate some version of the notion that pleasure is the Good. Associated with this is the view that pain is the Bad.
2. However, our formulation of Epicurean hedonism will have to respect his insistence that he is not advocating the life of "profligates and sensualists". We will have to avoid the idea that the good life is the life of "sex, drugs, and rock 'n' roll". Thus, we will want to avoid incorporating anything that would imply that ordinary sensual pleasures are the most desirable.
3. Instead of sensual pleasure, Epicureanism gives a central place to "static pleasure". We will have to try to give a clear account of the nature of this sort of pleasure, and we will have to formulate principles indicating values of various amounts of it. Furthermore, we will have to say something about the value of such pleasure as compared to the value of the more familiar "active" pleasure.
4. Finally, we will have to find some way to capture the Epicurean view that duration of pleasure does not matter; or does not matter as much as it does in Default Hedonism or other typical forms of hedonism.

I do not think it will be easy to formulate a complete and coherent axiology that incorporates all of the elements suggested in the above quotations. Some of them seem to rest uneasily together. Others are obscure or difficult to state coherently. Furthermore, the evidence is so sketchy that we will have to guess at what Epicurus might have said about a number of crucial elements. Thus, what follows is no more than a highly speculative proposal.

C.2. Static Pleasure

Since most of what is distinctive about Epicureanism is associated in one way or another with the doctrine of static pleasure, I turn to that first. In several passages (including some quoted earlier), Epicurus suggests a view about the nature of static pleasure. As I mentioned, one of these appears to be a definition. He says, 'By pleasure we mean the absence of pain in the body and disturbance in the soul' (LM6). Several other passages hint at a similar idea.

Commentators, focusing on these passages, typically say that Epicurus's view was that a person experiences static (or "katastematic", or "negative") pleasure at a time if and only if he does not suffer pain in body or mind at that time. They then proceed to claim that the Epicurean view was that such static pleasures are the most important pleasures a person can experience. Presumably, if we accepted this approach, we would attribute to Epicurus the notion that having lots of these static pleasures makes a life good in itself for the one who lives it.

This definition of static pleasure would make Epicureanism a very implausible view. In spite of the cited evidence, it is hard to imagine that Epicurus could have accepted it. As critics going back to ancient times have been quick to point out, it would imply, for example, that a dead person would be enjoying some of life's greatest goods. After all, such a person is not suffering any pain in body or mind. It is unlikely that Epicurus could have intended to say that such people are enjoying great goods, especially in virtue of the fact that he does not seem to think that being dead is any great good (though of course not a great evil, either). It also seems quite strange on the face of it to use the word 'pleasure' for such a state. Clearly, one can be in this state without feeling anything—more particularly, without feeling anything that would normally be called a pleasure, and without taking pleasure in anything.[2]

Additionally, there is the fact that Plato had discussed and decisively refuted the idea that pleasure can be defined as the absence of pain. In a well-known passage in the *Philebus*, Plato points out that someone may be located in any of three areas on the hedono-doloric spectrum: he can be enjoying pleasure; he can be suffering pain; or he can be in the neutral state where he feels neither pleasure nor pain.[3] A sleeping person, or a person in a coma, for example, might be said to be in the neutral state. Similarly, a person might be awake and fully conscious, yet find himself in a state in which he is neither suffering pain nor enjoying pleasure. Plato points out that these obvious and familiar facts about the neutral zone show that we cannot define pleasure as the absence of pain—for any such definition implies that anyone who is not suffering pain must therefore be enjoying pleasure. Indeed, if we defined static pleasure in this way, Epicureanism would then imply that anyone who is not suffering pain is enjoying a particularly valuable sort of pleasure. But this is wrong; the person might be in the neutral zone. I do not know whether Epicurus was familiar with the passage in Plato, but students and colleagues must have been aware of it, and the point seems so obvious in any case that it

---

[2] These objections are debated at some length in Book II of Cicero's *De Finibus*. The advocate of Epicureanism simply stands his ground, insisting that the objections fail. Further discussion together with a useful list of recent citations can be found in Stephen E. Rosenbaum's 'Epicurus on Pleasure and the Complete Life'.

[3] In this passage, Socrates is talking with Protarchus. They are discussing the idea that pleasure may be defined as the absence of pain. The conversation goes like this:

SOC. We may assume then that there are three lives, one pleasant, one painful, and the third which is neither; what say you?

PRO. I should say as you do that there are three of them.

SOC. But if so, the negation of pain will not be the same with pleasure.

PRO. Certainly not.

SOC. Then when you hear a person saying, that always to live without pain is the pleasantest of all things, what would you understand him to mean by that statement?

PRO. I think that by pleasure he must mean the negative of pain.

SOC. Let us take any three things; or suppose that we embellish a little and call the first gold, the second silver, and there shall be a third which is neither.

PRO. Very good.

SOC. Now, can that which is neither be either gold or silver?

PRO. Impossible.

SOC. No more can that neutral or middle life be rightly or reasonably spoken or thought of as pleasant or painful.

PRO. Certainly not.

is unlikely that he could have endorsed the definition often attributed to him and suggested in LM6.

Another possible interpretation would be this: we might say that a person enjoys static pleasure at a time if and only if he is alive and conscious at that time, but not suffering any pain. This is somewhat more plausible, but still strange. For one thing, a person in this state need not experience anything that would normally be called pleasure. He might be feeling nothing at all on the hedono-doloric spectrum. For another, if Epicurus were to say that such static pleasures are intrinsically good, then he would not really be a hedonist. He would be maintaining that something other than pleasure is intrinsically good. He would be maintaining that life without pain is intrinsically good (thus making him a "vitalist"), or that consciousness without pain is intrinsically good (thus making him a "consciousness axiologist").

Perhaps a better interpretation is possible. This interpretation depends essentially on the distinction between sensory pleasure and attitudinal pleasure. As I have explained these concepts, it is correct to say that a person has sensory pleasure at a time if he *feels pleasurable sensations* then, if he experiences the sensation of pleasure then, etc. On the other hand, a person has attitudinal pleasure at a time if he *takes pleasure in* some fact at that time, is pleased about something then, finds something pleasant.

Appeal to the concept of attitudinal pleasure opens the door to yet another interpretation of Epicurus's doctrine of static pleasures. We can say that a person enjoys static pleasure at a time if and only if he takes attitudinal pleasure at that time in the fact that he is not feeling pain or disturbance then.[4] This is to be understood in such a way as to entail that the person is in fact not feeling pain or disturbance then. A static pleasure, then, would be an event that consists in someone's taking attitudinal pleasure at a time in the fact that he himself is then feeling no pain or disturbance. Such a static pleasure could have a duration and an intensity. The duration of a static pleasure would be the length of time that the person goes on being pleased about the fact that he is not suffering pain. The intensity of a static pleasure would be the strength of the attitudinal pleasure the person takes in the fact that he is not suffering pain. Clearly, one person could be more pleased about the fact that he is not feeling pain than another person is in the fact that she is not feeling pain. Perhaps, though his extant words do not explicitly express this idea, Epicurus thought of static pleasure in something like this way.[5]

---

[4] For an extended, detailed discussion of this interpretation of static pleasure, see Clay Splawn, 'Updating Epicurus's Concept of Katastematic Pleasure'.

[5] It is interesting to note that something very like this idea might be expressed by Rist when he says that the Epicurean view was that 'when the body is enjoying complete absence of pain, it is already enjoying the greatest pleasure'. The problem here is that Rist never says anything to explain what he might mean by 'enjoying'. In all the associated passages he seems to mean to attribute to Epicurus the more standard view that a person experiences the greatest pleasure when he is simply not feeling any pain—without the further claim that he must *enjoy* the absence of pain. See Rist, *Epicurus, An Introduction*, p. 106.

This way of understanding static pleasure has a number of attractive features:

i. It leaves open the possibility that Epicureanism is a genuine form of hedonism, though not of the sensualist form. For on this view, static pleasures are genuinely pleasures, but not sensory ones. They are attitudinal pleasures taken in a specific sort of object—one's own lack of pain. So if Epicureanism is understood to incorporate the view that static pleasure is one of life's greatest goods, it may yet be a form of (attitudinal) hedonism.

ii. If we understand static pleasure in this way, Epicurean hedonism will not have the absurd implication that a dead person, or a comatose person, or a person in a painless trance who does not notice that he is in such a state, is enjoying one of life's greatest goods.

iii. The view admittedly is not entirely consistent with everything Epicurus says, but it is consistent with, and even sheds light upon, several of the remarks quoted above.

Epicurus clearly thinks that not all pleasures are static. He recognizes a more familiar sort of sensory pleasure, and he seems to think of sensory pleasures as involving some sort of "motion" of the atoms of the nervous system. Let us then say, by contrast, that a person enjoys *active pleasure* at a time if and only if he experiences sensory pleasure at that time. It is clear that Epicurus thought that active pleasures are good in themselves; but it is also clear that he thought that they are not as good as static pleasures. He suggests in several places that if a person has static pleasure, there is no further advantage to him in having any active pleasures. Furthermore, he sometimes suggests that ordinary active pleasures often lead to subsequent pains. On balance, then, such pain-inducing pleasures would not be worthy of choice. In spite of their positive intrinsic value, they have a negative overall value.

C.3. The Formulation of Epicurean Hedonism

We have seen evidence that suggests that Epicurus thought that all pleasures are intrinsically good, and we have seen further evidence that he thought that static pleasures are the greatest of intrinsic goods. He also thought that all pains are intrinsically bad. So far as I know, he never introduced any concept of "static pain" (which, by parity of definition, would be pain taken in the fact that one does not feel pleasure in the body or mind). Accordingly, we can take this as the first component of Epicurean Hedonism:

i. *Every episode of pleasure (active or static) is intrinsically good; every episode of pain is intrinsically bad.*

In this respect, Epicurean Hedonism is not very different from several of the forms of hedonism we have already discussed. It is like Default Hedonism in declaring every episode of active (sensory) pleasure to be intrinsically good. It is like Attitudinal Hedonism in declaring certain forms of attitudinal pleasure to be intrinsically good. It is like many forms of hedonism in declaring episodes of pain to be intrinsically bad. The important differences will arise when we turn to principles about the evaluation of pleasures and pains.

So far as I know, Epicurus does not say much about the importance of intensity and duration to the intrinsic values of active pleasures. This opens the door to lots of possibilities. In the absence of any firm evidence, I think it is permissible to say that the intrinsic value of an active pleasure is determined (as it is in Default Hedonism) by the intensity and duration of that active pleasure. It would be consistent with this to suppose that Epicurus also thought that the intrinsic value of a pain is determined in the familiar way by intensity and duration. We can make use of the concepts of the hedon and the dolor (introduced above in Chapter 2) in order to simplify our formulation.

In light of these assumptions, we can add a standard view about the evaluation of active pleasure and pain to our formulation of Epicurean Hedonism:

ii. The intrinsic value of an episode of active pleasure is equal to the number of hedons of pleasure it contains; the intrinsic value of an episode of active pain is equal to − (the number of dolors of pain it contains).

The evaluation of static pleasures is not so simple. Earlier I quoted several passages from the 'Principal Doctrines' that suggest that Epicurus thought that bigger static pleasures are no better in themselves than smaller ones— that when it comes to the evaluation of static pleasures, duration and intensity are simply irrelevant. (I allude here especially to the remark at PD18 where he says that 'As soon as the feeling of pain produced by want is removed, pleasure in the flesh will not increase but is only varied' and the remark at PD19 where he says that 'Unlimited time and limited time contain equal [amounts of pleasure], if one measures its limits by reasoning'.) I take these remarks to mean that if you genuinely do take pleasure in the fact that you are free of pain, then this episode of static pleasure is maximally good. It would be no better if it lasted for a month or a year. To take pleasure in the fact that you are free from pain for an instant is just as good as to take pleasure in the fact that you are free from pain throughout a limitless period of time. Similarly, although I am aware of no evidence to support this assumption, let us assume that intensity of static pleasure is also irrelevant—taking mild pleasure in the fact that you are not in pain is therefore just as valuable as taking intense pleasure in the fact that you are not in pain. We thus treat intensity and duration of static pleasure in the same way. Neither of them makes any difference to the intrinsic value of an episode of static pleasure. If these assumptions about duration and intensity are right, then we can add this to our statement of Epicurean Hedonism:

iii. Every episode of static pleasure is just as intrinsically good as every other episode of static pleasure.

The more interesting question concerns the relative intrinsic values of active and static pleasures. Again, I think the text is indeterminate.

Nevertheless, it is pretty clear that Epicurus wanted to give static pleasure a preeminent place in his axiology. He apparently claims (in LM7) that if you are enjoying static pleasure, you have no need of active pleasure. The addition of active pleasures in such a situation would not mark any improvement. We could therefore attribute to him the view that static pleasures are "lexically better than" active ones. In other words:

iv. Any episode of static pleasure (no matter how small) is intrinsically better than any episode of active pleasure (no matter how big).

So much for the fundamentals. I am interpreting Epicurean Hedonism in such a way that all the "atoms" of intrinsic value are episodes of pleasure and pain. I am also interpreting this view in such a way that active pleasures and pains are evaluated just as Default Hedonism evaluates them. In addition to these familiar themes, I have introduced a proposed interpretation of static pleasure, and I have added clauses indicating that episodes of static pleasure are equally valuable and lexically more valuable than episodes of active pleasure.

Now we have to introduce some principles concerning the evaluation of lives. Without such principles, the theory fails to constitute any view about our central topic—the Good Life. Earlier, when I stated Default Hedonism, I incorporated this aggregative clause:

iii. The intrinsic value of a life is entirely determined by the intrinsic values of the episodes of pleasure and pain contained in that life, in such a way that one life is intrinsically better than another if and only if the net amount of pleasure in the one is greater than the net amount of pleasure in the other.

It should be clear that we cannot make use of anything as simple as this in our formulation of Epicurean Hedonism. One problem is that we need to respect the idea that static pleasures are lexically better than active ones. Presumably a life containing some static pleasure should be ranked higher than any life containing only active pleasure, even if it contains a huge amount of active pleasure. Another, and perhaps even more troubling, feature of Epicureanism concerns duration. Epicurus says (p. 29) that a wise man does not seek a longer life, but a more pleasant one. He also says that a person who calculates the value of his life properly has no need of infinite time (pp. 33–4). My impression from all this is that Epicurus would say that the best life is one that contains an unbroken stream of static pleasure (and, obviously, no pain). My hunch is that he would say that such a life is maximally intrinsically good, no matter how long it lasts and no matter how much active pleasure it contains. Let us say that such a life is "purely statically pleasant". Such lives will count as the best possible. I doubt that any normal human being has much of a chance of leading a purely statically pleasant life.

Some of us lead lives containing some static pleasure, some active pleasure, and some pain. How are these to be ranked?

Epicurus says that 'when we are not in pain, then we no longer need pleasure' (LM7). I take this to be a remark about *active* pleasure; I take him to mean that when we do not feel any pain, we do not need any counterbalancing *active* pleasure—since we will then be able to enjoy the far more valuable *static* pleasure. I also suspect that the Epicurean view was that if a person has already suffered some pain, then he can improve his life, and make it "complete and perfect." This suggests that if a person has been feeling pain, then he can make the best of a second-class life by taking up a life of Epicureanism, banishing all unnecessary desires, and ending his life with a period of static pleasure. Let us say that a life is "terminally statically pleasant" if it ends with a period (of any length) of static pleasure. I do not know what Epicurus would say about such lives, but one natural thought is that it would be best to have a purely statically pleasant life; but if that is impossible, then the next best sort of life would be terminally statically pleasant. Furthermore, it would be natural to suppose that any terminally statically pleasant life would be better than any life that either contained no static pleasure at all, or that contained such pleasure but had it "spoiled" by being followed by a period of time in which the person was in pain, or was no longer pleased not to be in pain. Let us call such lives "temporarily statically pleasant". Such lives are third-best.

Suppose a person never enjoys any static pleasure. This might happen if he were never free of pain. It might also happen even if he were free of pain during some periods, but failed to notice or appreciate his painlessness. Then, it seems to me, the Epicurean would say that his life falls into a lower category. I propose that we evaluate all such lives just as Default Hedonism would evaluate them—so that one life in this category is deemed better than another if and only if it contains greater net (active) pleasure.

In order to incorporate all of these speculations, I propose to add the following principle about the evaluation of lives to Epicurean Hedonism:

v. The intrinsic value of a life is entirely determined by the intrinsic values of the episodes of pleasure and pain contained in that life, in such a way that (a) the best lives are purely statically pleasant; (b) the second-best lives are terminally statically pleasant; (c) the third-best lives are temporarily statically pleasant; and (d) of the remaining lives containing no static pleasure, each is less valuable than any life in group (a), (b), or (c), and one is intrinsically better than another if and only if the net amount of active pleasure in the one is greater than the net amount of active pleasure in the other.

I therefore am proposing that Epicurean Hedonism be understood to be the conjunction of principles (i)–(v). So understood, it is clearly a form of hedonism, since it is based on the idea that all the "atoms" of intrinsic value are episodes of pleasure and pain. It is also a form of universal hedonism, since it incorporates the notion that every episode of pleasure—active or static—is intrinsically good. Since nothing other than pleasure and pain affects the intrinsic value of a person's life, Epicurean Hedonism is also a form of pure hedonism. However, in spite of these similarities, it is clearly not equivalent to Default or Aristippean Hedonism. Nor is it equivalent to any other form of hedonism discussed in this book. No other form of hedonism discussed here makes such dramatic use of the concept of static pleasure, and no other form of hedonism is so cavalier about duration.

C.4. A Vision of the Good Life according to Epicurean Hedonism

So far I have been discussing the more abstract and theoretical aspects of a possible interpretation of the Epicurean view. But Epicurus's vision of the Good Life is richer than this. He also had detailed views about what sort of behavior would, given the actual circumstances of real people in the world, likely conduce to a good life. It seems to me that we get a clearer notion of Epicureanism if we take a look at some of these bits of practical guidance. Let us then briefly turn to some concrete elements of the Epicurean vision of the Good Life. While this sketch is intended to describe a pleasant life, it should be obvious that the life sketched is very different from the sort of life that Aristippus would describe as pleasant.

Epicurus thought that fear of the gods is a major source of unnecessary pain. People worry far too much about whether they will be punished or injured by the gods. So long as such fear is present, static pleasure is impossible. So Epicurus encouraged his followers to believe in the gods, but at the same time to realize that they do not interfere in human affairs.[6] A person living the Good Life, therefore, would not be terrorized by fear of the gods.

Epicurus thought that the fear of early death is another great source of unnecessary pain. He encouraged his students to grow accustomed to the fact that "death is nothing to us". He presented arguments intended to eradicate the terror of death. So if a person is to have a good life according to the Epicurean vision, he must have no fear of death. If he considers his impending death at all, he does so with complete equanimity.

It is natural for people to be worried about the pains that typically accompany illness. Perhaps in an effort to enable his students to overcome this fear, Epicurus claimed that such illnesses are usually of short duration. The pain will soon be gone. If one eats and drinks moderately, one is less likely to become ill in the first place. So Epicurus encouraged his students to be careful about their diets. Again, the aim seems to have been to enable his students to remain in, or to return as soon as possible to, a state of static pleasure. So an individual living the Good Life according to Epicurus will rarely be sick, and when he is sick, he will not be sick for long. He will never suffer any needless worries about illness.

If a person is leading the Good Life according to Epicureanism, he will have eliminated all unnecessary and unnatural desires. He will not long for luxuries. His desires will be for necessary goods such as healthful food and drink. These desires will be easily satisfied.

Epicurus encouraged his students to retire from the world and to live in small communities of like-minded people. The pleasures of communal living with dear friends make for a tranquil and happy life. Among the most important

---

[6] This idea is discussed at length in Cicero's *De natura deorum*. A brief hint of it appears in the first of the 'Principal Doctrines' in which Epicurus is quoted as saying, 'A blessed and indestructible being has no trouble himself and brings no trouble upon any other being; so he is free from anger and partiality, for all such things imply weakness.'

considerations is that one must be "just". If a person behaves in an unjust way, he will always be worrying about being found out or being punished. Such a person can never enjoy complete peace of mind.

So the life of pleasure takes on a new form in the thought of Epicurus. While we would clearly go wrong if we said that the Epicurean principle is that the Good Life is essentially the life of tranquillity, we must also recognize that to an outsider it might look like a life of tranquillity. The crucial fact here, however, is that the tranquillity is not seen as an end in itself. Mere absence of pain is not good. What makes the life so good according to Epicurus (as I have interpreted him) is a hedonic factor: the one living the life takes pleasure in the fact that he is not suffering any pain. It is this static pleasure that makes the tranquil life so outstanding, according to the Epicurean vision. Thus I think it would be more proper to say that Epicurus agreed with other hedonists that the Good Life is the pleasant life. It's just that he had a peculiar view about what sort of pleasure is best.

C.5. Why I Find Epicurean Hedonism Implausible

Epicurean Hedonism (at least when interpreted as I have interpreted it here) seems to me to be seriously implausible. Quite a lot of the implausibility arises in connection with the concept of static pleasure. While I am prepared to agree that static pleasure deserves a place in a hedonistic axiology, I am not prepared to say that it deserves to be assigned a value so great as to be worth more than any amount of active pleasure.

A concrete example may help to clarify my objection. The example involves two possible lives. The first life starts out badly. The person—we can call her 'Big Dolores'—suffers unremitting pain for 99 years, 11 months, and 29 days. Let us agree that the pain is severe. Let us agree also that this poor soul enjoys no compensating active pleasure during this long, miserable period. Then, on her final day, a miracle occurs. The pain suddenly vanishes. She spends her final day thoroughly enjoying her painless state. Then she dies. Note that this life ends with a period of static pleasure. That makes it a terminally statically pleasant life. And that, according to item (v) of Epicurean Hedonism, makes the life of Big Dolores a very good life indeed.

The second life also contains considerable pain. However, the pain in this case is very mild—almost negligible in intensity. It goes on for 100 years. The person who suffers this pain—we can call her 'Little Dolores'—in addition enjoys tremendous amounts of active pleasure at all times. Her hedono-doloric balance is always large and positive, though she always has at least a tiny pain. Since she is never entirely free of pain, she never has an opportunity to enjoy static pleasure.

The contrast between the life of Big Dolores and the life of Little Dolores is stark: Big Dolores has an overwhelmingly painful life that ends with a brief moment of static pleasure. Little Dolores has an overwhelmingly pleasant life that (unfortunately) is permanently marred by the presence of a tiny pain.

She never enjoys any static pleasure. Epicurean Hedonism implies that the life of Big Dolores is the better of the two—indeed, that it is so much better that there is no mathematical way of representing the amount by which its value exceeds the value of the life of Little Dolores.[7] This seems to me to get things exactly wrong. No matter how good a tiny blast of static pleasure may be, surely there must be some amount of active pleasure that would be equally good. Surely it would be reasonable to forgo a tiny bit of static pleasure in exchange for a lifetime of active pleasure. But if we accept lexicality, we must deny these very plausible claims.

Another source of implausibility in Epicureanism is to be found in his attitude toward time. As I indicated above, Epicurus insisted in several passages that duration is axiologically irrelevant. This view (whether authentically Epicurean) creates trouble.[8] Recall the life of Big Dolores. It starts with a more than 99-year-long period of unbroken pain, and ends with a one-day period of static pleasure. Compare that life to a second life that starts with a very brief period of pain—one that lasts just one day—and then concludes with a more than 99-year blast of unbroken static pleasure. Both lives are terminally statically pleasant. They differ in durations. In the life of Big Dolores, the period of static pleasure is very short. In the second life, it is very long.

In an effort to do justice to Epicurus's insistence that longer duration of static pleasure does not matter (as indicated in passages PD18–20 quoted above), I have formulated my interpretation of his theory in such a way as to ensure that all terminally statically pleasant lives are equally and outstandingly good. I took it that Epicurus wanted to defend this view in part because he did not want his students to fear early death. If a terminally statically pleasant life were less valuable merely because the period of static pleasure were shorter, then one could very well prefer a life containing a longer terminal period. In that case, one could fear early death. It might rob him of the better life. In order to be consistent with the Epicurean remarks about duration, I have formulated the doctrine in such a way as to imply that such lives would be of equal value. However, as the example is designed to show, lives with shorter terminal periods in fact do seem to be less good. Surely if a loving parent were given the opportunity to select a life for her child, she would choose the life with the shorter period of pain and the longer period of static pleasure. Contrary to Epicureanism (as formulated here), it would be the better life.

It might seem that we could retain what is distinctive about Epicureanism while watering down the offensive elements. We could eliminate the requirement of lexicality. We could say instead that each episode of static pleasure is

---

[7] Some philosophers would describe this situation by saying that the life of A is "incomparably" better than the life of B. That seems very odd to me. For if we can say that the life of B is better than the life of A, then we can compare them. One is better than the other. As James Griffin points out in *Well-Being*, it would be preferable to describe such cases by saying that the life of A is "incommensurably" better than the life of B.

[8] Objections concerning duration can be found in the critical literature going back all the way to Cicero. He raises objections of this sort in *De Finibus II*.

just *much more valuable than* corresponding episodes of active pleasure. We could also formulate the theory in such a way that longer durations of static pleasure would be more valuable than shorter ones. These alterations would require a certain amount of reorganization of the doctrine.

In connection with the formulation of Intrinsic Attitudinal Hedonism, I introduced the notion of an "amount" of attitudinal pleasure. I said that the amount of pleasure in an episode of attitudinal pleasure is based on the intensity and duration of that pleasure. When we speak of intensity in this context, we must not think of the intensity of any feeling. Attitudinal pleasure is an attitude, not a feeling.

Since static pleasure is attitudinal pleasure taken in the fact that one is not in pain, we can readily transfer this approach to the measurement of static pleasure. We can say that the amount of static pleasure in an episode of static pleasure is the product of intensity (of attitude) and duration. This implies that one episode of static pleasure contains a greater amount of static pleasure than another if the subject of the first episode is more pleased to be feeling no pain, or if he continues for a longer period of time to be pleased about feeling no pain.

In order to retain some element of the Epicurean doctrine of the outstanding value of static pleasure, we can say that attitudinal pleasure is always good in itself; but when such pleasure is taken in the fact that one is not suffering pain in the body or disturbance in the soul, then it is of especially great value. In ordinary cases the intrinsic value of an episode of attitudinal pleasure is equal to the amount of pleasure contained in that episode. Although the selection of the number is entirely arbitrary, let us say that the intrinsic value of an episode of attitudinal pleasure is *ten times* the amount of the pleasure when it is pleasure taken in the fact that one is not in pain. That means, in effect, that static pleasure is ten times more valuable than other sorts of attitudinal pleasure.

In Appendix B I introduced the idea that a person experiences sensory pleasure (pain) at a time if and only if he takes attitudinal pleasure in the fact that he is experiencing some feeling. If we make use of this idea we can eliminate all explicit talk of sensory pleasure from our formulation of Epicureanism. We can focus exclusively on attitudinal pleasure. The axiological impact of sensory pleasures (and pains) will not be lost, since they will in effect be counted when we count attitudinal pleasures (and pains) taken in one's own feelings.

Making use of these suggestions, we reach this revised formulation of the Epicurean view:

Semi-Epicurean Hedonism

i. *Every episode of attitudinal pleasure is intrinsically good; every episode of attitudinal pain is intrinsically bad.*

ii. *The intrinsic value of an episode of attitudinal pleasure is equal to the amount of pleasure it contains, except in the case of attitudinal pleasure taken in the fact that one is not suffering any pain (=static pleasure).*

The intrinsic value of an episode of attitudinal pain is equal to the amount of pain it contains.

   iii. The intrinsic value of an episode of attitudinal pleasure taken in the fact that one is not suffering pain (= static pleasure) is equal to ten times the amount of pleasure contained in that episode.

   iv. The intrinsic value of a life is equal to the sum of the intrinsic values of the episodes of attitudinal pleasure and pain contained in that life.

The resulting theory may evade the objections we have considered. The first objection, based upon the lives of Big Dolores and Little Dolores, seems to be ineffective against Semi-Epicurean Hedonism. It could be claimed that the huge amount of pain in Big Dolores's life is so great that its disvalue more than counterbalances the value of the last day's static pleasure, even when that pleasure is evaluated at ten times the rate of ordinary attitudinal pleasure. As a result, the total intrinsic value of her life for her, as calculated by Semi-Epicurean Hedonism, is less than the total intrinsic value of Little Dolores's life.

Similarly, we can claim to get more palatable results in the second case mentioned above. For the long (99-year) period of static pleasure in the second life is much more valuable according to Semi-Epicurean Hedonism than the short (one-day) period of static pleasure in the first life.

Semi-Epicurean Hedonism is thus slightly more plausible than Epicurean Hedonism. Nevertheless, I find Semi-Epicurean Hedonism to be an unattractive doctrine. It is formulated largely to capture the Epicurean notion that static pleasure is extra valuable. It gives this form of attitudinal pleasure ten times the value of otherwise similar attitudinal pleasures taken in objects other than one's own painlessness. But this strikes me as being dubious. The trouble can be seen by considering another pair of lives.

Imagine a man—we can call him 'Staticus'—who is fortunate enough to lead a truly blessed life. He lives 100 years and never suffers any pain at all. For quite a few years he notices that he is suffering no pain, and he takes attitudinal pleasure in this fact about himself. Thus, he has a substantial amount of static pleasure. I stipulate that he never takes attitudinal pleasure in anything other than (a) certain of his bodily sensations (these are his sensory pleasures) and (b) the fact that he is not feeling any pain. Semi-Epicurean Hedonism implies that Staticus leads a very good life. I have no quarrel with that.

Now consider a second man—'Atticus'. Atticus also leads a truly blessed life. He also lives 100 years and never suffers any pain at all. However, Atticus is so busy enjoying various other things that he never notices that he is suffering no pain. Thus, he takes no pleasure in the fact that he is feeling no pain. Instead, he takes attitudinal pleasure in many other things, including the fact that he has quite a bit of interesting knowledge, the fact that he sees many beautiful objects, the fact that he has so many good friends, the fact that there is peace in the world, etc. I stipulate that the amount of attitudinal pleasure that Atticus takes in this variety of objects is exactly equal to the amount of attitudinal pleasure that Staticus takes in the fact that he is feeling no pain. In addition, Atticus also takes pleasure in certain of his bodily sensations, exactly as Staticus does.

Atticus and Staticus are exactly alike with respect to pain: neither ever feels any. They are also alike with respect to attitudinal pleasure. They experience exactly the same amount of that, too. In each case, a certain amount of the attitudinal pleasure is taken in the fact that the subject is experiencing certain bodily sensations. That component of attitudinal pleasure plays the role of sensory pleasure in the two lives. The amounts are equal. They differ with respect to the remaining attitudinal pleasure. Staticus steadily takes pleasure in one object—the fact that he is feeling no pain. Thus, he gets a lot of static pleasure. Atticus never takes pleasure in the fact that he is feeling no pain. Instead, he takes an equal amount of attitudinal pleasure in a variety of other objects, including knowledge, beauty, friendship, and peace.

Semi-Epicurean Hedonism implies that the life of Staticus is many times better for him than the life of Atticus is for him. The difference is due to the fact that Staticus enjoys a lot of static pleasure while Atticus enjoys none. The static pleasure is assigned ten times the value of the attitudinal pleasure taken in other objects. This result seems to me to be implausible. While I recognize that static pleasure is a great good, and I agree that the life of Staticus is a good one, I cannot accept the notion that his life is significantly better than the life of Atticus. Atticus suffers no pain; he feels many sensory pleasures; he takes attitudinal pleasure in many things. The total amounts of attitudinal pleasure that the two enjoy are the same. It seems to me that their lives are of equal value. Some might even say that the life of Atticus is the better life, since it contains attitudinal pleasures taken in a much wider and more diverse array of objects.

Skeptical readers may reluctantly agree that these objections succeed, but they may feel that the objections succeed only because I have misrepresented the hedonism of Epicurus. They may think that if I had formulated the view more accurately, or more charitably, it would not have been so easily dismissed. I must admit that this objection could be right. Perhaps I have misunderstood Epicureanism.

However, I do feel confident that any accurate formulation of Epicurean Hedonism must be consistent with the four points I mentioned near the outset. It must be a form of hedonism—it has to imply that the atoms of value are episodes of pleasure and pain; it must not be equivalent to Aristippean Hedonism, or any sort of hedonism that implies that the life of sensual indulgence is the Good Life; it must assign a place of special importance to static pleasure, which in turn must have something to do with "the absence of pain in the body and trouble in the mind"; and it must not place too great a premium on longer duration of pleasures or lives. I am inclined to fear that any statement of Epicureanism consistent with these points would be open to objections like the ones I have stated.

CHAPTER 5

———

Replies to Some Objections

Earlier, in Chapter 3, I presented a catalogue of classic objections to hedonism. The catalogue contained seven items:

1. The Argument from Worthless Pleasures (Moore's bestiality argument)
2. The Argument from False Pleasures (the deceived businessman argument)
3. The Argument from Unconscious Pleasures (Plato's oyster argument)
4. Brentano's Cigar
5. The Argument from Nonexistent Pleasures (the Stoicus argument)
6. Moore's Heap of Filth
7. The Argument from Undeserved Pleasures (Ross's "Two Worlds" Argument)

I suggested there that some of those objections might constitute serious problems for traditional forms of sensory hedonism, such as our Default Hedonism or perhaps for Aristippean Hedonism. Then in Chapter 4, when I introduced Intrinsic Attitudinal Hedonism, I claimed that that theory would not be refuted by objection 5. I pointed out that even though Stoicus never feels any sensory pleasure, he does enjoy quite a lot of attitudinal pleasure. This might serve to explain our sense (if we have it) that his is not such a bad life after all. I also suggested in Chapter 4 that a variant form of IAH—one that I dubbed 'Altitude-Adjusted Intrinsic Attitudinal Hedonism'—might avoid the objection based on worthless or base pleasures. This theory was intended to be a coherent form of attitudinal hedonism that produces results relevantly like the ones Mill may have been seeking when he formulated his qualified hedonism. I did not mean to express any great enthusiasm for AAIAH. It seems to me to depend upon some fairly dicey assumptions.

My aim in this chapter is to reevaluate several of these objections in the light of IAH. While acknowledging that the objections might refute DH or AH or other forms of sensory hedonism, I will be trying to show that IAH might be less vulnerable. In the process, I will introduce some further refinements. The most important refinement, and the theory closest to my heart, is what I call 'Desert-Adjusted Intrinsic Attitudinal Hedonism'. It appears below in section 5.3. Let's start here with the deceived businessman argument.

5.1. *False Pleasures: A Problem for IAH?*

A number of philosophers (Nozick, Nagel, Kagan, etc.) have drawn attention to the phenomenon of "false pleasures". Perhaps the most well-known example concerns Nozick's "experience machine", though it is not clear that Nozick appealed to the experience machine in an effort to present an argument against hedonism.[1] Nagel's deceived businessman is also familiar. He enjoys many pleasures, but each is somehow predicated on some mistaken belief. For example, he enjoys the pleasures of family life, but his wife and children secretly despise him; he enjoys the companionship of his business colleagues, but they also misrepresent their attitudes. It is stipulated that the businessman would be miserable if he knew the truth about these matters.[2]

Since my aim is to defend a form of attitudinal hedonism, let us be sure to understand the case appropriately for present purposes. Let us stipulate that the businessman takes intrinsic attitudinal pleasure in many states of affairs, taking them all to be true. But they are all false. So, for example, this businessman is intrinsically pleased that he is respected by his colleagues, but in fact he is not respected by his colleagues. He is intrinsically pleased that he is loved by his children, but in fact he is not loved by his children, and so on. Let us agree that the businessman's mistake is crucial to his enjoyment. If he knew that these objects were false, he would not take pleasure in them.

The objection, as modified to apply to IAH, can take a number of forms. In one form we start by pointing out that IAH implies that the businessman's life is good in itself for him, yet none of us would want such a life; none of us would wish such a life for our loved ones; such a life is not easily thought to be ideal (as Kagan said). This suggests that IAH yields an incorrect evaluation of the businessman's life.

---

[1] Nozick, *Anarchy, State and Utopia*, 42–5.
[2] Thomas Nagel, 'Death', in *Mortal Questions*, 4.

It rates the businessman's life as being better in itself for him than it really is. Another version of the argument would invoke two businessmen. The first is the familiar deceived businessman. The second is his cousin, the undeceived businessman. The cousin takes pleasure in things just like the ones the first businessman enjoys: his colleagues' respect, the love of his wife and children, etc. We stipulate, however, that the second businessman is not deceived. The objects of his pleasure are all precisely as he takes them to be. IAH implies that the two lives are of equal value. This may seem unacceptable. It may seem that the life of the undeceived businessman is better than the life of his deceived cousin. If so, IAH is refuted.

As I mentioned earlier, it is not entirely clear that the objection succeeds in the first place. Perhaps the life of the deceived businessman is not so bad after all. Perhaps we can explain away our sense that something is amiss in the businessman's life by pointing out that we would not like to be deceived, and we would be pained to learn that our colleagues and family have been holding us in contempt for all these years. This helps to explain the fact that none of us would voluntarily choose the life of the deceived businessman. But that is because we know things about his life that he does not know. Since we know these things, we would not enjoy the experiences he enjoys. Hence, his life seems unattractive to us. But since he is in blissful ignorance, he does enjoy those things. His life is happy. Indeed, it is stipulated that he is just as happy as his cousin.

This may be another instance in which we have performed our thought experiment improperly. We were supposed to consider whether we would want to swap lives with the deceived businessman. Perhaps we imagined being surrounded by deceitful colleagues and family members. Perhaps we imagined being the butt of jokes and lies. Perhaps we imagined overhearing a vicious whispered conversation among colleagues at the water cooler. It seemed gruesome. We would not enjoy living a life like that. But if we engaged in that sort of imagining, our imaginings have no relevance to the case we are supposed to be considering. Instead of imagining the life of the deceived businessman, we were imagining a life that is a sort of hybrid between the businessman's life in his possible world and our life here in the real world. For we were taking bits of knowledge that we have here in the real world and grafting them onto the deceived businessman. If we imagine ourselves being unhappy as we live the life of the deceived businessman, then we are not imagining his life correctly. He is stipulated to be happy. His life contains no such moments of unhappiness.

Hence, it is not entirely clear that hedonism's implications for this case are indefensible. Perhaps considerations such as these help to explain away our intuitive sense that his life is not all a life could be.

But now that we have clearly distinguished attitudinal hedonism from sensory hedonism, certain previously unavailable options become more obvious. We can move to higher ground. We can take advantage of a feature provided by the attitudinal axiology. As in IAH, we can say that the fundamental goods are takings of intrinsic attitudinal pleasure in various states of affairs, but we can modify this by saying that such takings of pleasure enhance the value of a life more when they are takings of pleasure in *true* states of affairs. This single modification yields a view according to which the life of the deceived businessman is much less good in itself for him, even if internally indiscernible from the life of his cousin, the undeceived businessman, whose mental life feels to him just like his cousin's feels to his cousin, but whose family and colleagues are in reality as they appear to him to be.

In order to state this modified version of the theory, we will need to say something about pain, too. Shall we say that pain taken in *true* objects differs in intrinsic value from similar pain taken in *false* objects? I am puzzled by an apparent disanalogy between pleasure and pain here. On the one hand, I can readily sense the attractiveness of adjusting the value of pleasures for truth. Pleasure taken in things that are true does seem somehow better than equal pleasure taken in things that are false. Suppose the businessman is intrinsically pleased that his colleagues respect him. It is better if they in fact do respect him. But, on the other hand, I cannot so readily see the corresponding attractiveness of a similar adjustment of the value of pains for truth.

Suppose another businessman is unhappy about his personal relationships with his colleagues. He thinks they have contempt for him. This pains him. More exactly, he takes intrinsic attitudinal pain in the "fact" that his colleagues have contempt for him. As it happens, they do not have contempt for him. In fact, they respect him. It is all just a figment of his imagination. My puzzlement is this: I find that I have no clear intuitions concerning the impact of the falsity of the object of the businessman's pain. Is his pain made worse by the fact that it is pain taken in something that is not true? Or is it made better? Or perhaps the axiological value of his pain is unaffected by the truth-value of its object.

Consider a case in which I am pained by something that is independently evil. Suppose I have been told about the plight of some starving children in Somalia. Suppose I am a sympathetic person, and this information makes me sad. I am intrinsically pained that the children of Somalia are suffering. What difference does it make if the object of my belief is false? Is my pain worse if in fact there are no suffering children in Somalia? Or is it better? Or does the existence of the suffering children make no difference to the intrinsic value of my intrinsic attitudinal pain?[3] I simply don't know what to say.

In light of this difficulty, I will formulate the theory on the assumption that the truth value of objects has no impact in the intrinsic value of pains. I will leave that unadjusted. However, I do want to adjust the values of pleasures for truth. Let us say that the "truth-adjusted" amount of intrinsic attitudinal pleasure in an episode of intrinsic attitudinal pleasure is determined in this way: first find the intensity and duration of the pleasure in that episode. Then multiply to get the "raw amount" of intrinsic attitudinal pleasure. If the pleasure is taken in a true object, multiply by 1. If the pleasure is taken in a false object, multiply by 0.1. The result is the *truth-adjusted amount* of intrinsic attitudinal pleasure in that episode. I let the value of a pleasure depend upon the truth-adjusted amount of pleasure it contains. I make no similar adjustment in the value of an episode of intrinsic attitudinal pain. As before, it is straightforwardly determined by the raw amount of pain, and this is determined by intensity and duration. As a result, the theory has a sort of asymmetry. It goes like this:

Truth-Adjusted Intrinsic Attitudinal Hedonism

i. Every episode of intrinsic attitudinal pleasure is intrinsically good; every episode of intrinsic attitudinal pain is intrinsically bad.

ii. The intrinsic value of an episode of intrinsic attitudinal pleasure is equal to the truth-adjusted amount of pleasure contained in that episode; the intrinsic value of an episode of pain is equal to − (the amount of pain contained in that episode).

iii. The intrinsic value of a life is entirely determined by the intrinsic values of the episodes of intrinsic attitudinal pleasure and pain contained in that life, in such a way that one life is intrinsically better than another if and only if the net truth-adjusted amount of intrinsic attitudinal pleasure in the one is greater than the net truth-adjusted amount of that sort of pleasure in the other.

The resulting theory is a form of pure and universal hedonism. It implies (in light of clause (i)) that every episode of intrinsic attitudinal pleasure is good in itself. It also implies (in light of (iii)) that nothing other than such pleasure plays a direct role in increasing the intrinsic value of a life. Of course, this theory also implies that pleasure taken in

---

[3] Of course, the situation in the world as a whole is overall worse if the children are actually suffering. That's because their suffering is bad in itself. The question here is not about this overall value. It is a question about the intrinsic value of my attitudinal pain. My point is that it is hard to dredge up any clear intuitions about the axiological effect of truth in this sort of case.

true objects is ten times better in itself than otherwise similar pleasure taken in false objects.

Someone might think that TAIAH is not a form of hedonism. They might think this because they think it is a form of pluralism, and they think that if a theory is a form of pluralism, it is not a form of hedonism. I agree that if it is a form of pluralism, then it is not a form of hedonism. But I think TAIAH is not a form of pluralism. As I understand pluralism, what marks a theory as a form of pluralism is that it postulates the existence of a plurality of fundamental sources of intrinsic value. So, for example, imagine a theory according to which episodes of pleasure are intrinsically good, and in addition episodes of knowledge are independently intrinsically good. Imagine that, according to this theory, to find the value of a life, one must first find the total amount of value contributed by pleasure in that life, and then find the total amount of value contributed by knowledge in that life, and then sum (or otherwise combine) these values. That would be a form of pluralism. On that theory, pleasure and knowledge are independent ultimate sources of intrinsic value.

TAIAH is not like that. This theory does not imply that there is some independent source of intrinsic value in addition to pleasure. More precisely, the theory does not imply that *truth* has any intrinsic value. The mere fact that something is true does not have any value in itself according to the theory. The only ultimate bearers of positive intrinsic value according to this theory are episodes of pleasure. Truth functions here in something like the way intensity and duration function. The fact that some episode of pleasure has greater intensity makes it have greater intrinsic value. The fact that it has greater duration has the same effect. And similarly for truth. The fact that an episode of pleasure has a true object makes it have greater intrinsic value than it would have had if it had a false object.[4]

There is another reason for wondering whether TAIAH deserves to be called a form of hedonism. That concerns supervenience. It might be thought that one mark of hedonism is that it makes the value of a person's life supervene upon facts about that person's mental states. Hedonism seems to imply that if two people are alike with respect to mental states, then they are alike with respect to value. That would follow from the fact that episodes of pleasure and pain are mental states. But TAIAH might seem to violate this principle. The results

---

[4] My presentation here is somewhat informal. I write as if the bearers of intrinsic value are "episodes", and these may seem to be concrete events. In a more formal presentation I would make clear that I take the fundamental bearers of intrinsic value to be states of affairs—abstract and finely grained objects. For a more detailed and rigorous presentation of the view, see Ch. 8.

concerning the two businessmen might be thought to show that this theory implies that it is possible for two people to be alike with respect to mental states, but different with respect to value. The deceived businessman's life is alleged to be less valuable than his cousin's in spite of the similarity of their mental states. Does this show that TAIAH is not a form of hedonism?

The question is more complicated than it might at first appear. In the first place, one could doubt that the businessmen are in precisely the same mental states. After all, one of them is taking pleasure in facts about himself ('*I* have the love and affection of *my* wife and children'), whereas the other is taking pleasure in falsehoods about a different person, namely *himself* ('*I* have the love and affection of *my* wife and children'). The objects of their pleasure are therefore different. If their mental states are construed broadly, so that these objects are constituents of the mental states, then the two businessmen are in different mental states. The difference in value in that case would not have any relevance to the question whether the theory violates the supervenience thesis.

There is much more to be said about this issue. Since at least some of it turns on details of formulation that have not yet been introduced, I think it will be better to put off this discussion until Chapter 8, where those details are explained. For now, I leave it at this: TAIAH is an axiological theory derived from IAH; it makes the intrinsic value of an episode of attitudinal pleasure depend upon three main factors: the intensity of the pleasure, the duration of the pleasure, and the truth-value of the object of the pleasure. TAIAH yields the result that the deceived businessman's life is much less valuable than the life of his undeceived cousin.

My point here is to show that attitudinal hedonism has the resources to deal with the example of the deceived businessman. If you think that the deceived businessman's life is less valuable than the life of his undeceived internal duplicate (or perhaps *near duplicate*), then I offer TAIAH for you. If you think that the twin businessmen lead lives of equal value—that where pleasure is concerned, truth does not matter—then I offer IAH for you. Either way, there is a theory that evaluates lives by appeal to facts about pleasure and pain that will yield results consistent with your axiological intuitions about these cases.

5.2. *Unconscious Pleasures: A Problem for IAH?*

In the passage from the *Philebus* (21a) that I quoted earlier, Socrates describes an unfortunate person who has a life full of pleasure but devoid of *nous*. While the person who lives this life enjoys quite a lot of pleasure, he does not have any knowledge, memory, forethought, etc. Protarchus (the other character in the dialogue) at first seems to think that since the life would be full of pleasure, it would be a good one. But he is rendered speechless when Socrates points out that

if you had no memory you would not recollect that you had ever been pleased, nor would the slightest recollection of the pleasure which you feel at any moment remain with you; and if you had no true opinion you would not think that you were pleased when you were; and if you had no power of calculation you would not be able to calculate on future pleasure, and your life would be the life, not of a man, but of an oyster, or "pulmo marinus." Could it be otherwise?

Moore apparently took the point of the argument to be that hedonism implies that pleasures of which we are not conscious are just as valuable as ones of which we are conscious.[5] Moore himself recognized that, so construed, the objection turns on a dubious point. Perhaps it is somehow necessary that if a person is experiencing pleasure at a time, he must be conscious of that pleasure. I understood the point of the argument in a somewhat less contentious way. I assumed that we could get at this point by considering a pair of individuals, O and H. The lives of these individuals are stipulated to be hedono-dolorically indiscernible, but the life of H is in addition full of knowledge, memory, forethought, and other sorts of intelligence. Some of this knowledge and memory is directed upon H's experiences of pleasure. The life of O is as devoid of intelligence as is possible, consistent with the assumption that it is full of pleasure.

On this basis, I proposed the following argument:

1. If DH were true, then the life of O would be just as good in itself for O as the life of H is for H.
2. But the life of O is not just as good in itself for O as the life of H is for H.
3. Therefore, DH is not true.

Since I have no interest in defending any form of sensory hedonism, I am prepared to admit that in this form the argument refutes DH. I am much more interested in the question whether a suitably revised version of the argument would refute IAH. So let us consider the argument that we would get if we replaced 'DH' with 'IAH'. What shall we say about that?

[5] In *Principia Ethica*, ch. III, sect. 52.

Once we have introduced the idea that the value of a life is affected by *attitudinal* pleasures and pains, we have to give more detailed descriptions of the lives of the two protagonists, O and H. We have to provide the relevant information about their attitudinal pleasures and pains. It seems to me that there are two main cases to consider. In one case, after adding all the facts about attitudinal pleasures and pains, we find that their lives remain hedono-dolorically indiscernible. They take intrinsic attitudinal pleasure and pain in similar objects, for the same durations, and with the same intensities. In the second case, they begin to differ with respect to attitudinal pleasures and pains. Let us consider the first case first.

Case One. Assume that the oyster-like person, O, experiences some bodily sensations that he enjoys. He takes intrinsic attitudinal pleasure in the fact that he feels these sensations. He takes pleasure in nothing beyond that. He takes pain in nothing. He has no knowledge, memory, foresight, or other kinds of intelligence beyond whatever is required by the mere fact that he is feeling some sensations and enjoying them.

Assume that H, the more intelligent person, also experiences a bunch of bodily sensations that he enjoys. Let the total amount of intrinsic attitudinal pleasure that he takes in these feelings be equal to the amount that O takes in his corresponding feelings. In this respect, O and H are alike. But assume in addition that H has knowledge, memory, and foresight. He recalls his pleasures; he anticipates them; he understands them for what they are when they occur. *But we must be careful to insist that H does not enjoy any of this knowledge, memory, or foresight.* In Case One, H does not enjoy any attitudinal pleasures beyond those enjoyed by O. We have assumed that all of his attitudinal pleasure was directed toward some of his bodily feelings. As a result, he takes no pleasure in any of his recollections, foreseeings, or recognitions. If we were to ask him, H would say that these intellectual feats mean nothing to him. He is not glad to have this knowledge. (Though of course he is not pained to have it, either.)

It may be difficult to imagine how someone could recall his pleasurable sensations without some enjoyment. Surely, in real life, real people are generally pleased to recall their past pleasures. And furthermore any real-life person would gain various advantages and would take some pleasure in the fact that he has knowledge and memory and foresight. But in Case One we are assuming that H does not do this. In this case, we stipulate that all of his intellectual abilities yield nothing in terms of attitudinal pleasure. His hedono-doloric balance is exactly the same as O's. So his possession of knowledge and memory apparently does him no good.

My own reaction is that in this (hard-to-imagine) case, the life of H is no better in itself for H than the life of O is for O. Admittedly, H has some abilities that O lacks. But we have stipulated that he does not enjoy having these abilities and does not enjoy anything else as a result of having them. Perhaps our immediate inclination to rate his life as better comes from our natural assumption that intellectual abilities are just about always beneficial. When we properly resist that inclination in Case One, I think there is little justification for saying that the life of H is better in itself for H. Thus, the attitudinal hedonist can plausibly suggest that premise (2) is false in this case.

Case Two. Suppose that O and H are exactly alike with respect to sensory pleasures. They are hedon-for-hedon duplicates when it comes to feelings of pleasure. But suppose that they differ with respect to intellect. H has knowledge, memory, and foresight that O lacks. And suppose, furthermore, that H enjoys having these abilities. He is pleased to recall his past pleasures; he is pleased to anticipate his future pleasures; and he is pleased to recognize his current pleasures for what they are. Perhaps he takes pleasure in the sheer fact that he has these various intellectual abilities. In this case, H takes intrinsic attitudinal pleasure in many objects that are simply not available to O. As a result, IAH declares the life of H to be much better in itself for H than the life of O is for O. In this case, premise (1) of the argument is false.

In light of these considerations, I tentatively conclude that the oyster argument is ineffective against IAH. Part of its undeniable appeal, it seems to me, derives from the fact that ordinary people almost always are better off for having *nous*. I think the advantages provided by *nous* can be adequately explained by saying that ordinary people enjoy, or take pleasure in, their intellectual abilities and other things that are made possible for them by their intellectual abilities. Where intelligence produces no such benefits, it seems of little value in itself.

5.3. *The Objection from Worthless Pleasures*

One of the most popular anti-hedonistic arguments is The Argument from Worthless Pleasures. It comes in many forms. Of these perhaps the most striking is the version to be found in *Principia Ethica* in the passage I quoted earlier in Chapter 3. Moore there mentions 'the lowest forms of sexual enjoyment', and he says they might be 'the most pleasant states we ever experience'.[6] He speaks of 'a perpetual indulgence in bestiality' and says that if hedonism were true, then this perpetual indulgence in bestiality would be 'heaven indeed, and all human endeavors should be devoted to its realisation'.

I fleshed this out with the tale of Porky, who cavorts with the pigs in his pigsty. I stipulated that Porky enjoys a lot of disgusting pleasures and somehow avoids any counterbalancing pains. On this basis I constructed an argument against DH: if DH were true, Porky's life would be a good one. But it isn't. So DH is not true.

Let us now consider whether cases such as this cast doubt on Intrinsic Attitudinal Hedonism. In order to ensure that the example bears on IAH, we need to stipulate that Porky enjoys a lot of intrinsic attitudinal pleasure. Accordingly, let us assume that he takes quite a lot of intrinsic attitudinal pleasure in various facts—that he is feeling precisely *this* sensation in his private parts, that he is having sex with this muddy sow, that he is wallowing in the mud, etc. Let us also continue to assume that he is not suffering any attitudinal pains. If this sort of thing happens often enough and with enough intensity, IAH implies that Porky is leading an outstandingly good life. Many would find that hard to accept.

There are many replies available to the hedonist. One reply suggests that the objection might be based on confusion concerning the scale on which we are supposed to be evaluating Porky's life. We might grant that his life is ugly, immoral, unproductive, even disgusting. But none of this has any direct bearing on the question at issue: is the life of Porky good in itself for Porky? A hard-core hedonist might say that if Porky is happy with this life, and is taking pleasure in his activities, and is in no way harmed by his disgraceful behavior, then his life is good *for him*. This is not to suggest, of course, that a similar life would be good for anyone else. I suspect that many of us would find it difficult to endure being trapped in a pigsty with a lot of muddy sows. If so, IAH implies that such lives would not be good *for us*.

Another reply involves saying that critics might be confused because of a failure to imagine Porky's life properly. Maybe critics think they would find Porky's activities so disgusting that they would not be able to enjoy them. Thus, they think that they would never swap lives with Porky. They think they would find his life unbearable. But (as I suggested earlier in connection with the deceived businessman) this betrays a failure to perform the thought experiment properly. The critic is apparently imagining some sort of hybrid partial life swap. He is thinking of

---

[6] Moore, *Principia Ethica*, ch. III, sect. 56.

himself, complete with his actual tastes and preferences, engaging in activities relevantly like the ones described for Porky. The critic thinks such a life would be hell on wheels. Perhaps he is right. But this is entirely irrelevant to the case. What matters here is that Porky has *Porky's* tastes. He enjoys the life. To imagine a swap properly, the critic must imagine engaging in Porky's activities *while having Porky's tastes and preferences*. The life comes as a complete package.

I acknowledge that even after making suitable adjustments, and while performing the thought experiment properly, and while reflecting on the correct scale of evaluation, some critics may still insist that Porky is living a rotten life. Such critics might say that they are thankful that they do not have Porky's "whole package". Indeed, some might even say that they would rather be slightly dissatisfied professors of philosophy than fully satisfied Porkies. So perhaps we need to confront the case more directly.

A more adventurous reply starts by admitting that this sort of case might very well refute DH, AH, IAH, and even TAIAH. But hedonism has further resources. In this case, the resources are a product of the fact that in its attitudinal forms hedonism focuses on pleasures and pains that involve "objects". When I speak of 'objects', I mean the states of affairs that are the objects of attitudinal pleasure and pain. If we draw suitable distinctions among these objects, we can then draw corresponding distinctions among attitudinal pleasures and pains taken in those objects. (The general strategy is similar to the one I suggested for Mill when I introduced AAIAH in Chapter 4.) Let me explain one way in which this might work.

I think it is reasonable to describe certain states of affairs by saying that they 'deserve to be objects of pleasure'. In the case of such objects it is fitting, or appropriate, that someone take pleasure in them. Thus, for example, consider the state of affairs that consists in some painting's being genuinely beautiful. It is reasonable to say that this state of affairs deserves to be appreciated. In other words, it deserves to have someone take intrinsic attitudinal pleasure in it. Similarly, if some state of affairs is morally good, then it deserves to be admired or enjoyed. It too deserves to have someone take intrinsic attitudinal pleasure in it. So we can identify the objects worthy of pleasure as those states of affairs that deserve to have pleasure taken in them.

Other states of affairs may be described by saying that they 'deserve to be objects of pain'. In their case it is fitting, or appropriate, that anyone who considers them be pained by them. The suffering of innocent children seems to be such an object. The fact that some alleged work of "art" is truly atrocious might be another.

I think it is possible to modify our attitudinal hedonism by incorporating an adjustment of value to reflect pleasure-worthiness and pain-worthiness of objects. If we do this properly, we can make the resulting axiology generate results that will be consistent with the intuitions of those who think that the life of Porky (or any life full of cruel or disgusting pleasures) is not so good. The idea is to say that the intrinsic value of an attitudinal pleasure is determined not simply by the intensity and duration of that pleasure, but by these in combination with the extent to which the object of that pleasure deserves to have pleasure taken in it. More exactly, the value of a pleasure is enhanced when it is pleasure taken in a pleasure-worthy object, such as something good, or beautiful. The value of a pleasure is mitigated when it is pleasure taken in a pleasure-unworthy object, such as something evil, or ugly. The disvalue of a pain is mitigated (the pain is made less bad) when it is pain taken in an object worthy of pain, such as something evil, or ugly. The value of a pain is enhanced (the pain is made yet worse) when it is pain taken in an object unworthy of this attitude, such as something good or beautiful.[7]

For purposes of this theory, we should construe 'episodes of intrinsic attitudinal pleasure' broadly. We should take such episodes to be complex states of affairs in which some person takes intrinsic attitudinal pleasure at some time, of some intensity, for some duration, in some object, while that object deserves, to some degree, to be an object of pleasure. The amount of pleasure in such a complex state of affairs, adjusted for desert, is then determined by considerations of intensity, duration, and desert level of the object in which the pleasure is taken. The theory will then say that the intrinsic value of an episode of pleasure is equal to the desert-adjusted amount of pleasure it contains, rather than (as on IAH) the *raw* amount of pleasure it contains. Similar calculations will apply in the case of intrinsic attitudinal pain. The amount of such pain, adjusted for desert, is determined in a similar way.

The resulting theory may be called 'Desert-Adjusted Intrinsic Attitudinal Hedonism' (DAIAH). It is intended to generate the

---

[7] I speak loosely here. I do not mean to suggest that pleasures have variable intrinsic values—values that can be increased or decreased depending upon changes in the nature of their objects. Rather, what I mean is that the fundamental bearers of intrinsic value should be taken to be complex states of affairs involving not only the intensity and duration and truthfulness of a pleasure, but something also about the worthiness of its object—the extent to which that object deserves to be enjoyed. Thus, a basic value state, on this axiology, would be something of this form: *S takes intrinsic attitudinal pleasure of intensity n_1 and duration m_1 in state of affairs P, while P is worthy of pleasure of intensity n_2 and duration m_2.* The curious reader is encouraged to take a look at the more careful and extended discussion of these issues in Ch. 8.

desired results in the cases involving malicious and base pleasures. Here is a formulation of the theory.

Desert-Adjusted Intrinsic Attitudinal Hedonism

i. Every episode of intrinsic attitudinal pleasure is intrinsically good; every episode of intrinsic attitudinal pain is intrinsically bad.

ii. The intrinsic value of an episode of intrinsic attitudinal pleasure is equal to the desert-adjusted amount of pleasure contained in that episode; the intrinsic value of an episode of pain is equal to − (the desert-adjusted amount of pain contained in that episode).

iii. The intrinsic value of a life is entirely determined by the intrinsic values of the episodes of intrinsic attitudinal pleasure and pain contained in that life, in such a way that one life is intrinsically better than another if and only if the net desert-adjusted amount of intrinsic attitudinal pleasure in the one is greater than the net amount of that sort of pleasure in the other.

Like all the forms of hedonism so far introduced, DAIAH is a form of pure and universal intrinsic attitudinal hedonism. It implies that every episode of intrinsic attitudinal pleasure is good in itself, and that every episode of intrinsic attitudinal pain is correspondingly bad. It also implies that nothing other than such episodes contributes directly to the intrinsic value of a life for the person who lives it.

DAIAH differs from DH, AH, IAH, and many other forms of hedonism in at least one important respect: in its effort to explain what makes a life intrinsically good for the one who lives it, it makes essential use of another normative concept—the concept of *desert*. (The normative concepts of *truth* and *altitude* play similar roles in TAIAH and AAIAH.) But it may appear that the concept of desert is so obscure, or so intimately entangled with the concept of goodness, that this marks some sort of defect, or abnormality, in the theory. Critics might think there is some prohibition against adjusting the values of pleasures and pains for *desert*.

I think there is no such prohibition. I am inclined to think that there are several different ways in which we can justify the appeal to the concept of desert in this context.

In the first place, this sort of procedure has good historical precedent. Moore and others have made similar use of a variety of normative concepts in their accounts of intrinsic goodness. Thus, for example, Moore appeals to the normative concepts of *beauty* and *truth* in his axiology. Moore claimed, in passages that I discuss in detail in Chapter 7, that the love of beautiful things is intrinsically better than the love of ugly things. He also claimed that the love of beautiful things for their possession of properties that they *truly* have is better than the love of such things based on faulty perception. Brentano seems to have held similar views, as did Chisholm.[8] All such axiological views involve the notion that we can formulate principles about one kind of value (e.g., intrinsic goodness of emotions) by appeal in part to other sorts of value (e.g., truth, beauty). So the present procedure is nothing novel.

Secondly, the normative concept to which I appeal—desert—does seem to have at least some independent credibility. The concept plays a role in a number of normative domains, including epistemology, etiquette, and aesthetics. Thus, for example, we seem to have little difficulty accepting the notion that if a person has been insulted, he deserves an apology; or that if a certain work of art has shapes and colors arranged in a certain way, then it deserves to be completed in a certain other way. I merely propose to make use of this already familiar notion in a slightly different way. I propose to say that certain states of affairs deserve, or are worthy of, certain emotional reactions: some deserve to have pleasure taken in them; others deserve to have pain taken in them.

It would be good to have a fully developed theory of desert. That might serve to substantiate my claim that it is permissible to appeal to desert here. However, in the present context it may be just as well to say, 'That's a project for another book.'

And, finally, it seems to me that there is a pragmatic justification for the use of the concept of desert in this context. If we allow ourselves to adjust the values of pleasures and pains according to the extent to which the objects of those pleasures and pains seem to deserve to be enjoyed or disenjoyed, the theory as a whole will generate outcomes consistent with our axiological intuitions. We engage in something like the method of reflective equilibrium. We have strong, confident views about certain relatively clear cases. Thus, for example, some of us feel strongly that the life of Porky is not so good, while the life of Stoicus is at least pretty good. If we tweak our hedonism by adding some assumptions about the pleasure-worthiness and pain-worthiness of certain objects, we can get the theory to yield evaluations consistent with our firm and unshakeable pre-analytic assessments. The resulting theory then can be defended as an expression of a refined and thought-out version of our axiological scheme. In this way, the theory helps us to clarify, organize, and better understand what we take to be the Good Life. I see nothing shameful about the process.

---

[8] For a discussion of the views of Brentano and Chisholm, see Chisholm, *Brentano and Intrinsic Value*.

Let me now take a moment to say something about where we stand. In Chapter 3 I described seven main lines of objection to hedonism. These were:

1. The Argument from Worthless Pleasures (Moore's bestiality argument)
2. The Argument from False Pleasures (the deceived businessman argument)
3. The Argument from Unconscious Pleasures (Plato's oyster argument)
4. Brentano's Cigar
5. The Argument from Nonexistent Pleasures (the Stoicus argument)
6. Moore's Heap of Filth
7. The Argument from Undeserved Pleasures (Ross's "Two Worlds" Argument)

Subsequently, in Chapter 4, I tried to show that while some forms of sensory hedonism might be refuted by objection 5, that argument is not effective against forms of attitudinal hedonism. I also suggested that Altitude-Adjusted Intrinsic Attitudinal Hedonism provides a possible reply to objection 1. Porky's pleasures might be said to have very low altitude, and hence low value according to this form of hedonism. I also suggested that the oyster argument (objection 3) seems much less persuasive against IAH. In the present chapter I have suggested further variants. One of these (Truth-Adjusted Intrinsic Attitudinal Hedonism) was designed to accommodate our intuitions about false pleasures (objection 2). Another (Desert-Adjusted Intrinsic Attitudinal Hedonism) was designed to deal with the objection from Worthless Pleasures.

In all of this my aim has been to show that if we are open-minded and flexible, we can learn something useful from the objections. Instead of insisting that hedonism simply has to be something like DH or AH, we can seek new forms—especially forms of attitudinal hedonism. We can take the objections as opportunities for reflection and reconsideration—as suggestions of ways to advance our appreciation of the many forms that hedonism can take, rather than as door-slamming proofs that pleasure is not the Good.

CHAPTER 6

Hedonism and the Shape of a Life

A number of philosophers have claimed that something we can call the 'Shape of a Life Phenomenon' shows that the value of a person's life cannot simply be the sum of the values of the minimal-value constituents of that life. They apparently think that this fact casts doubt on many traditional value theories, including hedonism.

Although I accept some of the axiological intuitions that stand behind the Shape of a Life Objection, I do not think that these intuitions have the cited implications. They do not imply that the value of a life may be different from the sum of the values of its minimal value constituents; they do not imply that hedonism is false. More exactly, the intuitions that stand behind the Shape of a Life objection seem to me to be consistent with the forms of attitudinal hedonism that I have been describing. My aim in this chapter is to explain and defend these claims. In fact, I go a bit further than that. I try to show that attitudinal hedonism provides some helpful insight into the way in which the shape of a person's life may affect the value of that life.

The chapter is organized as follows: First (6.1) I give an account of the Shape of a Life Phenomenon and sketch in a general way the objection based on it. Then (6.2) I formulate a version of the argument designed to refute Intrinsic Attitudinal Hedonism. This requires a slight modification to IAH. Then (6.3) I try to show that at least one form of attitudinal hedonism is not refuted by the objection.

6.1. *The Shape of a Life*

David Velleman presents one of the clearest and most directly relevant instances of the Shape of a Life Phenomenon. He invites us to consider two lives:

One life begins in the depths but takes an upward trend: a childhood of deprivation, a troubled youth, struggles and setbacks in early adulthood, followed finally by success and satisfaction in middle age and a peaceful retirement. Another life begins at the heights but slides downhill: a blissful childhood and youth, precocious triumphs and rewards in early adulthood, followed by a mid-life strewn with disasters that lead to misery in old age. Surely, we can imagine two such lives as containing equal sums of moment-ary well-being.... Yet even if we were to map each moment in one life onto a moment of equal well-being in the other, we would not have shown these lives to be equally good.[1]

Velleman says that most people would think that the first life is the better of the two. He mentions that similar examples can be found in Michael Slote's 'Goods and Lives'. One of Slote's examples goes like this:

A given man may achieve political power and, once in power, do things of great value, after having been in the political wilderness throughout his earlier career. He may later die while still "in harness" and fully possessed of his powers, at a decent old age. By contrast, another man may have a meteoric success in youth, attaining the same office as the first man and also achieving much good; but then lose power, while still young, never to regain it. Without hearing anything more, I would think our natural, immediate reaction to these examples would be that the first man was the more fortunate.[2]

Although neither Velleman nor Slote cites Brentano in this context, it is interesting to note that Brentano mentioned the underlying phe-nomenon many years ago.[3] It appears to me that Brentano's point in describing this phenomenon was approximately the same as Velleman's and at least similar to Slote's. Brentano says:

Let us think of a process which goes from good to bad or from a great good to a lesser good; then compare it with one which goes in the opposite direction. The latter shows itself as the one to be preferred. This holds even if the sum of the goods in the one process is equal to that in the other. And our preference in this case is one that we experience as being correct.[4]

Chisholm reports that Brentano used some fairly fancy Latin terminology to describe these cases. He evidently said that the process from better to worse is a case of *malum regressus*, while the process from worse to better is a case of *bonum progressionis*. In spite of the obvious similarities of the cases, Brentano's view (which Chisholm seems to endorse) is that, other things being equal, a case of *bonum*

---

[1] Velleman, 'Well-Being and Time', 49–50.   [2] Michael Slote, *Goods and Virtues*, 23–4.
[3] Connie Rosati reminded me that William Frankena makes substantially the same point in his *Ethics*, 2nd edn., 92. Frankena there says that Plato also stressed the axiological importance of "form" or "pattern" in the evaluation of a life.
[4] Brentano, quoted in Chisholm, *Brentano and Intrinsic Value*, 71.

progressionis is better than the corresponding case of *malum regressus.* In his discussion of these views, Noah Lemos seems to be symp-athetic to Brentano's view.[5]

As I understand them, each of these philosophers is saying something relevant to the Shape of a Life objection.[6] Let's try to draw out the essen-tial elements of the phenomenon to which they call attention.

Assume that some feature, G, has been proposed as "the Good for man". Some other feature, B, is alleged to be "the Bad for man". Imagine that G and B are features that a person can have in "minimal bursts". Thus, if G and B were sensory pleasure and pain, then we could have a minimal burst of pleasure or pain—an episode in which someone feels some relatively uniform sensory pleasure or pain for a suitably short period of time. Each such burst is assumed to have a relevant magnitude. In the case of pleasure, as an example, perhaps the relevant magnitude is thought to be the intensity of the pleasure experienced. The value of the burst is thought to be entirely determined by its magnitude.[7]

Velleman, Slote, Brentano, and others[8] who present objections based on the Shape of a Life are imagining pairs of lives that are matched with respect to minimal bursts of G and B. For each burst of a given mag-nitude in one life, there is exactly one burst of that same magnitude in the other. The crucial difference is temporal order. One life contains

---

[5] Lemos, *Intrinsic Value*, 39, 200.

[6] Each may also have other fish to fry. Velleman seems mainly to be interested in showing that equal-sized bursts of welfare may have different "meaning", and hence different value, if they occur in different parts of a person's life. Slote's aim seems to be different both from Velleman's and from Brentano's, but I mention his example because it has been taken to illustrate the point I mean to discuss.

[7] I mean to be discussing a question about *intrinsic* values. I can't imagine why anyone would bother to argue about the relative values of lives that are "uphill" and "downhill" with respect to such things as wealth-at-a-time, or health-status-at-a-time, or quality-of-intimate-personal-relationships-at-a-time. These things are of extrinsic value at best. There is no saying how they might affect someone's intrinsic welfare. Obviously, there could be people who have intrins-ically downhill lives even though they get richer day by day.

[8] In their 'Death and Well-being', Bigelow, Campbell, and Pargetter mention cases of this sort, and they explicitly say that a person's global well-being is not simply the sum of his momentary well-beings. I cannot find a passage in which they unequivocally argue from the premise to the conclusion, but my impression is that they are sympathetic to the line of argument under con-sideration here. In 'Good Lives: Parts and Wholes', Johan Brannmark presents a number of closely related cases evidently in support of approximately the same conclusion. One case involves a pair of lives, each with a good half and a bad half. The only difference is that in one the good half comes first, whereas in the other it comes last. Brannmark asks (rhetorically, I assume), 'Would we not say that the second life is superior to the first one?' (p. 226). C. I. Lewis does not give specific examples of this form, but seems to endorse the general point when he says, 'If it be paradox that nevertheless the value of a whole of experience as such is not completely determined from the value[s] of its parts, each separately, then that paradox is one which we shall have to brook, because it expresses a fundamental fact' (*Analysis of Knowledge and Valuation*, 503). Many others could be cited.

a sequence of bursts with increasing magnitudes; the other contains a sequence with decreasing magnitudes. Let us call these, respectively, 'the uphill life' (or UHL) and 'the downhill life' (or DHL). In order for these lives to be relevant to our present concerns, they must be assumed to be alike in respects other than the order in which the bursts of G and B occur. In spite of their similarities with respect to sums of values of momentary bursts, many of us apparently are sympathetic to the idea that UHL is better in itself than DHL.

Let us then say that a pair of lives illustrates the Shape of a Life Phenomenon if they are relevantly like UHL and DHL—mirror temporal images with respect to minimal bursts of G and B, but one manifesting steady improvement through time while the other manifests steady deterioration through time.

I need one further bit of terminology. I need a term that will pick out the relevant feature of those axiological theories according to which the intrinsic value of a person's life is equal to the sum of the intrinsic values of the minimal episodes of G and B in that life. Some philosophers say that such theories are 'additive'. Others call them 'totalistic', or 'summative'. Others say they are 'aggregative', or that they embody 'sum ranking'. Brannmark uses the term 'non-compositional' apparently to indicate the relevant feature. For present purposes, let us agree to call such theories 'additive'.

In general, then, it apparently has been thought that the Shape of a Life Phenomenon casts doubt on all additive axiologies. For if there can be lives illustrating the Shape of a Life Phenomenon, then there can be lives that differ in value even though they are composed of minimal-value components whose values have the same sum. Since the Shape of a Life Phenomenon seems real, all such axiologies seem false.[9]

Every hedonistic axiology I have formulated in this book contains a clause that indicates that the value of a life is "entirely determined" by the values of the episodes of pleasure and pain in that life. I did not explicitly say that the value of each life is precisely the *sum* of the values of the episodes of pleasure and pain contained within the life, but I suggested that this was my view.[10]

The truth, however, is slightly more complicated. I wrote as I did in part because I wanted to put off dealing with some technical details. (I deal with them in Chapter 8.)

---

[9] Although I have mentioned quite a few philosophers (Brentano, Chisholm, Lemos, Slote, Velleman, C. I. Lewis, Bigelow, Pargetter, Campbell, Brannmark, *et al.*) I am not attributing precisely this argument to any of them. I mention these philosophers because they said things *suggestive of* this argument. I am interested in the argument, regardless of its provenance.

[10] The forms of Epicurean hedonism described in Appendix C are exceptions to this description.

In fact, it would be a mistake to say, on any of the proposed axiologies, that the value of a life is equal to the sum of the values of *all* the episodes of pleasure and pain contained therein. It would be a mistake largely because it would involve pervasive 'double counting'. This can be seen if we reflect on the fact that any temporally extended episode of pleasure contains many temporally smaller sub-episodes of pleasure. Thus, for example, consider a minute-long episode of pleasure lasting from t0 to t60. It contains sixty (or more) sub-episodes each lasting one second. It also contains fifty (or more) sub-episodes each lasting ten seconds. One of these starts at t0; one starts at t1; one starts at t2; one starts at t3; etc. It also contains hundreds of other overlapping sub-episodes. Clearly, if we simply added the values of all these episodes, utterly disregarding overlap, we would come up with a number that is much too high to serve as the value of the all-inclusive minute-long episode as a whole.

Later, in Chapter 8, I will describe a method for dealing with this problem. As a preliminary step, sufficient for present purposes, let us simply introduce the notion of a *minimal episode of pleasure (or pain)*. In order to do this, let us assume that time can be broken down into very short, nonoverlapping minimal intervals. A minimal episode of pleasure (or pain) will be understood to be one that occurs precisely through one of the minimal intervals of time. Longer episodes will be taken to be collections of these minimal episodes. By focusing exclusively on these minimal episodes, we take an important step toward avoiding the problems of double counting.

As a result, we will have to make a minor change in the way we understand our hedonistic theories. In each case, where the theory says that the value of a life is "completely determined" by the values of the included episodes of pleasure and pain, we will understand this to mean that the value of a life is equal to the sum of the values of all the included *minimal* episodes of pleasure and pain. To be frank, I have been understanding the hedonistic axiologies in something like this way more or less steadily throughout the preceding chapters. I now make this assumption explicit. Later, in Chapter 8, I will have more to say about these minimal episodes.

In any case, as a result of all this, it appears that the Shape of a Life Phenomenon constitutes a problem for all these forms of hedonism, including the ones I am inclined to defend. The problem is more blatant now that I have made the additivity of the axiologies more obvious. Clause (iii) in each case explicitly says that we find the value of a life simply by adding up the values of the minimal episodes of pleasure and pain contained within the life.

6.2. *Shape of Life and Intrinsic Attitudinal Hedonism*

In order to make our consideration of this problem more directly relevant to present concerns, let us construct a version of the objection designed to refute Intrinsic Attitudinal Hedonism. I choose IAH in part because it is one of my favorite forms of hedonism. That theory (modified so as to contain explicit reference to minimal episodes) says:

Intrinsic Attitudinal Hedonism(m)

i. Every episode of intrinsic attitudinal pleasure is intrinsically good; every episode of intrinsic attitudinal pain is intrinsically bad.

ii. The intrinsic value of an episode of intrinsic attitudinal pleasure is equal to the amount of pleasure contained in that episode; the intrinsic value of an episode of intrinsic attitudinal pain is equal to − (the amount of pain contained in that episode).

iii. The intrinsic value of a life is equal to the sum of the intrinsic values of the minimal episodes of intrinsic attitudinal pleasure and pain contained in the life.

Clause (iii) of this theory incorporates additivity. It says that the value of a person's life, in itself, for the person who lives that life, is the sum of the values of the minimal episodes of intrinsic attitudinal pleasure and pain in his life. The theory thus has the feature that Velleman, Slote, Bigelow, Campbell, Pargetter, Brentano, Chisholm, Lemos, Lewis, Brannmark, and the other critics have found objectionable.

Let us then give a more detailed account of the uphill life and the downhill life previously sketched. Let us stipulate that in his childhood and youth, Uphill experiences many episodes of intrinsic attitudinal pain. Perhaps he suffers from some painful disease, or is forced to live in poverty. At any rate, his life has a bad start from the perspective of pleasure and pain. As he grows older, the pains steadily decrease in magnitude until at some point he starts having episodes of intrinsic attitudinal pleasure. At first, the episodes of pleasure that Uphill experiences are small, each containing a tiny amount of intrinsic attitudinal pleasure. With each passing day, the episodes contain larger amounts of pleasure. When he finally reaches a ripe old age, he is enjoying pleasures wonderful for their intensity and duration. We must assume that he dies painlessly, perhaps in his sleep.

Downhill's life is the mirror image of Uphill's. He starts with wonderful pleasures. Things steadily deteriorate. By old age he is taking pain in many things, and the pain becomes worse and worse as he grows older.

Here are some diagrams showing the magnitudes of the minimal episodes of intrinsic attitudinal pleasure and pain experienced by Uphill and Downhill throughout their lives.

In diagram 1, a solid vertical line indicates the amount of pleasure in a minimal episode of pleasure. The dotted line just to the right of a vertical line indicates the amount of value in the episode of pleasure. It is intended that the part of the diagram representing Downhill's life be the temporal mirror image of the part of the diagram representing Uphill's life.

I stipulate that the sum of the values of the minimal episodes in Uphill's life is equal to the sum of the values of the minimal episodes in Downhill's life. The episodes differ only in the temporal order in

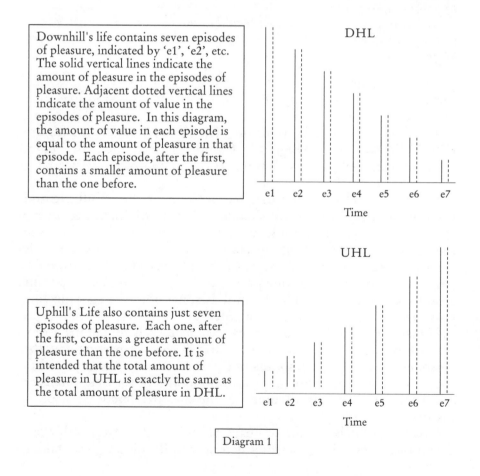

Downhill's life contains seven episodes of pleasure, indicated by 'e1', 'e2', etc. The solid vertical lines indicate the amount of pleasure in the episodes of pleasure. Adjacent dotted vertical lines indicate the amount of value in the episodes of pleasure. In this diagram, the amount of value in each episode is equal to the amount of pleasure in that episode. Each episode, after the first, contains a smaller amount of pleasure than the one before.

DHL

e1   e2   e3   e4   e5   e6   e7

Time

UHL

Uphill's Life also contains just seven episodes of pleasure. Each one, after the first, contains a greater amount of pleasure than the one before. It is intended that the total amount of pleasure in UHL is exactly the same as the total amount of pleasure in DHL.

e1   e2   e3   e4   e5   e6   e7

Time

Diagram 1

which they appear in the two lives. Now we have a specific version of the argument from the Shape of a Life:

1. If IAH(m) is true, then Uphill's life is just as good in itself for Uphill as Downhill's life is for Downhill.
2. It is not the case that Uphill's life is just as good in itself for Uphill as Downhill's life is for Downhill.
3. Therefore, IAH(m) is not true.

This is my interpretation of the argument, as modified so as to apply to Intrinsic Attitudinal Hedonism(m).

6.3. *Hedonism Unscathed*

You might think that after my tedious and detailed description of the two lives, no one could need further information about them. However, I think such information is needed. In particular, I think we need to know whether Uphill and Downhill noticed anything about the hedonic trajectories of their lives. Did Uphill ever notice that his life had an upward hedonic trajectory? Did Downhill ever notice that he was living a downhill life? And assuming that these individuals did take note of the hedonic trajectories of their lives, then I think we need to know if they cared. Was Uphill pleased to discover that his life was a life of improvement? Was Downhill disappointed about the corresponding feature of his life? Let's consider two salient possibilities.

Possibility One. "They care." We might assume that when he reaches early middle age, Uphill notices that things are improving for him. He might take pleasure in this, thinking that his later happiness makes his life as a whole more meaningful. Perhaps in old age he begins to think that his earlier pains served some purpose. Maybe he thinks that the earlier pains had instrumental value—they taught him important lessons, or were suffered in pursuit of goods that in fact were later achieved. He might think (to follow up on some remarks in Velleman's paper) that these later joys somehow serve to redeem his earlier sufferings. He might take pleasure in the thought that the earlier pains (though bad in themselves) were meaningful, or useful, or at least not utterly pointless. He might even take pleasure in the thought that those earlier pains helped to give his life as a whole a more beautiful aesthetic structure. 'Perhaps', he joyfully thinks, 'some modern-day Shakespeare will write a glorious drama about my uphill life.'

Downhill, on the other hand, might notice toward the end of his life that things are going downhill. He might be pained by this, thinking that this downward trajectory makes his life as a whole less meaningful. Maybe the fact that things turned out badly for him takes some of the luster off his earlier pleasures. Maybe he regrets the fact that he took all his pleasures while still so young. Maybe he thinks that the downward curve of his life is a less attractive aesthetic structure than the upward curve of a life like Uphill's. 'If anyone writes a play about my life,' he thinks, 'it will have to be a tragedy.' He might take pain in all these thoughts.

Possibility Two. "They don't care." In a different case, Uphill and Downhill might not notice that their lives have these hedonic trajectories; or they might notice but be unmoved. Neither takes any pain or pleasure in the fact that his life has the curve that it has. Perhaps each of them just lives in the moment.

My point in mentioning these possibilities should be obvious. If the first possibility is actualized, and Uphill and Downhill notice and care about the trajectories of their lives, then their lives contain some extra attitudinal pleasures and pains that were not previously recognized. The hedonistic axiology under consideration requires us to add a few points to the value of Uphill's life in virtue of the fact that UHL contains added pleasures such as the pleasure Uphill takes in the fact that his life is improving. Equally, the same axiology requires that some points be subtracted from the value of Downhill's life in virtue of the fact that it is now seen to contain some extra pains, such as the pain Downhill takes in the fact that his life is a life of downward trajectory.

Clearly, then, if Uphill and Downhill notice and care about the trajectories of their lives, then diagram 1 is seriously inaccurate. There is important hedono-doloric information that has been overlooked. Uphill's life contains extra intrinsic attitudinal pleasures, and Downhill's contains extra intrinsic attitudinal pains. When these are properly recognized, and their values added to the totals, the result is that Uphill's life is rated by IAH as being better in itself for Uphill than Downhill's life is for Downhill. Diagram 2 illustrates this case.

Notice that the heights of some of the vertical lines have been increased in the part of the diagram representing Uphill's life. This is intended to indicate the extra attitudinal pleasures and their associated values. These are the pleasures that Uphill experiences when he realizes that his life has such an attractive shape. Notice also that three extra 'e's' have been added to the part of the diagram representing Downhill's life. These indicate the extra attitudinal pains and their disvalues that

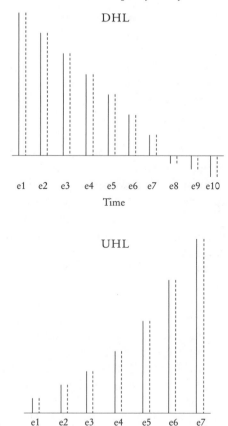

As in diagram 1, Downhill's life still contains just seven episodes of pleasure. Each one after the first contains a smaller amount of pleasure than the one before. But notice that in addition to the seven episodes of pleasure, there are now also three episodes of pain. The dot–dash lines indicate amounts of *disvalue*, or badness in those episodes. That indicates the pain that Downhill suffers when he realizes that his life has an ugly shape.

In this case, Uphill's life contains just seven episodes of pleasure and no episodes of pain. Each episode of pleasure, after the first, contains a greater amount of pleasure than the one before. Starting with e5, these episodes contain *greater* amounts of pleasure than the corresponding episodes in UHL in diagram 1. That indicates extra pleasure that Uphill gets when he notices the nice shape of his life

Diagram 2

Downhill suffered when he thought about his ugly life. As a result of the added pleasures and pains in this case, IAH generates precisely the result that Velleman and the others find interesting. The uphill life of Uphill is declared better in itself for Uphill than the downhill life is for Downhill. This does not *refute* IAH. It does not show that additivity fails. Rather, IAH gives us some insight into what makes UHL better than DHL. UHL is better in this case precisely because Uphill gets greater enjoyment out of his life than Downhill gets out of his.

Perhaps some critics of hedonism have thought that hedonism has got to be understood as *sensory* hedonism. Perhaps they have thought that if UHL and DHL are alike with respect to the total amount of *sensory* pleasure and pain they contain, then the hedonist will be unable to account for their apparent difference in value. This might constitute a sound objection to some forms of sensory hedonism. But it is important to notice that this problem does not affect the *attitudinal* hedonist (like me). For the attitudinal hedonist can say that even when two lives contain equal amounts of sensory pleasure, their values may diverge in virtue of the fact that they contain different amounts of attitudinal pleasure. Clearly, they would contain different amounts of attitudinal pleasure if Uphill took pleasure in the shape of his life while Downhill did not (and their lives were otherwise hedonodolorically indiscernible). That would be the explanation of the divergence in the first possibility.

Suppose the second possibility is actualized. Uphill and Downhill do not notice the trajectories of their lives, or do not care. Neither is pleased or pained by the shape of his life. There are no "hidden pleasures", either sensory or attitudinal. This case is adequately illustrated by diagram 1 above. All the attitudinal pleasures and pains have been accounted for, and there is no difference in their totals. In this case, attitudinal hedonism implies that their lives are of equal value.

My impression is that the implications of the proposed form of attitudinal hedonism for this possibility are correct as well. Thus, as I see it, premise (2) is false in Possibility Two. I see no reason to suppose that Uphill's life in fact is any better in itself for Uphill than Downhill's life is for Downhill. After all, Uphill does not get anything out of the fact that his life has this allegedly attractive shape. He does not enjoy it or take pleasure in it. It does not make him any the happier.[11] Downhill does not suffer from the fact that his life is getting worse with every passing minute. It doesn't matter to him. So why should we think Uphill's life is better for Uphill than Downhill's life is for Downhill?

Since some people apparently think that UHL is better in itself than DHL even when Uphill and Downhill take no pleasure in their trajectories, I would like to take that rhetorical question seriously. I would like to offer some suggestions about the propensity to think that UHL is better than DHL, even when the sums of values of the episodes of attitudinal pleasure and pain are equal in the two lives, and even when Uphill and Downhill remain unaffected by the shapes of their lives. So let us focus on the case illustrated in diagram 1, and consider why someone might think that UHL is better in itself than DHL. I have three suggestions to make about this.

Suggestion One. Consider what happens when a sensitive person first hears about the lives of Uphill and Downhill. He might think that he

---

[11] I realize that these remarks would be question-begging if offered as an argument.

would very much prefer to live the life of Uphill. He thinks he would be dismayed to find in middle age that his life was going to ruin. He would be pained to discover that his own life had a downward trajectory like Downhill's. Contrariwise, he thinks he would be delighted to find that things were getting better all the time, as they do in the life of Uphill. He imagines that, if given the choice, he would get more pleasure out of living UHL than he would get out of living DHL. So, naturally, he thinks that UHL is better in itself than DHL.

That sort of thinking embodies a fairly serious confusion relevantly like some confusions we have already discussed. The sensitive reader has imagined that if he were living UHL, he would take attitudinal pleasure in the fact that his life had an uphill trajectory. But this is impossible. Recall diagram 1. In the case at issue, we have stipulated that UHL does not contain any such extra attitudinal pleasures. We have stipulated that (aside from temporal order) UHL and DHL are exactly alike with respect to attitudinal pleasures and pains. If the sensitive reader were living UHL *as it has been described*, he would enjoy precisely the attitudinal pleasures that Uphill is stipulated to enjoy. In the case at hand, it has been stipulated that Uphill takes no pleasure in the fact that the life has an uphill trajectory.

Of course, there remains the fact that *the sensitive reader* gets more pleasure from the contemplation of UHL than he gets from the contemplation of DHL. This might show that UHL is extrinsically better than DHL—it has what is sometimes called 'inherent value'. It has the power to make the lives of contemplators better. But it does not show that UHL is better in itself *for Uphill* than DHL is *for Downhill*.

Suggestion Two. When the sensitive reader contemplates UHL and DHL, he might find that UHL exemplifies a sort of excellence, or beauty, or appropriateness that is missing from DHL. He might think that the world would be made better in itself by the presence in it of lives like UHL (other things being equal, of course). Thus he might think that even in the case in which Uphill himself does not notice the added value of his life, still that life makes the world better than it would be if DHL were lived in its place, and thus UHL is better in itself than DHL.

This suggestion embodies a certain other confusion. This is the confusion of the intrinsic value of a life *for the world* with intrinsic value of a life *for the one who lives it*. As I see it, these are two different scales of evaluation for lives. On the one hand, we can inquire into the value of a certain life *for the one who lives it*. When we do this, we inquire into the pure "quality of life" for that individual. Suppose you have a newborn baby. Suppose you are filled with love and hope for that baby. Suppose you want things to turn out well *for her*. Your hope, in this case, concerns the baby's welfare. You might, in addition, also hope that your baby will grow up to be someone whose life adds value *for the world*. But, fearing that making the world better might not be maximally advantageous for your baby, you might just stick with the earlier hope. In this case, you are thinking about the value of a life for the one who lives it.[12] That, I take it, is the relevant scale of value. I have proposed intrinsic attitudinal hedonism as a theory about that sort of value. Thus, even if UHL would make a greater contribution to the intrinsic value of *the world*, this would not show that UHL is better in itself *for Uphill* than DHL is *for Downhill*.

Those who prefer theoretical simplicity might hope that there would be one relevant scale of intrinsic value. They might hope that an axiological theory would assign amounts of intrinsic value to some basic units (episodes of pleasure and pain, for example) and then go on to assign intrinsic values to all larger things entirely on the basis of the amounts of intrinsic value in the components. Thus, the values of lives, possible worlds, and consequences of actions would all be straightforwardly composed of the values of their parts. A given episode of pleasure, on this scheme, would then make the same contribution to a life, a world, the consequence of some action, and anything else that needs evaluation in terms of intrinsic value.

I am rejecting this sort of conception. I am suggesting that there may be no necessary link between the amount of intrinsic value contributed by a certain episode of pleasure *to a life* and the amount of intrinsic value contributed by that same episode *to the world*. There are many reasons to insist on this distinction. Justice also calls for it.[13]

Suggestion Three. Let us imagine a slightly revised version of UHL and DHL. In this version, Uphill notices and takes some added pleasure in the fact that his has been an uphill life. But, in order to ensure that this added pleasure in Uphill's life does not introduce a difference in their totals, let us suppose that Downhill takes some added pleasure in some other things. Specifically, let us suppose that in his youth Downhill took added pleasure on several occasions in the fact that his beer was so frosty and his peanuts so salty. As a result of these alterations, let us agree, the sum of the values of the episodes of intrinsic

---

[12] Earlier, in sect. 1.2, I mentioned this "crib test". I pointed out that it is not entirely conclusive. Nevertheless, I find it suggestive.

[13] I discuss this idea at greater length in Ch. 9 in connection with an objection to hedonism due to W. D. Ross.

attitudinal pleasure and pain in UHL is equal to the sum of the values of the episodes of intrinsic attitudinal pleasure and pain in DHL. Nevertheless, someone might want to say that UHL is better in itself for Uphill than DHL is for Downhill. Would this show that intrinsic attitudinal hedonism is false?

This is a delicate question. The answer depends upon some details in the formulation of attitudinal hedonism. According to the simplest version of the theory—IAH(m)—we are required to say that the intrinsic value of a minimal episode of attitudinal pleasure depends entirely on the intensity of the pleasure.[14] Provided that the intensities are equal, pleasure taken in the temperature of your beer is just as valuable on this theory as pleasure taken in the shape of your life. In that case, IAH(m) implies that UHL is just as good in itself for Uphill as DHL is for Downhill.

But, as we have seen, since we are working with a form of attitudinal hedonism, we have certain options open to us that might otherwise be closed. One of these options is this: we can adjust the value of an episode of pleasure or pain to reflect features of the *object* of that pleasure or pain. Thus, we can say that certain states of affairs are more worthy of pleasure than others. We can say that it is better in itself for a person to take pleasure in a more pleasure-worthy state of affairs. It is less good in itself for a person to take pleasure in a state of affairs that is less worthy of having pleasure taken in it. If we modify the theory in this way, we get some form of Desert-Adjusted Intrinsic Attitudinal Hedonism.

Perhaps some who are intrigued by the Shape of a Life Phenomenon think that there is something especially axiologically important about pleasures taken in global features of one's life.[15] Perhaps they think that it is more important for a person to take pleasure in his life as a whole than it is for him to take pleasure in such local phenomena as the frostiness of his beer, or the saltiness of his peanuts. While it is not clear to me that I would want to defend this sort of view, I do want to point out that attitudinal hedonism can easily be extended so as to accommodate it.

As I have suggested, the attitudinal hedonist can say that pleasures taken in more pleasure-worthy objects are intrinsically better. He can also say, if he likes, that global features of one's own life are more

---

[14] Durations would not matter on this view, since we are assuming that each episode of pleasure is a temporally minimal "burst". In effect, we are stipulating that all pleasures and pains have the same minimal duration.

[15] Anyone who seriously wanted to defend this sort of view would have to explain what's meant by saying that a feature is 'global'. For present purposes I hope it will be permissible for me to proceed with a very rough and intuitive sense of the difference between "global" and "local" pleasures.

pleasure-worthy. When these two thoughts are combined, we have a view that looks something like this:

Globality-Adjusted Intrinsic Attitudinal Hedonism

i. Every episode of intrinsic attitudinal pleasure is intrinsically good; every episode of intrinsic attitudinal pain is intrinsically bad.

ii. The intrinsic value of a minimal episode of intrinsic attitudinal pleasure is equal to the globality-adjusted amount of pleasure contained in that episode; the intrinsic value of a minimal episode of intrinsic attitudinal pain is equal to − (the globality-adjusted amount of pain contained in that episode).

iii. The intrinsic value of a life is equal to the sum of the intrinsic values of the minimal episodes of intrinsic attitudinal pleasure and pain it contains.

Given the imagined assumptions about the globality-adjusted evaluation of the relevant attitudinal pleasures, this view implies that Uphill's mature pleasure in the fact that his has been an uphill life is more valuable in itself than Downhill's youthful pleasure in the frostiness of his beer, even if those pleasures are equal in intensity. The relevant features of the case are illustrated in diagram 3.

I assume that Uphill's pleasures are taken in objects that are more global, and thus more pleasure-worthy. Globality-adjusted hedonism implies that those pleasures are more valuable. The increased value is represented in the diagram by the fact that some of the dotted lines (representing value) are taller than the corresponding straight lines (representing amounts of pleasure). Correspondingly, some of Downhill's pleasures are taken in very local objects—the frostiness of his beer. Globality-adjusted hedonism says that such pleasures have mitigated value. The decreased value of these pleasures is represented in the diagram by the fact that some of the dotted lines (representing value) are shorter than the corresponding straight lines (representing amounts of pleasure). As a result of these adjustments for globality, the revised theory implies that UHL is better in itself for Uphill than DHL is for Downhill. Nevertheless, the axiology is still purely additive, as can be seen in clause (iii). The intrinsic value of UHL is still the sum of the values of the minimal bursts of pleasure contained therein—it is just that on this revised axiology the values of some of those minimal bursts are enhanced to reflect the greater globality of their objects, and the values of other minimal bursts are mitigated to reflect the greater locality of their objects.[16]

---

[16] I should be careful to acknowledge that some of this might be misleading. I do not mean to defend a view according to which an episode of pleasure has some intrinsic value, but that value may be enhanced or diminished depending upon the pleasure-worthiness of the object of the

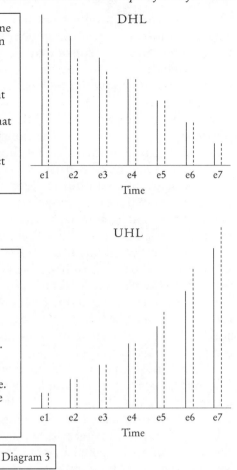

As in diagram 1, each solid vertical line indicates the amount of pleasure in an episode of pleasure, and the adjacent dotted vertical line indicates the amount of value in an episode of pleasure. In this diagram, the amount of value in the first three episodes is *less than* the amount of pleasure in that episode. That indicates that the value of the pleasure enjoyed in those episodes was mitigated due to the fact that it had a less global object.

In this diagram, the amount of value in some episodes, starting with e5, is *greater* than the amount of pleasure. This indicates that the value of pleasure is enhanced when it is pleasure taken in a more global object, such as the shape of one's life. The total amount of pleasure in Uphill's life is the same as the total amount of pleasure in Downhill's life. But when we adjust for globality, the result is that Uphill's life is deemed better.

Diagram 3

My aim here has been to show that there are forms of attitudinal hedonism that are purely additive but consistent with the apparent facts about the Shape of a Life Phenomenon. According to these theories, the value in itself of a life for the one who lives it is the sum of the values of the minimal bursts of good and evil in that life.

pleasure. On this sort of view, a given pleasure has its intrinsic value contingently. And its value depends upon some of its relations. My own view is different. I want to say that on the proposed view the bearers of the most fundamental sort of intrinsic value ("basic intrinsic value states") would be states of affairs of this form: 'Bob taking attitudinal pleasure at noon on Tuesday, October 16, 2001, of intensity 8 in the fact that his beer is frosty cold.' The intrinsic value of such a state would be necessary and fixed. It would be determined entirely by intrinsic features of the state. In this case, it would be fixed eternally by the intensity of the attitudinal pleasure that Bob takes and the pleasure-worthiness of the state of affairs of *Bob's beer being frosty cold*. I discuss all this in greater detail in Ch. 8.

On these theories, a minimal burst of good is taken to be a minimal episode of intrinsic attitudinal pleasure, and a minimal burst of evil is taken to be a minimal episode of intrinsic attitudinal pain. I suggested some possible explanations for the widespread thought that additive forms of hedonism would be falsified by cases like UHL and DHL.

One possible problem is that those contemplating the lives might inadvertently imagine that UHL contains some extra pleasures—pleasures taken in the fact that things are getting better all the time. Another possible problem is that those contemplating the lives might confusedly imagine that if they were living UHL, they would take extra pleasure in its uphill trajectory. I pointed out that even if we think that pleasure taken in global facts is more valuable than similar pleasure taken in local facts, forms of attitudinal hedonism are still not refuted by the Shape of a Life Phenomenon.

Finally, I indicated that some philosophers might think that pleasures taken in global features of one's life are better in themselves than equal pleasures taken in local facts. I tried to show that it is possible to construct a form of attitudinal hedonism that preserves this intuition, too. This form of hedonism is, like all the others discussed here, purely additive in the relevant sense. Thus, even real enthusiasts for globality can embrace additivity.

I have considered just one main form of the Shape of a Life Objection. This one is based on the example involving Uphill and Downhill. There are many variants of the objection. It might be suggested, for example, that it is better for a life to contain pleasures doled out in *more uniform* bursts.[17] It might be suggested, for another example, that it is better for the pleasures to be taken in objects that display *greater variation*.[18] Velleman apparently wanted to defend the idea that *better narrative structure* makes a life better, even when the sum of the values of the minimal-value constituents remains the same.

My reaction to such cases has been suggested here, but I have not presented it. Let me briefly summarize. Suppose some axiologist maintains that a life is better for the one who lives it if, in addition to the pleasures it contains, the life displays some holistic feature, F. Then I ask whether the one who lives the life cares about F. If he does care about F, and enjoys having a life with feature F, then I say that what makes his life better is the fact that he has greater enjoyment. If, on the other hand, he does not care about whether his life has feature F,

---

[17] Sen seems to suggest this idea in his 'Utilitarianism and Welfarism', 470–1.

[18] Brentano, and perhaps Chisholm, seem to suggest this idea. See Chisholm, *Brentano and Intrinsic Value*, 70–3.

then I say that the presence of F in his life does not make his life better in itself for him. After all, he doesn't "get anything" out of the fact that his life has feature F. Thus, the value of the life is determined ultimately by the amounts of enjoyment and disenjoyment—the holistic feature is of extrinsic value at most. The interested reader is invited to reflect on further cases, trying to see whether the strategy I have sketched would deal adequately with all such versions of the Shape of a Life Objection.

CHAPTER 7

G. E. Moore, Hedonist?

One of the attractive features of hedonism is its remarkable plasticity. By this I mean its capacity to take on many forms. In earlier chapters I tried to illustrate this plasticity by showing how Default Hedonism could easily be converted into Aristippean Hedonism merely by adding a couple of parenthetical remarks. I also tried to show how we could generate Attitudinal Hedonism by substituting some claims about attitudinal pleasures and pains for the original claims about sensory pleasures and pains.

In its turn, Attitudinal Hedonism opens the door to further modifications. One modification we have already seen involves the introduction of an adjustment reflecting the pleasure-worthiness or pain-worthiness of the objects of attitudinal pleasure and pain. Once we have made room for pleasure-worthiness, we can generate still more variants merely by adding suitable clauses in which we stipulate that experiences of such-and-such a sort are more pleasure-worthy than others.

I now want to turn to a more surprising thesis. I want to try to show that we can introduce relatively modest adjustments that will yield forms of hedonism that are equivalent (or nearly equivalent) to theories that, independently, might have seemed incompatible with hedonism. I illustrate this claim in this chapter. I try to show that there is a fairly straightforward modification to DAIAH that makes it nearly equivalent to the axiological system that Moore defended in chapter VI of *Principia Ethica*.[1] This seems to me to be an interesting result, since Moore attacked hedonism energetically in chapter III of the same book. He is not usually taken to be a hedonist. I am sure he did not take himself to be a hedonist in 1903. Yet, if my proposal is right, we can construct a form of hedonism that is extensionally equivalent to his allegedly pluralist axiology.

[1] Parenthetical page references in this chapter are all to Moore's *Principia Ethica*.

In an appendix, I consider whether a similar procedure would yield a form of hedonism equivalent to Darwall's "Aristotelian Thesis", according to which the Good Life is the life full of virtuous activity. But in this chapter we focus exclusively on Moore's own "official" axiology.

7.1. *Moore's Pluralism*

In chapter III of *Principia Ethica*, Moore presents an extended argument against hedonism. He seems to have in mind a fairly simple version (possibly similar to DH). He suggests that Sidgwick endorsed this sort of hedonism, and he attacks it on axiological grounds. After presenting the bestiality objection (discussed above in Chapter 2), he claims that hedonism is just false. 'I venture to think that this view is as false as it is paradoxical' (p. 95). He attributes a more complex hedonistic view to Mill. This view incorporates the notorious distinction between higher and lower pleasures. Moore's attack on what he takes to be Mill's position as a whole is somewhat heated. First he vigorously attacks Mill's argument in favor of hedonism. This, he concludes, is 'contemptible nonsense' (p. 72). He then presents his own arguments designed to show that Millian hedonism is false. He says at one point that he will 'try to produce an agreement that the fundamental principle of hedonism is very like an absurdity, by shewing what it must mean, if it is clearly thought out, and how that clear meaning is in conflict with other beliefs, which will, I hope, not be so easily given up' (p. 76). There can be little doubt about this: Moore was no fan of hedonism.

In chapter VI of the same book, Moore presents his own substantive views in axiology. At the end of the chapter he presents a sort of outline of the main points. According to that outline, the fundamental intrinsic goods and bads are as follows:

1. Great unmixed intrinsic goods:
   (a) The love of our friends for their goodness: personal affections.
   (b) The love of beautiful objects for their beauty: aesthetic appreciations.
2. Great intrinsic evils:
   (a) The love of what is evil or ugly: e.g., cruelty and lasciviousness.
   (b) The hatred of what is good or beautiful: e.g., malice, envy, and contempt.
   (c) The consciousness of pain.

3. Great mixed intrinsic goods:
   (a) The hatred of what is ugly or bad: e.g., courage and resolute defiance.
   (b) Compassion, or sympathy for those who suffer pain. (In the text, but not in the summary, Moore says that certain specifically moral emotions belong in category 3.)

We can introduce a little more order into all this by noting some general features of most of the items Moore discusses. In every case except the case of consciousness of pain, the "thing" involves an emotional attitude of love or hate; it also involves some sort of object, good or bad, ugly or beautiful, upon which the emotional attitude is directed. The general principles at work seem to be these:

LG: The love of the good and of the beautiful are very good (as in 1(a) and (b)).

LB: The love of the bad and of the ugly are very bad (as in 2(a)).

HG: The hatred of the good and of the beautiful are very bad (as in 2(b)).

HB: The hatred of the bad and of the ugly are very good (as in 3(a)).

In addition to this, we have one item that does not fit the scheme at all—the consciousness of pain (as in 2(c))—and one item that fits the scheme awkwardly—compassion for the suffering of others (as in 3(b)). (But Moore tells us that it is more important that the view be true than that it be neatly organized (p. 222).)

Although he places less emphasis on this point, Moore mentions that part of what makes the things on his "good list" so good is the appropriateness of the attitudes to the objects. And part of what makes most of the bad things so bad is the inappropriateness of the attitudes to the objects. He apparently thinks that in the case of the great goods (personal affections and aesthetic appreciations), a certain sort of love is the appropriate attitude. It is "fitting" that good friends and beautiful objects be loved. The same general idea holds in the case of courage and compassion, where hate is the appropriate attitude. It is equally fitting that ugly things and bad things should be hated. We might put this same point by saying that good things deserve to be loved, and bad things deserve to be hated. This makes complex states of affairs such as personal affections and aesthetic appreciations and "resolute defiance" extra good.

But in the case of cruelty and lasciviousness, the attitude is inappropriate. Bad and ugly things do not deserve to be loved; they deserve the opposite attitude. That helps to explain why the love of the evil or the ugly is so bad. A similar principle holds in the case of the hatred of the good. It is extra bad to hate the good, since that is the inappropriate attitude to have toward such things. They deserve to be loved. So where the attitude is inappropriate, the whole thing is bad.

Moore claims that the greatest intrinsic goods are "personal affections and aesthetic appreciations". He goes so far as to claim that it is the "ultimate and fundamental truth of Moral Philosophy" that these are the greatest of intrinsic goods, and that they form the rational and ultimate end of human action and the sole criterion of social progress (p. 189).

In order to have a clearer conception of his intent, I would like to consider in greater detail a couple of the things that Moore alleges to be among the most important items in his axiology. I will discuss one "great unmixed intrinsic good", aesthetic appreciation; one "great unmixed evil", the consciousness of pain; one "great mixed evil", cruelty; and one "great mixed good", resolute defiance. These illustrate the main categories of goods and bads.

First let us consider the case of aesthetic appreciations. Moore devotes sections 114–21 to the description of these complex states of affairs. What follows here is a brief summary of what he says. Moore seems to be thinking of something that contains an emotive attitude of love, or aesthetic appreciation; a cognitive attitude of judgment or belief about the existence of the object; the having of its qualities, and the beauty of those qualities; and an objective factor that concerns the actual existence and qualities of the object. He says that aesthetic appreciations are best when the observer has the right attitude toward the object; he judges the object to exist and to have a certain set of aesthetic qualities, and the qualities to be beautiful; and the object does exist and does have those qualities, and they are beautiful.

If we assume again that the bearers of intrinsic value are states of affairs, we may attempt to identify the things Moore has in mind as states of affairs with a certain fairly complex structure. Roughly, they look like this:

AA: i. S believing that there is an object, x, having qualities F1, F2, F3, ... , and
   ii. S believing x to be beautiful in virtue of having F1, F2, F3, ... , and
   iii. S feeling aesthetic appreciation for x in virtue of its having F1, F2, F3, ... , and

    iv. x actually existing,
     v. x actually having F1, F2, F3, . . . ,
      vi. x being beautiful in virtue of having F1, F2, F3, . . . ,
    vii. aesthetic appreciation being appropriate to F1, F2, F3, ...

The main elements of the state of affairs are these: it has a cognitive (more properly "doxastic") element (i, ii); an emotive element (iii); some objective ontological elements (iv, v); and some objective value-theoretical elements (vi, vii). In sections 114–20 of *Principia Ethica*, Moore discusses in detail how the absence of any of these elements affects the intrinsic value of the whole state of affairs. Thus, for example, if the object does not exist, then the intrinsic value goes down (section 117). Or if the properties in fact do not make it beautiful (in which case vi and vii would be false), then there is an error of taste, and the intrinsic value goes down (section 116). Or if the thing does not have those properties, then there is an error of judgment, and v and vi are false, and then the intrinsic value again goes down (section 116).

Moore says that such aesthetic appreciations are "unmixed" intrinsic goods. That is because they have good parts but no bad parts. He also says that these things are organic unities (section 113). His reasoning involves the idea that each part of such a state of affairs would be pretty worthless in isolation. For this reason he thinks that each part is of very low intrinsic value. For example, consider the mere existence of some beautiful object. It is good, he admits, but its value is minimal. Significant amounts of value emerge only when the object really exists, and really has the aesthetic properties, and is properly appreciated by some suitable subject. Similar reasoning shows, Moore thinks, that each part is of, at best, small intrinsic value. The sum of the small intrinsic values of these parts is much less than the intrinsic value of a whole aesthetic appreciation (section 120). Hence, as Moore sees it, each aesthetic appreciation is an organic unity.

Now let us consider the simplest of the alleged great intrinsic evils. Moore claims that the consciousness of pain is a great intrinsic evil. It is an organic unity because its parts are consciousness and pain, and neither of these is intrinsically bad (section 127). But when you put them together, you get a major-league evil. Moore claims that it is nowhere near as complex as the others to come.

The love of evil is alleged to be a great mixed evil. Since Moore mentions cruelty as an example, I suppose he must have had in mind the state of affairs in which someone loves, or is delighted by, the sufferings of another person. We may imagine, for example, that some innocent victim is suffering some pain, and the cruel one enjoys this. Translated into state of affairs talk, this is:

LE: i. S believing that there is a state of affairs, p, that consists in a person, x, suffering pain,
  ii. S believing p to be intrinsically evil in virtue of its being a case of someone suffering pain,
  iii. S feeling love for p in virtue of its being a case of someone suffering pain,
  iv. p actually occurring,
  v. p actually being a case of someone suffering pain,
  vi. p being intrinsically evil in virtue of being a case of someone suffering pain,
  vii. love being inappropriate to p.

The love of evil is said to be a mixed evil because (iii) contains a part (the pleasant feeling of love) that is good, while parts iv–vi are all bad. Moore also claims that it is an organic unity. Its value is much lower than the sum of the values of its parts. He also says that it is less bad if any component is false (sections 124–5).

Finally, let us consider an example from the category of mixed goods. The hatred of evil is a good example. This can be illustrated by resolute defiance as well as compassion, which Moore (strangely) thinks of as the hatred of the sufferings of others. This seems somewhat different from 'sympathy' literally understood. For, as I see it, one has sympathy for another when one "shares the other's pain". This would not be hatred of his pain so much as being pained by the fact that he is in pain. In any case, Moore seems to think that the fundamental state of affairs in this case would be of this general form:

HE: i. S believing that there is a state of affairs, p, that consists in a person, x, suffering pain,
  ii. S believing p to be intrinsically evil in virtue of its being a case of someone suffering pain,
  iii. S feeling hatred for p in virtue of its being a case of someone suffering pain,
  iv. p actually occurring,
  v. p actually being a case of someone suffering pain,
  vi. p being intrinsically evil in virtue of being a case of someone suffering pain, and
  vii. hatred being appropriate to p.

Suppose that p is a state of affairs consisting in the children of Somalia being conscious of pain; suppose that some person, S, knows about this state of affairs, and correctly believes that it is occurring and is evil. Suppose S hates it. Then we have a case of what Moore calls 'compassion'. Moore would say that though this whole state of affairs contains several bad components, taken as a whole it is one of the great goods. The existence of such a thing in complete isolation would be good.[2]

So there we have a few of the main elements in Moore's axiology. I think his views about the items I have not discussed are pretty similar in form to his views about these. Let these remarks suffice to illustrate the sort of thing he says about the others.

Before moving on, I should also mention that Moore makes one remark that may seem to doom my hedonistic plan. That, of course, is his remark about the consciousness of pleasure: 'the mere consciousness of pleasure, however intense, does not *by itself*, appear to be a *great* good, even if it has slight intrinsic value' (section 127).

Although Moore does not put it in this way, I think it would be fair to say that his view was that the things he has mentioned are the most important ultimate bearers of intrinsic value. If I were in Moore's position, I might want to go on to say that the intrinsic value of someone's life or a whole possible world is the sum of the intrinsic values of states of affairs like these true in that life or world. But Moore was far too cautious for this. He feared that lives and worlds might be organic unities. He feared that there might be great goods that are inconceivable. Thus, he was more cautious. He merely suggested (section 111) that the Good Life is the life filled with personal affections and aesthetic enjoyments and the other great goods he discerned, and devoid of cruelty, lasciviousness, pain, and the other evils. Similarly, he must have thought that a good world would be one of the same description.

7.2. *A Moorean Form of Hedonism*

As I mentioned earlier, Moore considered himself an anti-hedonist. Commentators sometimes take him to be a pluralist, though it has

---

[2] Moore's view seems to have been that a state of affairs such as this might be bad "on the whole" since it involves the actual suffering of the children of Somalia. That bad component contributes a lot of negative value to the whole situation. But if we consider the state of affairs "as a whole", we find that it is a great intrinsic good.

also been suggested that he could be described as a 'refined hedonist'.[3] I think Moore's view is approximately equivalent to a form of hedonism. First I will sketch the theory I have in mind. Then I will briefly consider the question whether it is equivalent to Moore's theory. I will also give some reasons to doubt the plausibility of the theory. In the next chapter, when I discuss the nature of hedonism in general, I will say a few words about the question whether the theory I here propose is legitimately considered to be a form of hedonism.

Earlier, in section 7.1, I presented a summary of Moore's axiology. According to that summary, there are some great unmixed intrinsic goods—the love of our friends and of beautiful things. There are some great intrinsic evils—the love of evil and of ugly things, the hatred of good and of beautiful things, and the consciousness of pain. There are some mixed goods—the hatred of bad and of ugly things.

If we make two uniform substitutions in Moore's outline, we will have the makings of a form of attitudinal hedonism. The substitutions in question should be obvious. Where Moore speaks of the "love" of something or other, we will speak instead of the taking of intrinsic attitudinal pleasure in that thing; and where Moore speaks of the "hatred" of something or other, we will speak instead of the taking of intrinsic attitudinal pain in that thing. (I also make a modest change in his account of the great evil that he calls 'the consciousness of pain'.) The resulting summary suggests a form of intrinsic attitudinal hedonism.

1. Great unmixed intrinsic goods:
   (a) The taking of intrinsic attitudinal pleasure in the goodness of our friends.
   (b) The taking of intrinsic attitudinal pleasure in things of beauty.
2. Great intrinsic evils:
   (a) The taking of intrinsic attitudinal pleasure in what is evil or ugly: e.g., cruelty and lasciviousness.
   (b) The taking of intrinsic attitudinal pain in what is good or beautiful: e.g., malice, envy, and contempt.
   (c) The taking of intrinsic attitudinal pain in our own feelings: e.g., sensory pains.
3. Great mixed intrinsic goods:
   (a) The taking of intrinsic attitudinal pain in what is ugly or bad: e.g., courage and resolute defiance.
   (b) The taking of intrinsic attitudinal pain in the suffering of others: e.g., compassion, or sympathy for those who suffer pain.

[3] Baldwin so describes him, in *G. E. Moore*, 131.

Since the substitutions are uniform, it will not be necessary to investigate all the cases. Let us focus here on one great good—aesthetic appreciations—and one great evil—cruelty. What I say about these should carry over to the other cases (with one uncontroversial exception—the consciousness of pain—which I will discuss later).

Moore took aesthetic appreciations to be cases in which someone engages in the proper appreciation of a beautiful object. He says (p. 189) that such appreciations include some kind of feeling or emotion toward the beautiful object. He identifies the emotion as "appreciation", and thus suggests that this emotion is the central identifying feature of the state. Mere cognition of beautiful objects is not enough. There must be some sort of appropriate emotional reaction to the beauty of the object. Precisely what emotion did he have in mind?

I do not think it farfetched at all to suggest that a person appreciates the beauty of an object if and only if he takes an appropriate sort of pleasure in the beauty of that object. This suggestion is borne out by Moore's use of the phrase '*enjoying* and appreciating' (p. 195) in his discussion of aesthetic appreciations. A bit later in the same context, when he performs the Isolation Test in order to check for the intrinsic value of aesthetic appreciations and personal affections, he asks us to 'imagine the case of a single person, *enjoying* throughout eternity the contemplation of scenery as beautiful, and intercourse with persons as admirable, as can be imagined' (p. 197, emphasis added). Clearly, Moore himself thought of aesthetic appreciation as a sort of enjoyment, which I understand to be the taking of pleasure.

I have been assuming that the objects of attitudinal pleasure are all states of affairs. Thus, when I gave examples to illustrate this sort of pleasure, I mentioned such things as Bob's taking pleasure in *there being peace in the world*. But the text suggests that Moore did not take such things as these to be the objects of aesthetic appreciation. He writes as if the objects of this attitude would be concrete works of art or nature—such things as a beautiful picture or some scenery or a musical performance (section 115).

It is not too hard to adapt Moore's conception to the present style of formulation. Imagine that someone is looking at and enjoying a beautiful painting. We might ask her what, in particular, she finds pleasing about the painting. Suppose she says that she likes the colors, the composition, and the looks on the faces of the characters depicted. Then it might be that she takes intrinsic attitudinal pleasure in the fact that *the painting has these colors, is composed in that way, and depicts the looks on the characters' faces like this* (where *this* indicates the particular aspect of the looks on the faces that the observer likes). Then we have a suitably propositional object for this person's aesthetic appreciation. I assume that in any case in which someone takes pleasure in some physical object such as a painting or some scenery, we can capture the enjoyed aspects of the object by formulating some appropriate proposition about the object. To find the proposition, ask the person what she likes about the object. Her answer will point you in the right direction.

Suppose that these facts about the painting enhance its beauty. That is, suppose that the painting is more beautiful in virtue of the fact that it has the particular colors our observer enjoys, and in virtue of the fact that it is composed in the manner she likes, and in virtue of the fact that it involves the depiction of those looks on the faces of the characters. Then the propositional objects of this observer's aesthetic appreciation are indeed worthy of such appreciation. They are facts about the painting that make it more beautiful. Moore would say that all this helps to make her enjoyment of the painting more valuable.

Other factors make the enjoyment more valuable, too. These include the truth of the propositional objects being enjoyed. If the painting actually does have those colors, and in fact is composed in that way, and if the faces do have those looks, then the things about it that please the observer are "accurate". She is pleased that the painting is a certain way, and it *is* that way. This also enhances the value of her pleasure.

Let us introduce a new term to capture all of these ideas. Let us say that if intrinsic attitudinal pleasure is taken in these facts about the painting—facts in virtue of which it really is beautiful—then that pleasure is 'properly directed'. It is directed toward a state of affairs that deserves to have pleasure taken in it. As a result, such episodes of aesthetic appreciation (or enjoyment) have great positive intrinsic value.

Moore was no enthusiast for sensory pleasures. He estimated their intrinsic values to be relatively low or even negligible (section 127). In order to produce a form of hedonism equivalent to Moore's axiology, we can stipulate that mere bodily sensations are *not* worthy objects of our attitudinal pleasure. Suppose someone is getting a massage. Suppose he takes intrinsic attitudinal pleasure in the fact that he is experiencing certain feelings in his sore and aching muscles. We can stipulate that he is taking pleasure in something that does not deserve to have much pleasure taken in it. (Not to suggest that it deserves to have *pain* taken in it, either.) As a result, the whole state of affairs is of negligible intrinsic value.

We now turn to the case of cruelty, which Moore took to be a great mixed evil. Moore said that evil and ugly objects do not deserve to be objects of our pleasure. If we take intrinsic attitudinal pleasure in such things, we thereby create intrinsically bad states of affairs. These are the states of affairs Moore characterized as cruelty and lasciviousness. Let us focus on cruelty. Suppose an innocent person is suffering. Suppose some cruel person observes this and takes pleasure in it, knowing it to be a case of an innocent person suffering.

Again, we need to make some trivial adjustments to Moore's formulation. We need to find a suitable propositional object for the cruel person's enjoyment. We can follow the procedure already introduced. We can ask the cruel person what he likes about the suffering of the innocent person. Perhaps what he likes is simply the fact that this innocent person is suffering. Then that fact is the object of his intrinsic attitudinal pleasure. He takes pleasure in the fact that this innocent person is suffering. Since the fact itself is bad, it is an inappropriate object for pleasure. The whole state of affairs that consists in this cruel person's taking intrinsic attitudinal pleasure in the fact that this other innocent person is suffering is very bad in itself. It essentially involves pleasure being taken in something that does not deserve to have pleasure taken in it. That object deserves to have pain taken in it.

Let us say that an episode of intrinsic attitudinal pleasure is "properly directed" if its object is something worthy of such pleasure. Following Moore, I stipulate that suitable facts about beautiful objects and good people are worthy of pleasure. I also stipulate that facts about mere bodily feelings (such as the feelings of pressure while getting a massage) are not worthy of such pleasure, and so attitudes of pleasure directed upon facts about these feelings are not properly directed. Let us say that an episode of such pleasure is "improperly directed" if its object is something seriously unworthy of such pleasure—and now, again following Moore, I stipulate that suitable facts about ugly objects and bad people fall into this category.

Concerning intrinsic attitudinal pain, let us say that an episode of intrinsic attitudinal pain is properly directed if its object is something worthy of pain, such as suitable facts about something evil or ugly or some other person's pain. Thus, we take compassion to occur when someone is pained by the fact that another person is suffering, rather than (as Moore had it) when someone "hates" someone's pain. We can also say that an episode of intrinsic attitudinal pain is improperly directed if it is directed toward something that deserves to be an object of pleasure, such as facts about something beautiful or good. We also need to incorporate something that will play the role of sensory pain, which Moore took to be a great evil. Although it may seem counter-intuitive, we can simplify matters considerably if we first identify the class of bodily sensations normally understood to be sensory pains. Then we can say that each of these sensations is something that does *not* deserve to be the object of intrinsic attitudinal pain on the part of the person who feels it. Then, if someone takes pain in such a feeling, his pain will count as *improperly directed*. As a result, such pains will *decrease* the welfare of the person who feels them, just as Moore intended.

Now I can state the specific form of DAIAH that I want to compare to Moore's "Ideal". It goes like this:

Moorean Desert-Adjusted Intrinsic Attitudinal Hedonism

i. Every properly directed episode of intrinsic attitudinal pleasure or pain is intrinsically good; every improperly directed episode of intrinsic attitudinal pleasure or pain is intrinsically bad.

ii. The intrinsic value of an episode of intrinsic attitudinal pleasure or pain is determined by the intensity, duration, and pleasure- or pain-worthiness of the pleasure or pain contained in that episode.

iii. The intrinsic value of a complex thing such as a life or a possible world is entirely determined by the intrinsic values of the episodes of intrinsic attitudinal pleasure and pain contained in the complex thing.

Note that the value of an episode of pleasure or pain is alleged by (ii) to be determined by three variables: intensity, duration, and pleasure- or pain-worthiness of its object. In order to explain precisely how these variables are supposed to determine the value of an episode of pleasure or pain, it would be necessary to assign numerical values to intensity, duration, and pleasure- or pain-worthiness. Then it would be necessary to describe mathematical functions from combinations of those values as inputs to some number as output. The output number would be the intrinsic value of the episode of pleasure or pain as a whole. Describing such functions would take us far afield. Instead, I will simply sketch a few of the principles governing the functions:

If e is an episode of properly directed pleasure, then increases in e's intensity, duration, or the pleasure-worthiness of e's object yield greater intrinsic value for e.

If e is an episode of properly directed pain, then increases in e's intensity, duration, or the pain-worthiness of e's object yield greater intrinsic value for e.

If e is an episode of improperly directed pleasure, then increases in e's intensity, duration, or the pain-worthiness of e's object yield lesser (more negative) intrinsic value for e.

If e is an episode of improperly directed pain, then increases in e's intensity, duration, or the pleasure-worthiness of e's object yield lesser (more negative) intrinsic value for e.

The first clause of MDAIAH specifies the fundamental sources of intrinsic value according to this axiology. As in every form of hedonism discussed in this book, these "atoms" of value are all episodes of pleasure and pain. In this case, they are episodes of intrinsic attitudinal pleasure and pain. Again, like all other forms of hedonism we have seen, this one implies that a life without pleasure or pain is a life without value. No matter how many friends one has, no matter how much knowledge, truth, virtue, consciousness of beauty, etc. there might be in one's life, MDAIAH implies that that life cannot have a value above zero unless there are some episodes of intrinsic attitudinal pleasure or pain within it. No matter how much ignorance, ugliness, vice, etc. there is in a life, that life cannot have a value below zero unless there are some episodes of intrinsic attitudinal pleasure or pain in it.

Earlier, I introduced the notion of a "pure" form of hedonism. I said that a form of hedonism is pure if it implies that nothing other than episodes of pleasure and pain directly affect the value of a life. Another way of putting this is slightly epistemic, but I hope not misleading: "If we know about the pleasures and pains in a life, then we can determine the value of that life in itself for the one who lives it. We don't need to know anything else about what goes on in that life." If we understand purity in this way, we can say that MDAIAH is a pure form of hedonism.

Thus, MDAIAH is very similar in some respects to the other forms of hedonism we have discussed. However, there are several respects in which this theory is strikingly different.

One important novelty is that MDAIAH does not imply that *every* episode of intrinsic attitudinal pleasure is good. Improperly directed pleasures are not good. Nor does it imply that *every* episode of intrinsic attitudinal pain is bad. Properly directed pains are not bad. Thus, it is not a form of universal attitudinal hedonism. It is much more restricted than that. It implies only that the properly directed pleasures are good, and that the improperly directed pains are bad.

A second, and perhaps even more important, point is this: MDAIAH implies that some episodes of intrinsic attitudinal pleasure are intrinsically *bad*, and that some episodes of intrinsic attitudinal pain are intrinsically *good*. These doctrines may seem to run against the fundamental hedonistic turn of mind. But, of course, that depends upon what one takes to be the "fundamental hedonistic turn of mind".

In *Brentano and Intrinsic Value*, Chisholm uses the term 'transvaluation' to indicate something like the phenomenon illustrated by the love of evil and the hatred of good in this Moorean axiology.[4] In the context of Chisholm's book, the term seems appropriate. That is because Chisholm was working with the notion that love would independently be intrinsically good; when it is the love of evil, it becomes an essential part of something that is extra intrinsically bad. Its intrinsic value seems to be transformed. The term is slightly less appropriate here, since there is nothing in MDAIAH to suggest that intrinsic attitudinal pleasure (considered in isolation) has any intrinsic value. The atoms of value on this theory are more complex things. They are indicated in clause (i) of the statement of the theory. Since these are the "smallest" items discussed in the theory, there is nothing whose value gets "transformed".

Nevertheless, MDAIAH does have an interesting feature: not all pleasures are good; some are bad. Not all pains are bad; some are good. This may raise some eyebrows. Some may wonder whether it is correct to characterize this theory as a form of hedonism. That is a deep and perplexing question. In order to answer it fully and responsibly, we would have to know in general what makes it correct to characterize any theory as a form of hedonism. I discuss that question in greater detail in Chapter 8.

7.3. *The Equivalence of MDAIAH to Moore's Theory*

There is a certain amount of "slack" or vagueness in my formulation of MDAIAH. I specified the fundamental bearers of intrinsic value on the theory pretty clearly. They are all pure attributions of a certain kind of intrinsic attitudinal pleasure or pain. They are either properly directed pleasures or pains, or improperly directed pleasures or pains. There is no slack there. And I said that the intrinsic value of each of these "atoms" of value is entirely determined by several factors: *intensity* of pleasure or pain taken; *duration* of pleasure or pain taken; and *pleasure-worthiness* or *pain-worthiness* of the object of the pleasure or pain. There is not much slack there, either.

---

[4] Chisholm, *Brentano and Intrinsic Value*, 83.

The problem is that I merely hinted at the way in which the three factors work together to generate a measure of the intrinsic value of the state of affairs as a whole. I discussed some sample cases. I said, for example, that it is "extra good" for a person to take intrinsic attitudinal pleasure in the fact that some painting has such-and-such features, when the having of those features makes the painting beautiful. But I did not specify precisely how good the taking of such pleasure would be for each possible combination of intensity, duration, and pleasure-worthiness. To do this, it would be necessary to describe a complex function that would take, as inputs, three amounts—one for intensity, one for duration, and one for pleasure-worthiness—and which would give as its output a single amount—the intrinsic value of the state of affairs as a whole. The specification of such a function would be difficult. It would also go well beyond anything that Moore provided for his own axiology. No such functions are specified in *Principia Ethica.*

To make up for this slack, I make use of a convenient assumption: I assume that my function from intensity, duration, and pleasure- or pain-worthiness yields the same ranking of outputs as whatever function Moore had in mind when he spoke, equally vaguely, of the value of an organic unity being somehow determined by facts about its parts (though, obviously, not merely by adding up the values of its parts).

With this assumption in place, the central difference between Moore's axiology and MDAIAH is this: where the Moorean axiology speaks of love and hate, MDAIAH speaks of intrinsic attitudinal pleasure and pain. But it seems to me that this difference is slight. In fact, I find it difficult to see precisely how these are supposed to differ in some cases. Consider aesthetic appreciations. Moore thinks of these as cases in which someone "loves" some work of art for its beauty. MDAIAH thinks of these as cases in which someone takes intrinsic attitudinal pleasure in the fact that the work of art has certain beauty-making features. What's the difference? Can a connoisseur love a work of art in the specified way without enjoying it? Can she enjoy it in the specified way without loving it?

If Moore's concept of *hate* corresponds in a similar to way to my concept of *intrinsic attitudinal pain*, the near equivalence of the theories is assured. I am inclined to think that insofar as these concepts differ—and I admit that they might—the results generated by MDAIAH are to be preferred. This is in part because I think that the proposed account of compassion is more plausible than Moore's. To feel sympathy, or compassion, for another's pain is to be pained by it, not to "hate" it.

7.4. *Problems for MDAIAH*

So much for the question whether MDAIAH is equivalent to the theory Moore presented in 'The Ideal'. Let us turn to the independently interesting question whether the theory is plausible. I think it is not. The problems concern the evaluation of improperly directed pleasures and properly directed pains, and the implications of these evaluations for the evaluation of lives.

I believe that it is a mistake to say that compassion and courage (as Moore understood these things) are great goods. I think that careful consideration of what MDAIAH implies concerning these things will make the problems apparent. Imagine the somewhat unrealistic case of a person—we can call her 'Anna'—living in Nazi Germany. Suppose Anna does not face any personal dangers; the Nazis are not going to give her any trouble. She is safe. However, Anna is well aware of the plight of the Jews, Gypsies, and homosexuals. She sees that they are suffering and dying. As a sympathetic person, Anna properly appreciates their huge misfortune. Let us assume that Anna is enormously pained by what she correctly takes to be the suffering of these oppressed people. More precisely, let us assume that there are many occasions on which Anna takes intrinsic attitudinal pain in the fact that the oppressed are suffering. Her pain is of great intensity, and it is directed upon an object that fully deserves this emotional reaction.

Let us also suppose (and this is somewhat unrealistic) that Anna has no other pleasures or pains. Her life is an emotional blank aside from the pain she endures when contemplating the suffering of the Jews, Gypsies, and homosexuals.

According to clause (i) of MDAIAH, Anna's pains are all intrinsically good. That is because they are properly directed. This is intended to reflect Moore's view that 'the appreciation of tragedy is a great positive good' (section 133). He explicitly says, in a discussion of this sort of compassionate pain, that 'the existence [of such things] must add value to any whole in which they are contained' (section 133).

MDAIAH implies that Anna's life is outstandingly good in itself for her. It implies that she is living one version of the Good Life. I find this hard to accept. I have stipulated that she is suffering and miserable. I recognize that her suffering and misery are all directed toward objects that are worthy of that emotional reaction, and I recognize that the whole state of affairs is much less bad than it would be if she were happy about the suffering; but I cannot see that things are going well for Anna. Surely she would be better off if she could find something to be happy about.

Recall the 'crib test' from Chapter 1. Suppose I am looking into the crib, checking on my newborn baby. Suppose I am filled with love for her, and want her life to go as well as possible for her. I certainly doubt that I would want her to have a life like Anna's. I cannot imagine hoping that my beloved child would go through her whole life feeling no emotion other than compassionate pain for the suffering of others. Admittedly, if I knew that she would have to confront suffering, then I would prefer to have her react to it with sympathy rather than indifference or some sort of perverted delight. Perhaps that is because I would want my daughter to be a morally sensitive person. But I would not think that large doses of compassionate pain would help to improve my daughter's welfare level, or help to give her a life well worth living. Yet this seems to be what MDAIAH implies.

It should be recognized that Moore himself says quite a bit more about cases such as this. He draws a distinction between value "as a whole" and "on the whole", and points out that the great disvalue of the suffering of others might in many cases more than counterbalance the value of the compassion. He mentions that it would surely be perverse to bring suffering into the world merely for the purpose of letting it serve as the object of someone's sympathy. He makes a number of related points. Yet the conclusion remains: he thinks the state of mind of a person hating (or "properly appreciating") the suffering of others is a complex organic unity; he thinks that such a state of mind is a great mixed intrinsic good; he seems to think that a whole (such as a human life?) is made better by the addition of such a thing. All of this is reflected in MDAIAH. When so understood, the view is implausible. It implies that certain lives would be good, though (speaking here just for myself) I find it difficult to see how such lives could be thought good in the relevant sense.

A similar thing happens in the other "transvaluation" case. To see this, we need to consider someone who enjoys a lot of improperly directed pleasures. Let us imagine a tasteless aesthete, Tom. Suppose Tom is a great lover of art, but suppose all of his aesthetic appreciation is directed toward works of art that are not beautiful. He likes the tackiest sort of kitsch. Suppose he goes through his whole life taking great intrinsic attitudinal pleasure in things such as paintings of florescent maidens on black velvet backgrounds, and statues of chubby gnomes and winking elves, believing them to be beautiful. (If you think these things are in fact worthy of admiring aesthetic contemplation, then I request that you make an appropriate substitution. In place of the winking elves, think of something that you take to be truly ugly.) Suppose, in addition, that the rest of Tom's life is an emotional blank. He does not take pleasure or pain in anything other than these truly ugly works of "art".

Moore thought that such pleasures as Tom's are odious. He says, 'When we admire what is ugly…, believing that it is beautiful…, this belief seems also to enhance [make even worse] the intrinsic vileness of our condition' (section 125). Clauses (i) and (ii) of MDAIAH incorporate my hedonistic analogue of this Moorean view. Since Tom's pleasure is improperly directed, clause (i) implies that each such pleasure is intrinsically bad. Clause (ii) suggests (but does not independently entail) that the stronger and longer the pleasure, and the uglier the gnome, the worse is Tom's pleasure. Since there are many such pleasures in Tom's life, and no other pleasures or pains, clause (iii) implies that Tom's life is very bad in itself for him. Better he should never have lived at all than to live in this vile manner.

This seems to me to be a bit harsh. I agree that there is something unfortunate about the fact that Tom has such bad taste. Maybe if he took a course in art appreciation he would learn to appreciate better art, and he would enjoy it even more than the art he currently enjoys. But it does not seem to me that his bad taste is so vile as to drive his overall welfare level into the negative range. In fact, I would be inclined to say that Tom is not doing badly at all. He is happy; he is enjoying things; he is an innocent fellow, doing no harm to anyone. His misguided aesthetic appreciations should not have been transvaluated. At worst, their value should have been somewhat mitigated.

However, my main point in discussing Moore's axiology is neither to attack it nor to defend it. Rather, it is to illustrate one of my main claims concerning attitudinal hedonism. That claim concerns the plasticity of the view. Attitudinal hedonism can take many forms. I have attempted to show that IAH is admirably well suited to serve as the basis for a number of variations. If we add clauses about pleasure-worthiness and pain-worthiness of objects, we can generate DAIAH. If we add clauses about properly and improperly directed pleasures and pains, we can generate MDAIAH. Other modifications will yield other variants. I discuss one of these in Appendix D.

Appendix D
Darwall on Valuing Activity

I think it is interesting to note a sort of "convergence" among axiologies. Some philosophers are gripped by the notion of 'flourishing'. They think the Good Life must somehow be a matter of the individual's flourishing as a human being. Other philosophers are gripped by the notion of "satisfaction". They think the Good Life must somehow be a matter of the individual's getting the things he desires, or would desire if fully informed. Pluralists focus on a number of items, thinking that the Good Life must somehow consist in the getting of the things on their lists. Hedonists, of course, think it depends upon pleasure. Philosophers of all stripes (if careful and responsible) recognize that the vision that originally attracted them needs clarification, refinement, and development if it is to capture a plausible view about the Good Life.

The noteworthy phenomenon is this: when they refine and clarify their views, these philosophers often tend to move toward common ground. The hedonist backs away from Default Hedonism, and begins to think that pleasures are better as they are taken in more deserving objects. The preferentist backs away from a view about the satisfaction of actual desires, and begins to think that it is more important that rational desires be satisfied, or that one satisfies desires whose satisfaction is sure to yield high-quality enjoyment. The pluralist begins to think that the things on his list are good—but only if the person who receives them gets some appropriate enjoyment from their possession. In the end, the views begin to look similar, and the visions of the Good Life begin to look like visions of the same life.

Furthermore, it seems to me that when this sort of convergence occurs, the views converge on a sort of desert-adjusted intrinsic attitudinal hedonism. Philosophers may disagree about the sorts of objects that deserve pleasure and pain, but they seem to agree that when one enjoys objects that deserve to be enjoyed, one's life is made better.

In this appendix I discuss one example of this phenomenon. It concerns a view sketched by Stephen Darwall in 'Valuing Activity'.[1] I suggest that the view in question is surprisingly similar to a form of intrinsic attitudinal hedonism. This may be worth considering, since Darwall does not seem to be interested in defending any sort of hedonism.

Darwall characterizes his view as being a version of what he calls the 'Aristotelian Thesis'. This is the view that the Good Life consists of excellent, or virtuous, distinctively human activity (p. 176). One who engages in such activity flourishes as a human being and is happy. Although Darwall mentions pleasure, and pleasure plays a role in the theory, his view is not intended to be a form of hedonism. Roughly, Darwall's idea is that a person

---

[1] Darwall, 'Valuing Activity'. Parenthetical page references in this appendix are all to this article. Ch. 4 of Darwall's *Welfare and Rational Care* is a trivially revised version of the 1999 paper.

has a good life if (a) he engages in a variety of activities that involve the valuing, or appreciation, of various good things, and (b) he properly values the things in question as well as his own activity.

Darwall's main thesis is suggested by these passages:

'we flourish through (meritorious) activities such as parenting and music-making, because these activities involve an appreciation of things that matter, things with worth' (p. 179).

'a good human life consists of activities that involve the appreciation of worth and merit. I do not claim that appreciating these values is the only source of human good. I only claim, somewhat vaguely, that it is the major source' (pp. 179–80).

'a life of virtuous activity is best *for the person herself*, what benefits *her* most' (p. 181).

Darwall makes use of a phrase with a double meaning as his title. 'Valuing Activity' can be understood in two ways. (a) It indicates a certain sort of activity—activity in which we are valuing something. That type of activity is important here, since Darwall says that the Good Life is the life chock full of this sort of activity. In addition, (b) the phrase indicates something that we can do to some activity—we can value it, or take it to be valuable. That is another element in the Good Life. He identifies a certain sort of activity (activity in which someone is valuing something), and then he claims that this sort of activity is valuable (thus he is valuing valuing activity).

I propose to formulate something that Darwall never quite says, and maybe something a bit more blatant than he would want to say. I acknowledge his remark (quoted above) designed to withhold his endorsement of this overly strong version. I state it in this way in order to highlight the distinctive features of the view.

In order to understand Darwall's view, we need to understand some technical terms that he uses. Let us start with 'merit' and 'worth'. Darwall explains these by appeal to a Kantian analogy (p. 178). To say that a thing has *worth* is apparently to say that it is important or significant in itself. A Kantian might say that every human being has worth, simply in virtue of being a human being. Some philosophers use the term 'moral considerability' to indicate approximately the same idea. When a thing is morally considerable, we are required to take it into consideration when making moral decisions; we can't just walk all over these things, for such things are deserving of at least some moral respect. But worth is not restricted to persons. A beautiful work of art or an ecosystem might have worth, too.

A thing has *merit* when it is worthy of being admired, or emulated. We credit, praise, admire, encourage, and desire to emulate meritorious things. So, on the Kantian analogy, a person with an outstanding Good Will would have merit. We are humbled or filled with admiration for such a person. Any ordinary person has worth, but only the morally outstanding person has merit.

The notions of merit and worth are linked. A person comes to have merit because of the way she responds to things that have worth. Suppose some things have worth—imagine they are some people, some works of art, and some ecosystems. Suppose a person responds appropriately to all of these things. Imagine that she shows proper respect and consideration for the other people, and that she properly appreciates the beauty and importance of the works of art and the ecosystems. Then this person has merit. Someone has merit because she appropriately responds to things with worth. Darwall goes so far as to suggest that merit 'consists in being properly oriented to or guided by [worth]' (p. 179).

Darwall also claims that whatever is meritorious is worthy. As a result, we have a sort of hierarchy. Suppose something, X, has worth. Let it just be a beautiful painting, or a nice piece of music. Then suppose S_1 responds appropriately to X. S_1 might admire the beauty of X, for example. Then the proper response of S_1 toward X is also worthy, because it is meritorious, and it would be nice if S_2 responded appropriately to it. Suppose S_2 does this. S_2 says, 'Isn't it wonderful that S_1 has appreciated X as is appropriate!' Then S_2's response to S_1's response to X is also meritorious, and hence worthy. Darwall hints at this when he says that merit ramifies both "up" and "out" (p. 192).

The appropriate response to a worthy or meritorious thing is *appreciation*. What is involved in appreciating something of merit or worth? It is not merely a matter of judging that the thing is good. An observer might *feel* nothing about a work of art, but since the experts tell him it is a good one, and he believes them, he might still *judge* that it is a good one. But looking at the painting leaves him cold. In this case, he does not appreciate it. To appreciate a meritorious thing, one must "esteem" its meritorious traits (p. 186). One must "see or feel" the thing itself and its traits; it has to seem to one as if it is meritorious. A similar thing happens in the case of worthiness. The appreciation of such a thing is not simply a matter of judging that it has worth. Rather, the object must seem important, as if it matters. Appreciation is thus "quasi-perceptual" (p. 186). When you appreciate a thing, it seems almost as if you are seeing or feeling its importance. Darwall says that in such cases, the observer stands in an 'experienced valuing relation to the thing itself' (p. 186).

Appreciation involves pleasure. Darwall reminds us of an untypical remark in the *Nicomachean Ethics* where Aristotle is talking about virtuous activity. He says that 'pleasure completes the activity…as an end that supervenes as the bloom of youth does on those in the flower of their age'.[2] Darwall incorporates something like this idea into his account of appreciation. When you properly appreciate some worthy or meritorious thing, you will enjoy doing so. 'Virtuous activity is actively enjoyed' (p. 188).

Darwall makes a couple of comments on this doctrine of enjoyment. In all these cases, he is talking about the enjoyment that goes along with the proper appreciation of some evaluative activity.

(a) The object of enjoyment is not merely some proposition to the effect that the activity is good or meritorious. The object of enjoyment is the activity itself. A merely continent person could be pleased that he is doing something

---

[2] Aristotle, *Nicomachean Ethics*, 1174b33–5, (bk 10, ch. 5; translation by Darwall on p. 176).

meritorious; he could find the act itself a bit onerous. But a virtuous person would actually enjoy the act.

(b) Before engaging in some evaluative activity, one may have "favorable regard" for it. He may believe it to be meritorious. This mere favorable regard "turns into" enjoyment when he is doing the act (p. 187). It "becomes enjoyment" when the action turns out as he envisioned (p. 188).

(c) The virtuous person does not merely feel some pleasure that happens to be produced by doing the act. Rather, he takes a sort of pleasurable appreciation in the merit of his object. This is illustrated by the case of a music-lover who revels in the beauty of the music.

(d) The Sign Theory: the pleasure you take in virtuous activity is a sign, not the substance, of the virtuousness of your activity (p. 189). You don't virtuously raise children because of the pleasure you get out of it; you virtuously raise children because you appreciate their worth; you then enjoy doing it, and this enjoyment is a sign of your virtue (p. 189).

Darwall speaks about the 'quality of the appreciation'. By this he evidently means to suggest that when you appreciate something, it is best if your appreciation matches its object properly. So, for example, if you deeply appreciate what you take to be the beauty in some work of art, but it isn't beautiful, then your appreciation misfires and is of low quality. There must be a proper relation between the subjective element (your appreciation) and the objective element (the actual merit of the object of your appreciation). I take this to mean that it is better to appreciate objects that in fact deserve to be appreciated (pp. 190–1).

Darwall does not specify much more about the way in which the intrinsic value of an act of valuing is determined by the merit or worth of its object and the appreciation lavished upon it. I will make some assumptions about this. I assume that it is better in itself to appreciate things in proportion to their actual merits. Too much is less good; too little is less good. If you appreciate things in exact proportion to their merits, your appreciation is most valuable. Furthermore, it would seem natural to suppose that it is better to be engaged in the great appreciation of outstandingly meritorious things, rather than in the tiny appreciation of trivially meritorious things. We might put this by saying that, other things being equal, properly proportioned appreciation of more valuable things is more valuable.

It is not difficult to understand the general picture of the Good Life that emerges from all this. On this view, a person would be living the Good Life if he were frequently engaged in activities that involve the deep appreciation of meritorious and worthy things. So, for example, imagine a person who participates wholeheartedly in family life, raising and nurturing his children. Suppose he appreciates the worthiness of his children and of his child-rearing activities. He enjoys being a father. Suppose, in addition, that he works hard at his job as a professor of philosophy. He appreciates the worthiness of the task as well as the merits of his students. And in addition to all this, he has some active hobbies. Imagine that he practices and performs with a musical group. Suppose he is fully engaged in the music and takes great pleasure in it and his musical activities. Suppose this sort of virtuous activity continues for many happy years, until the children are grown and the professor is retired.

As I understand it, Darwall's view is that this sort of life would be good in itself for the one who lives it.[3]

Following Darwall, I will use the term 'valuing activity' to indicate activity in which something is appreciated, or valued. If a father devotes a half-hour to reading with his daughter, and he appreciates the worth and merit of his daughter and his activity, then he is engaged in an episode of valuing activity. If an amateur musician spends the better part of the morning practising with her musical group, and as she does this she appreciates the worth of the music, her fellow musicians, and the activity itself, she is also engaged in an episode of valuing activity. With this concept in hand, I will state in my own words what I take to be the core of the theory:

An Axiology of Valuing Activity

i. Every episode of valuing activity is intrinsically good.

ii. The intrinsic value of an episode of valuing activity is determined by the amount of appreciation it contains and the merit or worth of the objects of the appreciation in such a way that episodes containing greater amounts of appreciation, directed upon objects of greater merit or worth, have greater intrinsic value.

iii. The value of a life for the one who lives it is determined [largely] by the intrinsic values of the episodes of valuing activity performed within that life.

This is my reinterpretation of a view suggested by Darwall when he said, 'a life of virtuous activity is best *for the person herself*, what benefits *her* most' (p. 181).

One could raise a number of objections to this view. One serious problem is that the view as so far stated contains no information about the Bad. There is nothing here to indicate what makes a life worse in itself for the one who lives it. But, of course, Darwall was discussing the Good Life. He apparently was not attempting to give an account of the principles for evaluating every possible life. There is also some obscurity in the account of the way in which the values of the episodes of valuing activity determine the value of the life. Do we sum the values of these episodes to find the value of the life? What about subtracting to reflect the disvalue of bad episodes within the life? Or is there some sort of holism at work here?

I am not interested in pursuing any of these questions. I am more interested in considering the question whether this axiology is similar to a form of attitudinal hedonism. I think it is. In fact, I think it is equivalent to (a fragment of) a specific variety of desert-adjusted attitudinal hedonism.

---

[3] Assuming, I guess, that there are no serious "negatives" to be subtracted. I also assume that the person must not suffer any terrible misfortunes, that his health must not interfere, etc. Darwall does not devote much attention to these matters in the paper under consideration.

Let me first state a form of desert-adjusted intrinsic attitudinal hedonism that appeared earlier in Chapter 5.

Desert-Adjusted Intrinsic Attitudinal Hedonism

i. Every episode of intrinsic attitudinal pleasure is intrinsically good; every episode of intrinsic attitudinal pain is intrinsically bad.

ii. The intrinsic value of an episode of intrinsic attitudinal pleasure is equal to the desert-adjusted amount of pleasure contained in that episode; the intrinsic value of an episode of pain is equal to − (the desert-adjusted amount of pain contained in that episode).

iii. The intrinsic value of a life is entirely determined by the intrinsic values of the episodes of intrinsic attitudinal pleasure and pain contained in that life, in such a way that one life is intrinsically better than another if and only if the net desert-adjusted amount of intrinsic attitudinal pleasure in the one is greater than the net amount of that sort of pleasure in the other.

In clause (i), DAIAH expresses the idea that every episode of intrinsic attitudinal pleasure is good. In clause (ii), it makes the evaluation a bit more precise by saying that the value of such an episode is affected by the extent to which the object of the pleasure deserves such a response. We could modify the first of these features by saying instead that episodes of intrinsic attitudinal pleasure are intrinsically good—*but only when the pleasure is taken in some worthy or meritorious object.* If the pleasure is taken in some worthless and meritless object, the episode has no value. And we could modify the second feature by saying that the value of an episode of intrinsic attitudinal pleasure is determined by the amount of pleasure in that episode, *adjusted to reflect the extent to which the amount of pleasure fits the merit or worth of the object of the pleasure.* We can abbreviate this last point by say-ing that the relevant feature is 'merit-or-worth-adjusted amount of pleasure'. Finally, we can simply delete all the components of the theory that concern pain and intrinsic badness.

Now consider this form of hedonism:

Merit-or-Worth-Adjusted Intrinsic Attitudinal Hedonism

i. Every episode of intrinsic attitudinal pleasure that has a worthy or merit-orious object is intrinsically good.

ii. The intrinsic value of an episode of intrinsic attitudinal pleasure that has a worthy or meritorious object is equal to the merit-or-worth-adjusted amount of pleasure contained in that episode.

iii. The intrinsic value of a life is entirely determined by the intrinsic values of the episodes of intrinsic attitudinal pleasure that occur in that life and that have worthy or meritorious objects, in such a way that one life is intrinsically better than another if the merit-or-worth-adjusted amount of intrinsic attitu-dinal pleasure in the one is greater than the amount of that sort of pleasure in the other.

MWAIAH is a form of hedonism. All the fundamental "atoms" of intrinsic value according to this theory are episodes of pleasure. It is not a form of *universal* hedonism, since it does not imply that *all* episodes of pleasure are intrinsically good. (Only the episodes with worthy or meritorious objects are intrinsically good.) But it is a form of *pure* hedonism, since it does imply that nothing other than these episodes of pleasure serves to enhance the intrinsic value of a life for a person. If we know the relevant facts about the pleasures in a person's life, the theory enables us to determine the value of that person's life, even if we know nothing else about the person.

I am inclined to think that MWAIAH is extensionally equivalent to the theory I extracted from Darwall's remarks. If this is right, then, after all is said and done, this Darwallian Aristotelian theory of flourishing turns out to be equivalent to a form of hedonism.

Any life that would be judged good on the Darwallian theory (as I understand it) would be judged good on MWAIAH. Darwall's theory might base its evaluation on one factor (the life contains a lot of "valuing activity"), whereas MWAIAH bases its evaluation on another (the life contains a lot of properly directed attitudinal pleasure). So I am happy to agree that the theories are based upon different conceptions of the "substance of a person's good". They are distinct theories. My claim is just that, in spite of their differences, the theories yield nearly equivalent evaluations of lives.

Perhaps it will be easy to see why the theories yield similar outcomes if we take note of the fact that one can be engaged in valuing activity of the right sort if and only if one is taking intrinsic attitudinal pleasure in some worthy or meritorious object. Even if pleasure is no more than a mere sign of virtuous activity (like the bloom of health on the cheek of one in the flower of his age), if the pleasure occurs when and only when the virtuous activity occurs, we can take either as our guide to the value of the life. Given that these items occur in equal amounts within any life, it seems to make little difference whether we select the activity or the pleasure as the foundation of value. The ranking of lives will be the same.

There are further differences that must be acknowledged. Darwall went out of his way to emphasize the fact that, as he sees it, one's motivation for engaging in meritorious actions is not that one hopes thereby to get some pleasure. As he sees it, one engages in such activities for their own sake, simply because one sees that the activities themselves, as well as the objects appreciated in those activities, are worthy of appreciation. MWAIAH does not have these implications concerning motivation. It allows that a person might be motivated by a desire for pleasure. Is that not a difference between the two theories?

If this doctrine about motivation is an essential feature of Darwall's theory, then we can add a parenthetical remark to clause (ii) of MWAIAH to ensure that it is an essential feature of the proposed form of hedonism, too. The parenthetical remark would be this: 'when some valuing activity is the object of someone's intrinsic attitudinal pleasure, then that valuing activity is more worthy or meritorious if it is performed for its own sake'. As a result of the addition of this remark, the theory now implies that an episode of valuing activity is more meritorious or worthy if it is undertaken for its own sake. Since the value of the pleasure depends upon the degree of merit or worth in the object, it follows that it is better in itself to take pleasure in an episode of valuing activity that is undertaken for its own sake. Lives full of that better sort of valuing activity will accordingly be given a higher evaluation.

I should be clear about my aims here. I have not been trying to show that Darwall is "really" a hedonist. My point is much more modest. I merely mean to be claiming that there is a form of hedonism—MWAIAH—that is at least nearly extensionally equivalent to a simplified version of Darwall's view. I do not think that MWAIAH is a plausible theory. I think there are serious gaps in it. One very serious gap is that there is no explanation of the way in which various amounts of merit and worth combine with various amounts of attitudinal pleasure to yield determinate amounts of intrinsic value. Another, perhaps even more serious, gap concerns the complete lack of any account of the Bad. Neither Darwall's own theory, nor MWAIAH, contains clauses specifying the items that serve to make a life worse in itself for the one who lives it.[4] As a result, clause (iii) as it currently stands, is unacceptable. It implies that one life is better than another whenever the one contains more of the right sort of pleasure than the other. But of course, one life could contain more pleasure *but also a lot more pain* than another. In that case, the one would probably not be better than the other.

However, I do think that a fully developed version of MWAIAH might be considerably more plausible. Formulating such a theory is a project for another day and another philosopher. My impression is that if the theory were fleshed out, it would begin to look much more like Moore's theory in 'The Ideal' than it would like anything Aristotle ever said.[5] But such speculations carry me far afield. My main aim here is simply to illustrate once more that attitudinal hedonism can take a lot of forms, and in some of them it is equivalent to views not normally thought to be hedonistic.

[4] The following case illustrates the problem. Suppose two twins, Stefan and Steven, enjoy very many exactly similar episodes of intrinsic attitudinal pleasure for fifty years. Suppose they take pleasure in similar objects, and each object is highly worthy or meritorious. So far, MWAIAH would rate Stefan's life as very good in itself for Stefan, and Steven's life just as good for Steven. Now suppose Stefan dies peacefully in his sleep, but Steven continues to live for another fifty years. Suppose that in the latter half of his life, Steven never enjoys any pleasure. Suppose he suffers unremitting intense pain. Suppose he becomes a nasty, hate-filled monster, constantly miserable with envy and spite. His life becomes a horror. MWAIAH implies that nothing that happens in the second half of Steven's life has any bearing on the value of that life in itself for Steven. His life remains just as good in itself for Steven as Stefan's life is for Stefan. That seems absurd.

[5] Darwall briefly alludes to Moore at the very end of his book. He says that Moore's view 'has something approaching the ring of truth' (*Welfare and Rational Care*, 102).

CHAPTER 8

But is it Really "Hedonism"?

In earlier chapters of this book I have described an array of axiological theories. I described some of them as forms of sensory hedonism. The Default Hedonism and Aristippean Hedonism of Chapter 2 fall into this category. Although I did not try to formulate it with care, I think Mill's Qualified Hedonism can be interpreted as a form of sensory hedonism. The other theories are forms of attitudinal hedonism. This group includes Intrinsic Attitudinal Hedonism (introduced in Chapter 4) as well as several "adjusted" versions. Altitude-Adjusted, Truth-Adjusted, and Desert-Adjusted Intrinsic Attitudinal Hedonism (Chapter 5) fall into this category. I formulated an axiology intended to be relevantly like the hedonism of Epicurus. That appeared in Appendix C. I also described (in Chapter 7) another variant intended to be extensionally equivalent to the axiology presented by G. E. Moore in 'The Ideal'. In Appendix D I formulated a kind of hedonism that is, I claimed, nearly extensionally equivalent to the Aristotelian theory that Darwall discusses in 'Valuing Activity'.

In some cases, I formulated a theory in an effort to show that hedonism has the resources to answer certain classic objections. I claimed that every one of these theories is a form of hedonism. Some, I said, are forms of sensory hedonism. Others are forms of attitudinal hedonism. But they are all forms of hedonism.

Critics might find this approach problematic. Such critics might acknowledge that the proposed axiologies generate the desired evaluations, but they might wonder whether this suffices to answer the objections. After all, they might reason, the objections were objections to *hedonism*; they were supposed to show that *hedonism* generates the wrong results in certain cases. Merely producing *some axiology* that generates the right results in these cases does not suffice to answer the objection. The new axiology has to be a form of *hedonism*. Otherwise, it is not relevant to the original objection. How can I defend hedonism against these objections by producing axiologies that are not forms of hedonism?

Furthermore, there are some reasons for thinking that the proposed theories are not forms of hedonism. Some have said that these theories are forms of pluralism. If they are forms of pluralism, they are not forms of hedonism. Others have said that these theories violate the principle of the supervenience of value upon mental states. They have said that this principle captures an essential feature of hedonism. So they have concluded that the proposed theories are not forms of hedonism.

In this chapter I address these questions. I try to show that the axiological theories I have presented in this book are forms of hedonism, and that they are not in violation of the arguments from pluralism and supervenience. First, obviously, we have to know what makes a theory a form of hedonism.

8.1. *A Historical Account of Hedonism*

We might start out by thinking that what marks a theory as a form of hedonism is that it is relevantly like the theories defended by the great unquestionable hedonists of the past: Aristippus, Epicurus, Bentham, Mill, and Sidgwick. Mere accidental extensional equivalence cannot be sufficient. It must be that the theory explains the goodness of a life by appeal to something about pleasure (rather than by appeal to the satisfaction of desires, or virtue, or perfection, or the possession of items from any list containing items other than pleasure).

This historical approach is clearly suggestive, and would vindicate my claims about the theories discussed in this book; but in the end it is unsatisfactory. Part of the problem is that there might be some debate about which great axiologists of the past have been hedonists. A prime example is Mill. I claim that he is a hedonist. I am sure he would categorize himself in that way. If I accepted the historical approach, I would claim that certain of the views discussed in this book are forms of hedonism precisely because they are so similar to the view defended by Mill. I would try to show this in the case of Mill's Qualified Hedonism and my Altitude-Adjusted Intrinsic Attitudinal Hedonism in Chapter 4. However, if I were to argue in this way, my line of argument might backfire. Recall that a central part of Moore's attack on Mill turned on precisely this point. Moore claimed that Mill's theory is *not a form of hedonism!*[1]

---

[1] Moore, *Principia Ethica*, ch. III, sect. 48.

Critics of this historical approach might take the same line. They might agree that some of my theories are in important ways similar to the theories of Epicurus, Aristippus, Bentham, Mill, Sidgwick, and others whom I take to be hedonists, but that since several of these philosophers were not hedonists in the first place, the comparison casts doubt upon my claims. The similarities demonstrate that my theories are *not* forms of hedonism, they might say.

In order to prove them wrong, I would have to bring in some independent argument to show that the philosophers whose names appear on my list of "Great Unquestionable Hedonists of the Past" really were hedonists. The historical approach simply assumes it. The upshot is that we need some less question-begging way of identifying a theory as a form of hedonism.

8.2. *Moore's Criterion of Hedonism*

In chapter III of *Principia Ethica*, Moore sets out to refute hedonism. Before turning to the attack, Moore takes a moment to identify the target. He says:

By Hedonism, then, I mean the doctrine that pleasure alone is good as an end—'good' in the sense which I have tried to point out as indefinable. The doctrine that pleasure, *among other things*, is good as an end, is not Hedonism; and I shall not dispute its truth. Nor again is the doctrine that other things, beside pleasure, are good as means, at all inconsistent with Hedonism: the Hedonist is not bound to maintain that 'Pleasure alone is good,' if under good he includes, as we generally do, what is good as means to an end, *as well as* the end itself. In attacking Hedonism, I am therefore simply and solely attacking the doctrine that 'Pleasure *alone* is good as an end or in itself'. (*Principia Ethica*, 62)

We might extract a simple criterion of hedonism from this passage. It is this:

H1: A theory, T, is a form of hedonism if and only if T entails that pleasure is the only thing that is intrinsically good.

Unfortunately, this approach is not acceptable. As formulated here, it seems to imply that hedonistic theories entail that there is *exactly one thing* that is intrinsically good. What else could 'the only thing' mean? But any coherent hedonistic theory would have to be consistent with the idea that the supply of intrinsically good things is potentially limitless. For any such theory implies that something intrinsically good happens whenever someone experiences a pleasure (of the right sort). A typical sensory hedonist, for example, would say that something intrinsically good happens every time a person feels sensory pleasure: your experience of pleasure yesterday while drinking champagne, my experience of pleasure last week while smelling roses, etc. All of these, and many more, are intrinsically good according to typical forms of hedonism.[2]

A trivial variant of H1 might appear to solve this problem. We could say:

H2: A theory, T, is a form of hedonism if and only if T entails that episodes of pleasure are the only things that are intrinsically good.

Here we confront again a problem discussed earlier in Chapter 2 in connection with my commentary on Frankena's formulation of hedonism.[3] Of course it seems right to say that every form of hedonism implies that certain episodes of pleasure are intrinsically good. But every form of hedonism (if coherent) implies in addition that a person's life could also be intrinsically good, and would be intrinsically good if it contained a suitable balance of the right sort of pleasures over the right sort of pains. Hence, hedonistic theories do not imply that episodes of pleasure are the *only* things that are intrinsically good. They imply that certain human lives (and perhaps other complex, pleasure-containing things such as total consequences of actions and possible worlds are intrinsically good). Any coherent form of hedonism would have to be like this. One of the central goals of the theory is precisely this: to provide a systematic way of determining when a person's life is intrinsically good. No person's life "is a pleasure". As a result, H2 is unacceptable as it stands. It entails that no human life is good in itself. Surely that is a mistake.

I will have some further remarks to make about this Moorean criterion of hedonism later.

8.3. *Hedonism and "Pleasant Lives"*

A natural approach here would be to appeal to very general considerations about the sorts of life deemed good by a theory. We might say that if a theory implies that the Good Life is the pleasant life, then that

---

[2] This may seem a very trivial, almost nit-picking point. But I think it is not. Notice that if there is really only one intrinsically good thing, it follows that there is no case in which there are two good things, one better than the other. It also follows that we cannot determine the value of a life by adding up the values of the intrinsically good things in that life; for there could at most be *one* such thing.

[3] I discussed a similar objection in connection with Brandt's formulation in Appendix A.

theory is a form of hedonism. If it does not have that implication, then it is not a form of hedonism. In other words, we might endorse this criterion of hedonism:

H3: T is a form of hedonism if and only if T implies that a life is good in itself for the one who lives it if and only if that life is on balance pleasant.

This criterion might seem attractive, but it is also unacceptable. The central problem is that there are lots of different ways in which a life might be "on balance pleasant". Some forms of hedonism are intentionally formulated in such a way as to imply that lives that are pleasant in certain of those ways may fail to be good in themselves for the ones who live them. All such forms of hedonism are incorrectly categorized by H3. Let me explain one clear instance of this problem.

Consider, for example, a form of hedonism according to which pleasure taken in sufficiently disgraceful objects is worthless. Imagine a life that is on balance pleasant because it is full to the brim with such worthless pleasures. The imagined form of hedonism implies that this life, pleasant though it may be, is intrinsically worthless. That is because this form of hedonism implies that the pleasures of which it is full are worthless. As a result, this form of hedonism does not imply that *every* life that is on balance pleasant is good in itself for the one who lives it. Thus the imagined form of hedonism is judged not to be a form of hedonism by H3. If Altitude-Adjusted, or Truth-Adjusted, or Moorean Desert-Adjusted Intrinsic Attitudinal Hedonism were formulated in such a way as to allow for worthless attitudinal pleasures, then each of those theories would be incorrectly categorized by H3 as well. For each of those theories implies that some lives that are on balance pleasant are nevertheless not intrinsically good. Yet at least some of those theories are clearly forms of hedonism. Our criterion of hedonism should be broad enough to include them.

8.4. *Basic Intrinsic Value States and Hedonism*

H3 tries to identify forms of hedonism by their common *output*. The suggestion is that what marks a theory as hedonistic is that it implies (roughly) that the good life is the pleasant life. As we have seen, this approach is problematic. Not all forms of hedonism imply that every pleasant life is good. We can come at the problem from the other end. We can consider trying to identify forms of hedonism by their common *input*. More exactly, the suggestion is that we can identify a theory as a form of hedonism by the sorts of thing it takes to be the ultimate and most fundamental 'atoms' of intrinsic value. The guiding intuition will be this: if the "atoms" are all pleasures and pains, the theory is a sort of hedonism. Since I take these "atoms" to be *basic intrinsic value states*, I need to take some time to explain what these are.[4]

Every axiology (if fully and properly formulated) specifies some items that have their intrinsic values in the most fundamental way. In earlier chapters of this book, I spoke somewhat vaguely of "episodes" of pleasure and pain, and my formulations presupposed that it would be these "episodes" that have their values in the most fundamental way. On all those axiologies, the values of larger things are determined by the values of the included episodes, but the values of episodes are not determined by the values of any smaller items. *Episodes* were always fundamental. In earlier chapters, however, I did not say precisely what I take an *episode* to be. The time has come to supplant this vague concept of the episode with a more precise notion—the notion of the basic intrinsic value state.

The basic intrinsic value states according to each axiology are the items that the axiology takes to be the most fundamental bearers of intrinsic value. Each of them has its intrinsic value in a completely nonderivative way. They are not concrete events, or mere properties. Nor are they sets or sentences. Rather, they are intended to be finely grained propositional entities—states of affairs. More precisely, they are states of affairs that have their intrinsic values in the most fundamental way according to the axiology in question.

When I say that these states of affairs have their intrinsic values in "the most fundamental way", part of what I mean is that they do not have their intrinsic values because they are conjunctions or other combinations of smaller items that are intrinsically good. Thus, if some state of affairs, P, is intrinsically good, and some other state of affairs, Q, is intrinsically good, then their conjunction, P&Q, might also be intrinsically good. The value of P&Q might just be the sum of the value of P and the value of Q. In that case, P&Q would not have its value "in the most fundamental way". It would have its value in virtue of the fact that it is composed of these parts, and they have their specified values. So P&Q could not be a basic intrinsic value state.

Another way in which a state of affairs might have its value derivatively involves duration. Suppose a person feels pleasure throughout a stretch of time that lasts five minutes. (Earlier, when speaking of episodes, I would have spoken of an episode with a duration of

---

[4] I discussed the concept of the basic intrinsic value state in my 'Basic Intrinsic Value'.

five minutes.) The person must also feel pleasure at many shorter intervals during the five-minute period. Since there are many ways to divide the period into smaller intervals, and many of these are temporally overlapping, there are indefinitely many intervals during which he feels pleasure. If we count each of these intervals, we will overestimate the amount of pleasure he feels by counting overlapping pleasures as distinct. We must not allow for this sort of double counting.

I propose to deal with this problem by making a simplifying assumption about time: I will assume that time can be "discretized". To say that time is discretized is to say that time is broken down into a sequence of tiny intervals. Each of the intervals is of very tiny duration; the collection of them is exclusive, in the sense that no two of them overlap temporally; and the collection is exhaustive, in the sense that there is no period of time that falls outside the collection. If you have all the minimal intervals, you have all the time there is. I prefer to let a basic intrinsic value state be a state of affairs about pleasure or pain experienced at one of these minimal intervals. In this somewhat artificial way I hope to avoid problems of double counting. From now on, when I speak of someone's feeling pleasure "at a time", I intend that the time in question be one of these minimal intervals. Episodes of pleasure with longer duration, then, can be taken to be nonbasic states containing large collections of basics.

If we allow every basic intrinsic value state to be about someone's pleasure at a precise, named, minimal unit of time, we can drop all talk of durations. Basics are all alike with respect to duration. In each case, the duration is some tiny temporal extent. Old-fashioned "episodes", with their varying durations, can be seen as collections of basic intrinsic value states. But this alteration alone is not sufficient to identify the basic intrinsic value states.

Consider a generalized state of affairs such as *everyone feeling lots of pleasure at t*, where 't' indicates one of the minimal units of time. On many hedonistic axiologies, this would be counted as intrinsically good. But it does not have its intrinsic value in the most fundamental way. It is intrinsically good in virtue of the fact that specific facts about the pleasures of specific individuals are true, and the specific individuals are "everyone". Thus, *everyone feeling lots of pleasure at t* is not a basic intrinsic value state.

Furthermore, the basic intrinsic value states on an axiology must not contain any information beyond the essentials: who is feeling this pleasure? how much pleasure is he feeling? when is he feeling it? If the relevant pleasures on that axiology have objects, then a basic intrinsic value state on that axiology must also identify the object of that pleasure. The basic intrinsic value states on an axiology must contain no more than the core bits of information (such as the ones indicated) that bear on intrinsic value according to the axiology in question.

Perhaps I can make this clearer by focusing on a simple example. Let's consider Default Hedonism. Consider a state of affairs like this:

B1: Bob feeling sensory pleasure of intensity M at time t while taking a hot soapy shower.

B1 tells us more than we need to know according to DH. Not only does it tell us about the *who*, the *when*, and the *how much* of Bob's pleasure, it also tells us something more—it tells us that he experiences this pleasure while taking a shower. That is an irrelevant bit of information as far as DH is concerned. It has no effect on the value of the episode of pleasure. As we have seen, DH implies that the intensity of a pleasure affects its intrinsic value, but its cause, effects, and concomitants (such as that it takes place while taking a shower) do not. Thus, B1 is not a basic intrinsic value state on DH. It tells us more than the theory thinks we need to know.

As I see it, the basic intrinsic value state in this example would be something relevantly like this:

B2: Bob feeling sensory pleasure of intensity +7 at noon on October 16, 2001.

B2 is a "pure" attribution of sensory pleasure. It mentions the intensity of that pleasure (+7), the recipient of the pleasure (Bob), and the time of the receipt of the pleasure (noon on October 16, 2001). Each of these other things is indicated in B2 by a mere tag, or name, devoid of further conceptual content. Since other bits of information could be smuggled in via descriptions of the central items, I insist that the basics contain no such descriptions. All other elements are introduced via mere tags.

If some state of affairs is a basic intrinsic value state on some axiology, then it must have a fully determinate intrinsic value on that axiology, and it must have it intrinsically. In the case of B2 and DH, we can say that the amount of pleasure in B2 according to DH is precisely 7 hedons. As a result, the intrinsic value of B2 according to DH is also a determinate, fixed amount, also +7. By contrast, consider a state of affairs such as this:

B3: Bob feeling quite a lot of sensory pleasure at noon on October 16, 2001.

Though some hedonists might want to say that B3 is good in itself, they would be hard pressed to say precisely how good it is. It just does not say. It seems to have an indeterminate amount of goodness. For this reason, B3 is not a basic intrinsic value state on DH. Note that whenever something like B3 is true, there must be some basic (like B2) that is also true, and in virtue of which B3 is true. This fact explains why it is permissible to disregard nonbasics when calculating the value of a life. The value of the life is determined by the values of the basics true in the life. The nonbasics are, for purposes of calculation, irrelevant. Whatever impact they may appear to have will be accounted for by some collection of basics.

Clearly, what counts as a basic intrinsic value state will vary from axiology to axiology. B2 would count as a basic on DH, but it would not be a basic on any sort of attitudinal hedonism. The basics on IAH, for example, are all fully determinate, precise, "pared down" attributions of intrinsic attitudinal pleasure. They are all relevantly like this:

B4: At noon on Tuesday, October 16, 2001, Bob takes intrinsic attitudinal pleasure of intensity +8 in the fact that Bob's beer is frosty cold.

If we let 'c' stand for the state of affairs of *Bob's beer being frosty cold*, and we let 't' stand for the indicated date, and we let 'b' stand for Bob, and we introduce 'P' as a four-place relational predicate indicating the taking of intrinsic attitudinal pleasure by someone to some degree at some time in some object, then we can represent the underlying logical structure of B in this way:

B4′: Pb, t, +8, c.

The state of affairs expressed by B4′ is thus shown to be an attribution of intrinsic attitudinal pleasure to a person, at a designated minimal time, to a precise and designated degree, in a precisely specified object. I say that it is a "pure" attribution of intrinsic attitudinal pleasure, since the other constituents of the state of affairs are all picked out by mere tags. The conceptual content of B4′ is exhausted by the meaning of 'P'. The intrinsic value of B4′ is determined (according to IAH) entirely by the amount of pleasure it contains.

You might wonder why I include a reference to the object of Bob's pleasure in B4. (I might have said that the basic is expressed by 'Bob takes 8 units of intrinsic attitudinal pleasure in *something* at t'.) The answer is simple. If Bob is taking intrinsic attitudinal pleasure in several different things at the same time, I want each of them to make an independent contribution to his total welfare. As a result, I want there to be a distinct basic intrinsic value state for each of these objects. In order to ensure that it works out this way, I simply include the object of pleasure in the basic intrinsic value state, and thereby guarantee a suitable plurality of basic states.[5]

In addition to pure attributions of pleasure, as in B4, there are also pure attributions of pain. Consider this as an example:

B5: At noon on Tuesday, October 16, 2001, Bob takes intrinsic attitudinal pain of intensity +3 in the fact that Bob's peanuts are soggy.

Anything relevantly like B5 is a pure attribution of intrinsic attitudinal pain. The amount of such pain in B5 is +3. Intrinsic Attitudinal Hedonism therefore declares B5 to have an intrinsic value of −3. Its inclusion in any life would have the direct effect of making that life worse by three units.

According to IAH, all basic intrinsic value states are relevantly like B4 and B5. They are all pure attributions of intrinsic attitudinal pleasure or pain. Each such state of affairs has a precise amount of intrinsic value, and it has that value in virtue of its intrinsic features. According to IAH, the value of a life for a person is entirely determined by the values of the things like these that are true in that person's life.[6] Other theories would identify the states that they take to be the basics in a similar way. In each case, the basics are pure attributions of the types of pleasure and pain the theory takes to be important for the evaluation of lives.

With this concept of the basic intrinsic value state in hand, we may now state what I take to be a somewhat more satisfactory general characterization of hedonism:

H4: T is a form of hedonism if and only if all the basic intrinsic value states according to T are pure attributions of some sort of pleasure or pain.

Let me illustrate the application of H4 by showing how it generates correct results in a couple of typical cases. I have already mentioned

---

[5] I should mention that the basic intrinsic value state contains a *reference* to the object of pleasure. It does not contain any conceptual material deriving from that object. So it would be best to imagine that all mention of the object of Bob's pleasure in B4 or B5 should really take place via contentless *names* of those objects.

[6] When I say that such a thing is "true in a person's life", what I mean is that (a) the thing is true, and (b) the person himself is the subject of the state—he is the one said to be experiencing the pleasure or pain.

DH and IAH. According to DH, every basic intrinsic value state is a state of affairs relevantly like:

B2: Bob feeling sensory pleasure of intensity +7 at noon on October 16, 2001.

Each such state attributes sensory pleasure or pain of some specific intensity and date to some specific recipient. Hence, all the basics on DH are pure attributions of a sort of pleasure or pain—in this case straightforward sensory pleasure or pain.[7] This means that DH is a form of hedonism according to H4. Similar considerations apply to IAH, though IAH takes the basics to be a different set of states of affairs. On IAH, the basics are all relevantly like:

B4: At noon on Tuesday, October 16, 2001, Bob takes intrinsic attitudinal pleasure of intensity +8 in the fact that Bob's beer is frosty cold.

It is a little more difficult to explain why H4 generates the correct results in the case of non-hedonistic axiologies. That is largely because there is less consensus about the correct formulation of such axiologies. Advocates of such theories do not always tell us precisely what they take to be the basic intrinsic value states on their views. In order to proceed, we would have to sketch our own account of the nature of the basics on the non-hedonistic axiologies.

Consider a form of preferentism according to which a person's life is made better in itself for that person by the satisfaction of that person's actual desires. As I understand such views, they take the basics all to be states of affairs of this sort:

B6: Bob desiring at noon on Tuesday, October 6, 2001 with intensity +6 that there be peace in the world; and his desire being satisfied.

On the preferentist axiology that I am imagining, something like B6 would be an "atom" of intrinsic value. It would be good in itself—presumably to degree +6—for it to be true. Bob's life would be made better in itself for Bob if things like B6 were true. If there were many facts like this in Bob's life, and few frustrations, then Bob could be said to have a good life on this axiology.

---

[7] I am assuming that we can tell when a relation (such as the one indicated by 'P' in B4') expresses a form of pleasure. Each such relation is a determinate form of the determinable expressed by 'x is pleased in some way at t'. It might be a bit tricky to explain this in any greater detail. The relation of determinates to determinables is a matter of controversy, going well beyond the scope of the present project (I sincerely hope).

B6 seems to be an attribution of *satisfied desire* to a person, at a time, with an intensity, for an object. It is clearly not an attribution of pleasure of any sort. The truth of B6 is consistent with no one's ever being pleased in any way about anything. As a result, H4 implies that this imagined form of preferentism is not a form of hedonism. That, it seems to me, is a clearly correct result.

Consider a form of pluralism according to which a person's life is made better in itself for the person by the presence in it of sensory pleasure but also by the presence in it of knowledge. On this view there are two main ultimate sources of value—pleasure and knowledge. Instances of each independently help to make a person's life better. This axiology will acknowledge two main sorts of basic intrinsic value state. On the one hand, it will admit hedonic atoms like B2. But in addition it will admit epistemic atoms like:

B7: Bob knowing at noon, October 6, 2001, that there is peace in the world.

On the pluralistic theory I am imagining, the value of something like B7 would have to be stipulated. Perhaps it would be just as good as a 10-hedon sensory pleasure. Perhaps its value would be a function of the importance of the object of the knowledge, or the strength of Bob's belief. Spelling that out would be a job for any advocate of the suggested form of pluralism. In any case, the value of Bob's life in itself for him would then be determined in some way by consideration of the values of the hedonic and epistemic basic intrinsic value states contained in his life.

Again, it is obvious that H4 generates the correct result in this case. Since not all of the basic intrinsic value states are attributions of pleasure (some are attributions of knowledge), H4 declares that this form of pluralism is not a form of hedonism. Another correct result.

The results of the application of H4 to certain of the other, more complicated allegedly hedonistic axiologies is of greater interest. Since it may be the subject of considerable doubt and controversy, let us take a look at Desert-Adjusted Intrinsic Attitudinal Hedonism. I intend it to be a form of hedonism. What does H4 say about this?

In my original formulation of DAIAH, I indicated (though I did not quite say it) that the fundamental atoms of value on this view are states of affairs in which someone takes intrinsic attitudinal pleasure (or pain) in some object. I specified that the attitudinal pleasure must have a precise intensity. I also specified that the object of the pleasure must deserve to some particular degree to be the object of someone's pleasure. In Chapter 5 I suggested that these things are to be understood as "episodes". That might have suggested some sort of concrete event. I now want to clarify this by specifying that these episodes are proposition-like entities—states of affairs. I intend them all to be relevantly like this state of affairs:

B8: Bob taking intrinsic attitudinal pleasure at noon today of intensity +8 in *there being peace in the world*, when *there being peace in the world* deserves, to degree +6, to be the object of someone's pleasure.

I want to rewrite this in order to clarify my intent. I propose to use 'b' as a meaningless rigid designator, or tag, for Bob. I propose to use 'n' as a similar tag for the relevant time, noon today. Let 'q' serve as a name for the proposition *there is peace in the world*. And let the numerals +8 and +6 indicate, respectively, the intensity of Bob's pleasure and the pleasure-worthiness of the object of Bob's pleasure. I use the predicate letter 'P' followed by five variables to indicate the five-place relation of *x taking intrinsic attitudinal pleasure at time y of intensity z in object w when w deserves to degree n to be an object of pleasure*. Using this notation, I can express the fact about Bob this way:

B9: Pb, n, +8, q, +6.

B9 is a sample of the sort of thing that would be a basic intrinsic value state according to DAIAH. It seems clear to me that B9 is an attribution of a kind of pleasure (intrinsic attitudinal pleasure) to a person, at a time, to a degree, in an object, while the object deserves to a certain degree to be an object of pleasure. I intend to understand DAIAH in such a way that all basic intrinsic value states on DAIAH are relevantly like B9. Attributions of attitudinal pain will be like B9 except that they are attributions of intrinsic attitudinal pain. Thus, every basic intrinsic value state on DAIAH is a pure attribution of some kind of pleasure or pain. Therefore, DAIAH is a form of hedonism according to the proposed criterion.

I could go further. In light of the fact that every basic according to DAIAH is of this form, DAIAH is a form of pure attitudinal hedonism. Nothing other than these pleasure-attributing and pain-attributing basics serves directly to make a life better or worse. And in light of the fact that every state of affairs of the illustrated form is declared by DAIAH to be intrinsically good, we can say that DAIAH is also a form of universal attitudinal hedonism. There is nothing pluralistic about it. It is as much a form of hedonism as our old Default Hedonism, or the uncontroversially hedonistic Aristippean Hedonism. What entitles us to call it 'hedonism' is precisely the same thing that entitles us to call those simpler theories 'hedonism': all the basic intrinsic value states on the theory are pure attributions of some sort of pleasure or pain.

Let me now return to the two objections I mentioned earlier but did not pursue. The first of these is an objection concerning the supervenience of value upon mental states. It is often said that this sort of supervenience is a necessary condition of something's being a form of hedonism. In other words, it is said that if a theory is a form of hedonism, then that theory implies that intrinsic values supervene on mental states.[8] It might be thought that some of the suggested axiologies fail this supervenience test, and thus are not properly categorized as forms of hedonism.

There are several different forms of supervenience. According to one form, the thesis amounts to this: if two individuals experience all the same mental states, then even if they are in two different possible worlds, their lives must be of equal value. This is the strong supervenience of value on mental states. Given some natural assumptions, most of the allegedly hedonistic theories that I have discussed satisfy this requirement. Consider IAH, for example. Suppose two individuals experience episodes of intrinsic attitudinal pleasure and pain of the same intensities and durations. Then IAH implies that their lives are of equal value even if they are in different circumstances. Nothing about their circumstances bears in any way on the values of the basic intrinsic value states involving these two individuals, and since the values of the lives depend entirely on the values of these basic intrinsic value states, their lives remain of equal value no matter what goes on around them.

DAIAH satisfies this strong supervenience requirement, too, assuming that the pleasure-worthiness and pain-worthiness of objects does not vary from world to world. Assume that two individuals take intrinsic attitudinal pleasure of the same intensity and duration in the same objects. Then the basics true about the one individual must have the same values as the basics true about the other, no matter how much their circumstances differ. As before, DAIAH entails that their lives are of equal value.

One form of hedonism violates this supervenience thesis. That is Truth-Adjusted Intrinsic Attitudinal Hedonism (TAIAH). A given set of attitudinal pleasures might have one value in a certain possible world partly because the objects of those pleasures are true in that world. The same pleasures would have a different value in another

---

[8] Although he does not use precisely this terminology, Kagan seems to endorse the central point. See, e.g., his *Normative Ethics*, 34.

possible world where the objects of the pleasures are false. Thus, strong supervenience could fail.

However, it is still possible that even TAIAH satisfies a version of the supervenience requirement. If we interpret the supervenience thesis in another way, it yields a different result. We might take it to mean that if two individuals *in a given possible world* experience all the same mental states, then their lives must be of equal value. This is the doctrine of the weak supervenience of value on mental states. So long as we stick to a single possible world, and we stick to individuals who take pleasure in the same objects, the values of their pleasures cannot be differentially affected by a difference in truth-value of their objects. Recall the case of the deceived businessman and his cousin. If the cousins are in the same world, and their pleasures have the same objects, then the truth-values of the objects of their pleasures must be the same. The basic intrinsic value states concerning one cousin will have the same intrinsic values as the corresponding basic intrinsic value states concerning the other cousin. TAIAH then implies that the values of the lives of such cousins must be equal. So if the supervenience thesis is understood in this second way, TAIAH does not violate it.

A deeper point concerns the supervenience requirement itself. Although many philosophers seem to accept it, it is not clear to me that it must be true. Suppose we have identified some axiological theory according to which some sort of pleasure is the Good. Suppose that this theory violates some version of the supervenience thesis. It is not entirely clear to me that this would establish that the axiology is not a form of hedonism.

8.5. *Some Hard Cases*

I have to acknowledge that my proposal (as so far formulated) permits some odd ducks into the hedonistic category. Let us consider one particularly outrageous axiology. This is a form of "dolorism"—the view that *pain* is the Good and *pleasure* is the Bad. More exactly, I have in mind a view just like DH except that all sensory pleasures are said to be intrinsically bad, and bigger ones are said to be worse; all sensory pains are said to be good, and bigger ones are said to be better. Strangely, H4 implies that this is a form of hedonism. That may be a bit hard to swallow.

We could avoid this surprising result merely by requiring that if a theory is a form of hedonism, then it has to entail that the *good* basic intrinsic value states are pure attributions of some kind of pleasure, and the *bad* basic intrinsic value states are pure attributions of some kind of pain. Call the resulting criterion 'H5'. H5 would eliminate dolorism while maintaining almost every form of hedonism we have recently discussed. It might seem that this is the natural fix.

However, there is a possible problem. The problem (which was mentioned in Chapter 7) concerns transvaluation. Recall that in the case of the Moorean axiology discussed in Chapter 7, certain episodes of pleasure were deemed to be bad, and certain episodes of pain were deemed to be good. Moore himself said as much when he described cruelty. As he saw it, cruelty consists in the enjoyment of the suffering of others. Moore declared this to be a great mixed evil—an evil because it is a kind of pleasure that involves such a serious mismatch between emotion and object. In the opposite direction, Moore also claimed that compassionate suffering is a good, even though it is the suffering of pain. In this case, because the object of the pain is another's suffering, and that is a completely appropriate object to be pained about, the state of affairs as a whole is good.

I carried these ideas over into my formulation of Moorean Desert-Adjusted Intrinsic Attitudinal Hedonism. I pointed out that on that axiology only *some* episodes of intrinsic attitudinal pleasure are good—those are the ones that are "properly directed". Episodes that involve "improperly directed" attitudinal pleasure are said to be bad. And similarly, episodes of properly directed pain are also said to be good. So MDAIAH involves two sorts of transvaluation. On this theory, there are some bad pleasures and some good pains.

This puts us in a sort of bind. We could stick with H4. This would enable us to say—as I want to—that the Moorean theory is a form of hedonism. But if we take this route, we will also have to say—somewhat awkwardly—that dolorism is a form of hedonism. On the other hand, we could turn to H5. This would enable us to say that dolorism is not a form of hedonism. But we would lose the Moorean theory in the bargain.

Personally, I prefer H4. My sense is that it is reasonable to use the term 'hedonism' to refer to any theory that takes all the atoms of intrinsic value to be pleasures and pains. In light of the fact that this has some unexpected implications (dolorism is a form of hedonism!), we might use the term 'hedono-dolorism' to refer to the general family. We could use this new term to indicate theories that take pleasures and pains to be the atoms of value.

8.6. *'Pleasure is the Good'*

In an earlier era, philosophers often spoke of 'the Good'. The terminology may derive from the ancient Greek *to agathon*, which would naturally be translated as 'the Good'. Our branch of moral philosophy is often characterized as 'the search for the Good', or 'the attempt to identify the Good'. Hedonism might be said to be the thesis that 'pleasure is the Good'.

What would it mean to say that pleasure is the Good? Surely it does not mean that pleasure is (identical to) goodness—the property of being intrinsically good. A philosopher can be a hedonist while rejecting the claim that the property of *being a pleasure* is the very same property as the property of *being intrinsically good*. Indeed, I have already given reasons to conclude that these properties are not even coextensive. Some whole lives are intrinsically good; those lives do not have the property of *being pleasures*.

I am inclined to suspect that when our predecesors said 'Pleasure is the Good', the core of what they meant was this: the fundamental sources of positive intrinsic value in a person's life are all episodes of some sort of pleasure. I would rephrase this by saying: every good basic intrinsic value state is a pure attribution of some sort of pleasure. If this does not capture what the ancients meant, then I guess I don't know what they meant.[9]

8.7. *Monism and Pluralism in Axiology*

This appeal to basics has another value. It enables us to answer the objection based on the idea that some of these theories are forms of pluralism, and hence not correctly categorized as forms of hedonism.

This objection is trickier than it might at first appear. The problem arises because it is not entirely clear what is meant by saying that a theory is a form of pluralism. So I think I have to deal with a preliminary puzzle first: I need to explain the difference between pluralism and monism in axiology. Then I will be able to turn to the more immediate issue: are the theories discussed in this book forms of monism, or are they forms of pluralism?

---

[9] This account of the meaning of 'Pleasure is the Good' has an interesting implication. It implies that if you think that some pains are good (as Moore thought), then you should not say 'Pleasure is the Good'.

I think that the essential feature of monism in axiology is this: the monist says that there is exactly one property such that all intrinsically good basic intrinsic value states are pure attributions of that property. In other words, the monist says that all the good atoms of value are pure attributions of the same single property. Pluralists, on the other hand, say that there are several different properties such that some good atoms of value are attributions of one of them and other good atoms of value are attributions of others.

Given this account of monism, we can see that typical hedonists are monists. They answer 'one' to a certain question. Pluralists answer 'several' to that same question. The question is this:

Q: How many properties are there such that intrinsically good basic intrinsic value states are pure attributions of those properties?

The Default Hedonist is a monist because he answers Q by saying, 'One. And it is the property of *feeling sensory pleasure of intensity n at time t.*' The Intrinsic Attitudinal Hedonist is also a monist. In his case, it is because he answers Q by saying, 'One. And it is the property of *taking intrinsic attitudinal pleasure of intensity n in object x at time t.*' The advocate of Desert-Adjusted Intrinsic Attitudinal Hedonism is also a monist. In his case, he is a monist because he answers Q by saying, 'One. And it is the property of *taking intrinsic attitudinal pleasure of intensity n in object x at time t while x deserves to degree m to have pleasure taken in it.*' Pluralists answer Q by mentioning more than one property. For example, the advocate of the theory discussed by Socrates in the *Philebus* answers Q by saying, 'Two. One of them is the property of *feeling pleasure* and the other is the property of *knowing*.'[10]

These reflections on monism may help to shed some light on the Moorean remark quoted earlier. In a passage I quoted in section 8.2, Moore said, 'By Hedonism, then, I mean the doctrine that pleasure *alone* is good as an end.' Many others have said similar things, suggesting that every form of hedonism implies that there is exactly one intrinsically good thing, and that thing is 'pleasure'. As I said earlier,

[10] Theories that incorporate transvaluation, such as MDAIAH, remain problematic. If we assume that attitudinal pleasure and attitudinal pain are two distinct properties, then the proposed criterion implies that MDAIAH is a form of pluralism. That is because it involves the claim that while most good basic intrinsic value states are pure attributions of attitudinal pleasure, some pure attributions of attitudinal pain are intrinsically good basic intrinsic value states. If this implication seems counter-intuitive, one could pursue the notion that pleasure and pain are nothing more than positive and negative degrees of one and the same property. That would permit us to say that even on MDAIAH, there is exactly one property such that all basics are pure attributions of it.

if taken literally and at face value, these remarks seem wrong. Every form of hedonism implies that there are many intrinsically good things, and none of them is named 'pleasure'. These intrinsically good things are the various episodes selected by these forms of hedonism as the atoms of intrinsic value, as well as the larger items such as human lives and possible worlds that have favorable balances of pleasure over pain.

Perhaps when Moore said that hedonism is the view that pleasure is the sole intrinsic good, he meant that hedonism is the view that the sole property, such that pure attributions of it are the basic intrinsic goods, is pleasure. If he meant that, then (as I see it) he was right. That is a fair characterization of hedonism. I recognize, of course, that attributing precisely this meaning to him is a bit of a stretch.

8.8. *Axiological Taxonomy*

I have given an account of the nature of hedonism. According to this account, what marks a theory as a form of hedonism is that all the basic intrinsic value states on that theory are pure attributions of some kind of pleasure or pain. I have pointed out that this casts the net of hedonism fairly widely. DH, AH, IAH, DAIAH, TAIAH, and other clearly hedonistic theories are included. But theories that accept transvaluation are also accepted. Theories that incorporate consideration of such values as "altitude" and "desert" are also included. Even dolorism is included.

I recognize that my account of hedonism will strike some as being too generous. Some critics apparently want to reserve the name 'hedonist' for someone like Aristippus—a man on the hedonistic fringe—out there with the publishers of girlie magazines and other extremists. But that is unfair. Moderate hedonists such as Epicurus and Mill have been insisting for years that their commitment to pleasure is not to be confused with a commitment solely to the pleasures of profligates and sensualists. Mainstream hedonists have almost always recognized that there are "higher pleasures" or "static pleasures" or "pleasures of the mind". I think that some of these classic figures may have been trying to express the idea that I have called 'intrinsic attitudinal pleasure'. In any case, I think it is appropriate to use the term 'hedonism' to refer to theories according to which not only sensory pleasures, but attitudinal pleasures as well, might be included in 'the Good'. And that is what my criterion does.

The whole issue is largely verbal anyway. There is not much point in debating what 'hedonism' *really means*. There is considerable arbitrariness in the taxonomy no matter how we work it out. I prefer to do things as I have, in part because I feel sorry for poor old Epicurus, who knew all this 2,000 years ago, and yet was a voice crying in the wilderness. No one would pay any attention to him. 'Yeah, yeah, yeah,' they would say, 'Hedonism shmedonism. If it's really hedonism, it's a doctrine worthy only of swine. It's gotta say that sex with pigs is great. If it is something more worthy of our attention, it's gotta be a form of pluralism.' Such narrow-minded critics misunderstood the limits of hedonism then, and, if their descendants continue to say such things, they continue to misunderstand those limits today.

CHAPTER 9

Problems about Beauty and Justice

Two classic objections to hedonism were mentioned earlier in Chapter 3, but have not yet been addressed. One of these concerns beauty. The other concerns justice. Because of certain important similarities between these objections and the replies that I intend to give to them, I have put off consideration of them until this chapter, where I discuss them together. First, let us reconsider the objections.

9.1. *Moore's Heap of Filth*

In a memorable passage that I quoted earlier, Moore describes two possible worlds.[1] One is filled with a harmonious array of beautiful scenery; the other is just a disgusting heap of filth. No one is present in either of the worlds. As a result, no one enjoys the beauty of the first, and no one is disgusted by the foulness of the second. Moore says that he thinks it would be rational to hold that the beautiful world is better than the ugly one. But since the amounts of pleasure and pain in the two worlds are equal (there is no pleasure or pain in either one), hedonism seems unable to account for any difference in value. This is apparently intended to show that hedonism is false.

There is a question about the precise target of Moore's criticism. He said he was talking about "hedonism". He said that the central thesis of hedonism is that 'pleasure alone is intrinsically good'.[2] When I introduced this argument in Chapter 3, I suggested that it could be understood as an attack on Default Hedonism, though, of course, Moore never mentioned Default Hedonism. We will have to clarify the target.

---

[1] Moore, *Principia Ethica*, 84.   [2] Ibid., ch. III, sec. 37.

9.2. *A Problem about Justice*

In *The Right and the Good*, Ross presents another argument against hedonism. The argument is like Moore's Heap of Filth in one respect: it essentially involves a comparison of two possible worlds that are alike with respect to pleasure and pain. But Ross's example does not involve differences in beauty and ugliness. Rather, the worlds in Ross's example differ with respect to *justice and injustice*.[3]

Ross wants us to imagine two possible worlds, W_j and W_k. The worlds are supposed to be exactly alike with respect to several important features—amounts of virtue and vice, amounts of pleasure and pain. So the worlds are very similar. The central difference concerns who gets what. In W_j, the virtuous people get to live the lives filled with pleasure, and the vicious people get to live the lives filled with pain. It is the reverse in W_k. In W_k, the vicious people live the lives filled with pleasure, and the virtuous people live lives filled with pain.

I took Ross's point to be that hedonism implies that these worlds are equally valuable in themselves. Yet Ross clearly thinks that the just world, W_j, is much better in itself than the equally pleasant but unjust world, W_k. This might seem to show that hedonism is false.

The arguments of Moore and Ross are interesting and insightful. Each of them draws our attention to an important consideration. Nevertheless, neither argument refutes any form of hedonism that I have presented up to this point in this book. That is because none of the forms of hedonism discussed so far says anything about values of *worlds*. These theories speak only about the values of individual episodes of pleasure and pain, and about *lives*. Yet the two arguments just described are not based on any alleged misevaluation of *lives*. Moore did not say that the *lives* of people in the filthy world are less good. In fact, he stipulated that there were no people in the filthy world. Similarly, Ross did not say that the *lives* of the happy vicious people were misevaluated by hedonism. (Indeed, it seems to me that some of the forms of hedonism we have discussed might get this right. Perhaps the lives of the thieves in W_k are pretty good in themselves for those thieves. That might be part of the reason why we find the world so distressing: bad people get to live good lives there.) Rather, Ross's claim concerns the evaluation of *worlds*. Since the forms of hedonism so far discussed give no evaluation of worlds, they cannot be guilty of giving the wrong evaluation of the worlds described by Moore and Ross.

[3] Ross, *The Right and the Good*, 138.

It seems to me that an axiological theory should give an account of what makes a life worth living. Every form of hedonism we have discussed does this. Each of these theories tells us that the value of a life is determined by the net extent to which the one who lives that life experiences sensory pleasure, or attitudinal pleasure, or object-appropriate intrinsic attitudinal pleasure, or whatever sort of pleasure the theory takes to be important. The arguments just discussed do not raise any serious trouble for these theories. But an axiological theory should also give an account of what makes a world worth creating, or aiming for. It should give some account of the factors that make a world good in itself. So all of the theories so far considered appear to be incomplete. We should address this issue.

9.3. *A Hedonistic Reply to the Heap of Filth*

The anti-hedonist can make use of Moore's Heap of Filth as the basis of a somewhat different challenge to the hedonist: 'Granted, your theory as so far formulated is not refuted by the Heap of Filth. But the example shows that your theory is incomplete. It says nothing about the evaluation of worlds. How, as a hedonist, do you evaluate worlds?'

The simplest response, of course, is for the hedonist to say that he will evaluate worlds hedonistically. The hedonist will say that the value of a world is determined in the same way that the value of a life is determined—by the total net amount of pleasure it contains. Since there are several different forms of life-evaluating hedonism, there are several different forms of world-evaluating hedonism. Let us consider one of these.

For purposes of discussion, let us make use of Intrinsic Attitudinal Hedonism (IAH)[4] as our starting point. I propose that we simply add a world-evaluating phrase (here in roman type) to the theory. The resulting theory looks quite a lot like its predecessor:

Intrinsic Attitudinal Hedonism +

i. Every episode of intrinsic attitudinal pleasure is intrinsically good; every episode of intrinsic attitudinal pain is intrinsically bad.
ii. The intrinsic value of an episode of intrinsic attitudinal pleasure is equal to the amount of the pleasure contained in that episode; the intrinsic value of an episode of intrinsic attitudinal pain is equal to − (the amount of the pain contained in that episode).

---

[4] Introduced in sec. 4.3.

iii. The intrinsic value of a life or a possible world *is entirely determined by the intrinsic values of the episodes of intrinsic attitudinal pleasure and pain contained in the life or world, in such a way that one life or world is intrinsically better than another if and only if the net amount of intrinsic attitudinal pleasure in the one is greater than the net amount of that sort of pleasure in the other.*

Since I have already discussed IAH at some length, and IAH+ is just a simple extension of the same idea to worlds, it will not be necessary to explain IAH+. The question is whether this theory is refuted by Moore's argument about the beautiful world and the ugly world.

It must be acknowledged that IAH+ does have the allegedly offensive implication. It does imply that the depopulated ugly world is just as good in itself as the depopulated beautiful world. The net amount of pleasure in each is exactly zero. Moore said that the beautiful world is better. If Moore is right, IAH+ is false.

There are certain possible mistakes that would make it easy for critics to think that they are "intuiting" that the ugly world is worse in itself than the beautiful world. The most natural of these mistakes occurs if we imagine what it would be like to live in one of these worlds. A critic of IAH+ might reason as follows: 'If I had to live in one of those worlds, I would vastly prefer living in the beautiful world rather than in the heap of filth. If I had a beloved child, and I had to choose a world for her to live in, and I were concerned about nothing beyond the quality of her life, I would vastly prefer that she should live in the beautiful world rather than in the heap of filth. This indicates that I think the beautiful world is somehow intrinsically better than the ugly world.'

It should be obvious that this sort of reasoning is confused. The critic is performing the thought experiment incorrectly. He is imagining what it would be like to live in the beautiful world, and he is comparing this to what it would be like to live in the ugly world. Strictly speaking, of course, it is impossible for anyone to live in the beautiful world. It was stipulated, as part of the essential description of the world, that it had a population of zero. Any world with people in it would be a different world. At best, we can imagine a world similar to the beautiful world, but with people in it.

The hedonist can readily admit that it would be much more pleasant, and therefore much better, to live in a world like the beautiful world. If you are looking for real estate to occupy, it is better to find beautiful real estate than it is to find ugly real estate. But this is compatible with hedonism. The hedonist can explain the greater value of living in the beautiful world by pointing out that those living there would get a lot of pleasure from viewing the rivers, sunsets, stars, mountains, and other beautiful scenery. But this fact should not confuse us about the question at issue here. The question here is whether the beautiful world is better *even though in fact no one is living there, and no one is enjoying the pleasures that would be produced by living in a world like that.* When we consider the case fairly, it is harder to see why the beautiful world should be preferred.

Another possible mistake is this: it might be that when we reflect on the two worlds, we find ourselves pleased by the thought of the beautiful world, and disgusted by the thought of the heap of filth. We see that the beautiful world is somehow more pleasant and the ugly world somehow more unpleasant. Since, as hedonists, we tend to admire and approve of pleasant things, we then declare the beautiful world to be better in itself.

But that sort of thinking is also confused. Perhaps it suggests that the beautiful world has greater "inherent" value—it has the capacity to serve as the object of good experiences. But inherent value is not the same as intrinsic value. The world has the capacity (if only it could be populated!) to produce pleasure in those who contemplate it. But since there are no contemplators there in the world, its capacity remains unactualized. No pleasure is produced. Thus, when considered in itself, devoid of population as it is stipulated to be, the beautiful world is intrinsically no better than the ugly one.

My conclusion, then, is that hedonism, in the form of IAH+, is not refuted by Moore's Heap of Filth. It remains reasonable to say (following Sidgwick) that the value of beauty lies primarily in its capacity to give pleasure to those who observe and enjoy it. Let us turn, then, to Ross's objection.

9.4. *A Hedonistic Reply to Ross's "Two Worlds" Objection*

Ross's objection is a tougher nut to crack. Whereas we can reasonably say that in itself the beautiful world is no better than the ugly one, it may seem somewhat unreasonable to say that the just world, W_j, is no better than the unjust one, W_k. I am prepared to acknowledge that the more fitting allocation of pleasures and pains in W_j makes it better in itself than W_k. (I grant that in real-life cases such fitting allocations often have good consequences. In the cases described by Ross it is stipulated that the consequences balance out. Nevertheless, it still seems to me that the just world is better.) As a result, Ross's case presents real difficulties for IAH+, since IAH+ implies that the intrinsic value of W_j is exactly the same as that of W_k.

I think that Ross's example calls for further refinements in our formulation of hedonism. I now turn to that project.

Earlier, when I introduced Desert-Adjusted Intrinsic Attitudinal Hedonism (DAIAH), I described a way in which we could adjust the value of a pleasure to reflect the extent to which the object of that pleasure deserves to be enjoyed. Roughly, the idea was that attitudinal pleasures taken in objects that deserve to have pleasure taken in them would be rated as intrinsically better than otherwise similar pleasures taken in objects that do not deserve to have pleasure taken in them. Similar adjustments for desert were made in the evaluation of attitudinal pains. This adjustment for desert (I claimed) solves the problem of worthless pleasures (and worthwhile pains) and gives the proper basis for the hedonistic evaluation of lives. DAIAH incorporates those adjustments. They are adjustments designed to reflect the extent to which *objects* of pleasure and pain deserve to be objects of pleasure and pain. I propose that we perform a similar sort of desert adjustment again, this time to reflect the extent to which the *subjects*—the ones who experience the pleasures—deserve to be experiencing them. I also propose that we make a corresponding adjustment in the evaluation of pains. These adjustments for the pleasure- and pain-worthiness of *subjects* will give the proper basis for the hedonistic evaluation of worlds and will solve the problem set by Ross.

Let us take IAH as our starting point. Thus, as before, the fundamental bearers of intrinsic value will be episodes of intrinsic attitudinal pleasure and pain. But this time, instead of adjusting the value of a pleasure or pain to reflect the extent to which the *object* of that pleasure or pain deserves to be enjoyed, let us adjust the value of the pleasure or pain to reflect the extent to which the *subject*—the person who enjoys the pleasure or suffers the pain—deserves to be enjoying or suffering it. The guiding intuitions will be that it is better for good people to enjoy good things; worse for good people to suffer bad things; better for bad people to suffer bad things; worse for bad people to enjoy good things. Let us consider four of the main cases.

i. Suppose a person has been good and has not yet been rewarded for his virtue. We can say that he has "positive desert", thereby indicating that he deserves some goods. Suppose that this positively deserving person then enjoys some intrinsic attitudinal pleasure. For example, suppose that he takes pleasure in the observation of a pretty painting.

We want to say that positive desert enhances the value of pleasure. So, in the case described, we want to say that the intrinsic value of this episode of pleasure adjusted for subject's desert is extra high—higher than it would be judged to be by IAH.

To make this more concrete, let us imagine some numbers. Suppose a person has been good and deserves to have some pleasure. Let us say he deserves 10 units of pleasure. Suppose that he then sees a pretty painting and takes 10 units of intrinsic attitudinal pleasure in the fact that the painting is so beautiful. While on IAH we might say that the intrinsic value of this episode is +10, we can now say that the intrinsic value of this episode *adjusted for subject's desert* is +20.

ii. Suppose a person has been bad and has not suffered any penalties for his vice. We can say that he has "negative desert", thereby indicating that he is due for a fall. Suppose this negatively deserving person then enjoys some intrinsic attitudinal pleasure. We can even suppose that he enjoys the same pleasure as his more virtuous friend, just discussed. This vicious fellow looks at the pretty painting and enjoys its beauty. We can say that his negative desert mitigates the value of his pleasure. Again we can make this more precise.

Let us assume that the vicious fellow enjoys 10 units of pleasure in the observation of the painting. Let us assume that he has been so rotten that he deserves 10 units of pain. In this case, we can say that the intrinsic value of his episode of pleasure *adjusted for subject's desert* is +5. Thus, it is still good in itself. It is just much less good than a similar pleasure enjoyed by a more virtuous person.

iii. Now imagine a virtuous or good person who unfortunately suffers some pain. The thinking here is that it is extra bad for good people to suffer. Suppose he suffers intrinsic attitudinal pain to the tune of 10 units in the fact that there is so much injustice in the world. Suppose he has 10 units of positive desert. Then we can say that the intrinsic value of this episode of pain, *adjusted for subject's desert* is −20. It is much worse than a similar pain suffered by a less deserving person.

iv. Now imagine a vicious person who suffers a pain of the same raw magnitude. Suppose he suffers 10 units of intrinsic attitudinal pain in the fact that he is in jail. The thought here is that it is not so bad for bad people to suffer. Then we can say that the intrinsic value of this episode of pain, again *adjusted for subject's desert*, is −5. So the pain is still bad in itself, it is just much less bad than a similar pain suffered by a good person.

In all these cases we have been thinking about a new measure of value. I have been calling it 'subject's desert-adjusted intrinsic value'. Subject's Desert-Adjusted Intrinsic Attitudinal Hedonism (SDAIAH) is the view that the value of a world is the sum of the subject's desert-adjusted values of the intrinsic attitudinal pleasures enjoyed and pains suffered in that world. The theory as a whole looks like this:

Subject's Desert-Adjusted Intrinsic Attitudinal Hedonism

i. Every episode of intrinsic attitudinal pleasure is intrinsically good; every episode of intrinsic attitudinal pain is intrinsically bad.

ii. The subject's desert-adjusted intrinsic value of an episode of intrinsic attitudinal pleasure is equal to the amount of pleasure contained in that episode adjusted for subject's desert; the subject's desert-adjusted intrinsic value of an episode of intrinsic attitudinal pain is equal to − (the amount of pain contained in that episode adjusted for the subject's desert).

iii. The intrinsic value of a possible world is entirely determined by the subject's desert-adjusted intrinsic values of the episodes of intrinsic attitudinal pleasure and pain contained in that world, in such a way that one world is intrinsically better than another if and only if the net amount of intrinsic attitudinal pleasure adjusted for subject's desert in the one is greater than the net amount of that sort of pleasure in the other.

It is important to recognize that this theory is not intended as a replacement for IAH. That theory offers evaluations of *lives* by appeal to net amounts of attitudinal pleasure. It does not offer any evaluation of worlds. This latest theory offers an evaluation of *worlds*. The evaluation is by appeal to the net amounts of attitudinal pleasure *adjusted for subject's desert*. It does not offer any evaluation of lives. So this theory should be seen as a possible partner for IAH. When used jointly, the two theories will generate evaluations of lives and worlds.

I am therefore proposing that the evaluation of worlds and the evaluation of lives make use of different considerations. If we want to know how well a person's life is going for him, we want to know the net extent to which he is enjoying things.[5] On the other hand, if we want to know how well things are going in a world, we want to know something about the extent to which people are enjoying good things and suffering bad things, taking account of the extent to which those people deserve to be enjoying the good things and suffering the bad ones.

---

[5] Those who are impressed by the argument from worthless pleasures might want to make use of DAIAH here. Partly because it makes things simpler, I am sticking with IAH for purposes of exposition.

A perhaps surprising implication of this approach is that it becomes possible for there to be worlds in which people's lives are going well for them, but nevertheless the worlds are not very good. Let me give an example to illustrate this. Suppose there is a small world in which everyone is rotten and vicious and has behaved miserably. No one in the world deserves to be happy. But suppose that it turns out that everyone is quite happy. Each of them takes pleasure in many things. Then every inhabitant of the world is living a life that is good in itself for him as determined by IAH, but the world itself might be much less good as determined by SDAIAH.

The description of the world can be made more intuitive: the rotten vicious inhabitants live lives that are good for them. They enjoy lots of pleasure and not much pain.[6] They are happy. But since they don't deserve to be happy, there is a failure of fit. The world is not very good.

Consider another surprising case. Suppose again that the world is full of rotten, vicious monsters. They don't deserve any pleasure. They have been so bad that they deserve some punishment. Suppose they all suffer—each in proportion to his miserable deserts. In that case, IAH implies that these rotten individuals are living rotten lives. Each is suffering pain and so has low welfare according to IAH. IAH says nothing about the world. SDAIAH, on the other hand, evaluates worlds. In this case, it says that the world is not very bad, since all of the suffering is being doled out to people who deserve it. When we adjust the intrinsic values of all those episodes of pain for subject's (negative) desert, the result is that the intrinsic values are mitigated (made less bad). The intrinsic value of the world, then, is determined by consideration of all of these not-so-low numbers.

We can now see the general form of the proposed answer to Ross. Recall that he described two possible worlds that were alike with respect to pleasure and pain, virtue and vice, but which differed with respect to apportionment. In W_j, the good people enjoyed the pleasure, and the bad people suffered the pain. It was the reverse in W_k. I acknowledge that IAH+ and perhaps other forms of hedonism entail that such worlds are equal in value. But SDAIAH does not have this implication. It implies that W_j is much better than W_k. My answer to Ross is this: 'Yes, Ross, you have presented a problem for some possible forms of hedonism. You have shown that we would go wrong if we evaluated worlds strictly in terms of unadjusted intrinsic

---

[6] If you like, you can additionally imagine that they get their pleasure from pleasure-worthy objects. Since I am appealing to IAH here, I don't need to make this stipulation in the text.

attitudinal pleasures and pains. You have shown that IAH+ is wrong. But hedonists are not forced to evaluate worlds in that way. Instead, we can evaluate worlds by intrinsic attitudinal pleasures and pains, *adjusted for subject's desert*. When we evaluate worlds in this way, we get precisely the ranking you seem to prefer. You have not shown anything wrong with SDAIAH.'

9.5. *Atomism*

Some work in axiology seems to presuppose that there must be just one set of atoms of value. It furthermore seems to presuppose that the intrinsic value of any larger thing—a human life, a possible world, the consequence of some action—would just have to be determined by the intrinsic values of those atoms *as measured on a single scale*. We can call this the presupposition of atomism. The basic units would serve many roles. They would be the atoms of value in all sorts of complex situations. It would just be a matter of sorting and collecting them into different bundles. The idea of atomism is both attractive and easily overlooked. It seems so natural that it often goes completely unnoticed.[7]

But it seems to me that reflection on Ross's "Two Worlds" Argument shows that atomism must be questioned. For the argument suggests that it is possible to have situations in which we have worlds full of lives constructed in such a way that the lives are all very good for those who live them, but the worlds are not so good. Similarly, Rossian considerations suggest that there can be cases in which there are lives that are not so good for those who live them, but in which the lives combine to form worlds that are quite good.

I have attempted to deal with this puzzle by recognizing two distinct sets of atoms and two scales of evaluation, one for each set of atoms. On the one hand, when we are attempting to evaluate human lives, we focus on episodes of intrinsic attitudinal pleasure and pain, and we evaluate these by appeal to raw amounts of intrinsic attitudinal pleasure and pain. We say that the intrinsic value of one of these atoms

---

[7] I overlooked this assumption for many years. Following certain strands in Moore's thinking, I just assumed that "intrinsic value" was *one thing*. I assumed that more of it would have to be better, whether we were thinking about lives, or worlds, or consequences of actions. It now seems to me that there are many different sorts of intrinsic value, each relevant to the evaluation of a different sort of thing. If we want to evaluate human lives, we can evaluate them by appeal to unadjusted intrinsic value (or perhaps object's desert-adjusted intrinsic value). If we want to evaluate worlds, we can evaluate them by subject's desert-adjusted intrinsic value.

is determined by that raw amount. The evaluation of a life depends entirely on the values *on this scale* of these atoms. This evaluation tells us little about the value of the world containing these lives. If we want to evaluate the possible worlds in which these lives are lived, we focus on slightly more complex atoms. These are episodes of intrinsic attitudinal pleasure and pain together with information about the extent to which the subjects deserve pleasure and pain. We evaluate these atoms in terms of subject's desert-adjusted intrinsic value. We then determine the value of the world by consideration of this evaluation of these (distinct) atoms. On this proposal, the idea that there is just a single set of atoms is rejected.

CHAPTER 10

Themes and Puzzles

Throughout this book I have been trying to develop and defend a number of views about pleasure and the Good Life. In this final chapter, I restate and comment on some of these views. I also give a sketch of the sort of life I take to be the Good Life. Finally, I am aware of quite a few deep and troubling problems that might have been addressed but which were not discussed in this book. In an effort to be open about my deficiencies, I list and comment on them, too.

10.1. *Themes*

a. Hedonism is intended to be an answer to the question, 'What makes for a good life?' But there are many distinct questions that could be asked with those words. They could be used to ask about the basis of the *morally* good life, or the *beneficial* life, or even the *beautiful* life. As I understand it, and as I think it was traditionally understood, the question is not to be understood in any of these ways. Instead, the question should be understood as an inquiry into what makes a person's life good in itself for him—what makes for individual welfare. I think some criticism of hedonism is based on a misconception concerning the scale of evaluation. One central theme of this book has been that it is important at the outset for us to be clear about the scale of evaluation such that hedonism is intended to provide the basis for a ranking on that scale.

   b. A review of formulations in encyclopedias, in textbooks, and in the relevant literature reveals a surprising amount of disagreement and confusion about the formulation of a typical hedonistic doctrine. Some take it to be a theory about happiness; others take it to be a theory about what ends we ought to pursue; yet others take it as a proposed analysis of the concept of goodness. I think it is most reasonable to take hedonism to be a theory in the heart of substantive axiology, about what makes for a good life (or world). I have steadily tried to understand it in this way throughout the book. If discussion of a hedonistic theory is going to be useful and enlightening, we have to understand our topic, and we must have a clear, coherent statement of the proposed doctrine. Thus, a second main theme of this book is that it is important for us to state various forms of hedonism coherently, so as to avoid confusion and misunderstanding.

c. I think quite a lot of the literature on hedonism is marred by confusion and obscurity about the nature of pleasure and pain. Some people seem unquestioningly to take pleasure to be some sort of feeling. Others seem almost as unquestioningly to take it to be something other than a feeling. "Pleasure talk" in ordinary language blurs important distinctions. These make a difference to the content of the hedonistic thesis. The theory means one thing if it says that *feelings of pleasure* are the Good. It means something completely different if it says that *taking pleasure in things* is the Good. A third main theme of this book has been that it is important for us to recognize the distinction between sensory and attitudinal pleasures, and the accompanying distinction between the corresponding forms of hedonism.

d. Quite a few of the classic objections to hedonism seem to me to be fairly effective against forms of sensory hedonism. Such forms strike me as implausible. But those objections are much less effective against forms of attitudinal hedonism. Thus, I am more inclined to defend some form of attitudinal hedonism. Attitudinal hedonism has other advantages. Once we recognize that pleasures have objects, we are free to draw distinctions among those objects and to claim that pleasure taken in objects of one sort may be more valuable than pleasure taken in objects of another sort. In this way we can maintain our hedonism but get different evaluations of lives and worlds. At any rate, another main theme of this book has been that while sensory hedonism may be naive and implausible, there are forms of attitudinal hedonism that deserve serious consideration.

e. Hedonism comes in many forms. Many of these are forms of attitudinal hedonism, differing primarily with respect to the preferred objects of attitudinal pleasure. Objections that succeed against one form of hedonism may be ineffective against another. A form of life ranked high on one may be considered worthless on another. Yet they are all forms of hedonism. Indeed, I have attempted to show that even some theories not traditionally taken to be forms of hedonism can be reconstructed as forms of hedonism. Another main theme of this book has been the plasticity of hedonism.

f. Critics of some of the views presented here have sometimes been prepared to agree that the theories I have proposed do manage to evade classic objections to hedonism, but they have claimed that this is irrelevant to the debate, since my theories are not forms of hedonism. Others have taken them to be *obviously* forms of hedonism. Yet, after the dust settles, we may still be in doubt. Precisely what does it take to make a theory be a form of hedonism? One of the main themes of this book has been that this is an important question. I have proposed an answer, and that answer turns essentially on the concept of the basic intrinsic value state. Yet another central theme of the book has been that it is important (for a variety of reasons) to recognize the concept of the basic intrinsic value state.

10.2. *My Vision of the Good Life*

Many of the great axiologists of the past (and present) have offered "visions of the Good Life". They have described, sometimes in considerable detail, the important features of the sort of life they take to be best. In some cases, they have given the description but no theory. We are left to construct the theory on the basis of the sort of life they seem to admire. In other cases, philosophers have focused mainly on more abstract considerations. They have given us a formulation of the theory, and we are left to fill in the details.

If we are to take the report of Diogenes Laertius seriously, Aristippus maintained that the Good Life is the life of sensory pleasure. He apparently did claim that if you want to achieve the best sort of life, you should aim for near-term, physical, "selfish" pleasures. Perhaps Aristippus would have been delighted to hear about the swingin' magazine publisher I described at the beginning of chapter 2.

Aristotle seems to have given us a general theory and a more detailed sketch of his conception of the Good Life. It may even appear to the casual reader that the theory conflicts with the sketch. Perhaps Aristotle has given us *two* visions of the Good Life. In Book I of the *Nicomachean Ethics*, he seems to be maintaining that the Good Life is the life of flourishing and virtue. It is the life in which the person displays the peculiarly human excellences. Of course, it is a bit more complicated than that, especially since Aristotle has a distinctive view about virtue. But after some twists and turns he seems to say that a person has a good life if and only if he lives a full, sufficiently rich life throughout which he is active in accord with the moral virtues (courage, temperance, liberality, pride, friendliness, ready-wittedness, justice, etc.) and the intellectual virtues (intuitive reason, science, "philosophical wisdom", art, and practical wisdom). In addition, the person should be adequately supplied with the necessaries—plenty of money, respectable children who won't ruin things for him even after he dies, and a modicum of honor.

Aristotle also held that when a person engages in virtuous activities, he gets pleasure out of them. He says, in a somewhat untypical passage, that 'pleasure completes the activity like the bloom of youth in those who are in their prime'. So it is pretty clear that Aristotle would say that the life of a morally (in his sense) and intellectually virtuous person would have to be pleasant, because the person would always be acting in accord with one virtue or another, and all these virtuous activities would have their "bloom". But, of course, Aristotle did not think that the virtuous person performs the virtuous acts simply as a means to achieve the pleasure. The pleasure is just a happy by-product of the virtuous activity, and a sign of virtue (as the bloom of youth on a cheek might be a sign of health).

According to this vision, the Good Life would be a fully engaged, active, public life. Perhaps the life of a vigorous, intelligent, successful senator or a military man would make a good example.

Toward the end of the *Nicomachean Ethics* Aristotle seems to return to the same topic: the Good Life. But in this context he seems to have a different vision. Now he says that the best life is a life of *theoria*, or philosophical contemplation. This seems to boil down primarily to a life consisting mainly of the exercise of one of the intellectual virtues— philosophical wisdom. This has as its object necessary, unchanging truths. An important feature of this life is that the one who lives it engages in philosophical contemplation for its own sake, and not as a means to anything else. One who engages in practical contemplation, by contrast, apparently does so in order to achieve various goals, either for himself, or for his family, or for his nation.

So in this context he seems to say that the best life for a person is a full life throughout which the person is deeply and permanently engaged in philosophical contemplation. Given his extraordinary productivity, it is likely that Aristotle himself led a life well filled with philosophical contemplation. But what I want to emphasize here is that this seems to be a different vision of the Good Life.

The later Stoic, Seneca, often mentions an idealized character identified as 'The Sage'.[1] The Sage is supposed to illustrate this late Stoic

---

[1] See, e.g., the 75th of Seneca's 'Moral Epistles', where he describes the life of the sage as "unspoiled by pleasure".

conception of the Good Life. According to this conception, the best life is a life marked by wisdom, tranquillity, withdrawal from the world, mastery of the passions, and eventually *ataraxia*—the condition in which one is not troubled by unruly desires or emotions.

Although Mill does not devote much attention to precisely this topic, the reader may come away from *Utilitarianism* with the sense that Mill would most admire a life filled with the "higher pleasures" and as far as possible devoid of pain. A person living such a life would enjoy various intellectual, moral, and aesthetic experiences. Perhaps he would study and write—maybe even a book on logic. Perhaps he would serve in the legislature, there trying to pass legislation that would better the lives of others, especially the oppressed and downtrodden. Perhaps he would attend concerts and art exhibits. In order to make his life a good one, he would have to take pleasure in all these intellectual, moral, and aesthetic activities. Perhaps not so surprisingly, the life Mill describes is in some respects similar to the life he tried to lead.

Those with a more theological turn of mind might think that the Good Life would have to include relatively large doses of worship and prayer. Perhaps, like Robert Adams, they would say that the best life is the life in which one takes pleasure in the love of God.

So now we come to the present question: What is the vision of the Good Life that is supported by my favored forms of intrinsic attitudinal hedonism? Would it be the life of the sage, or the rake, or the scholar, or the vigorous man of the world? Or would it be something else entirely?

The simple answer is that my view implies that the Good Life could be a life of virtually any of these sorts. If we are interested in the goodness in itself of a life for the one who lives it, then, on my view, the whole issue comes down to one thing: Does the one living the life take intrinsic attitudinal pleasure in the things he is doing, the life he is living? If he does this, and does it with intensity, and for a long time, and does not take counterbalancing attitudinal pains in other things, then my view implies that he is living a good life—no matter where he takes his pleasure.[2]

As a result, the Stoic sage might be living the Good Life, and then again he might not. It depends upon whether he enjoys his style of life. If he takes great pleasure in his wisdom, meditation, mastery

---

[2] Intrinsic Attitudinal Hedonism has these implications. If we prefer Desert-Adjusted Intrinsic Attitudinal Hedonism, we will have to add another factor—the extent to which the objects of pleasure deserve to be enjoyed.

of desires, etc., then his life is good for him. If he doesn't, then even if he is otherwise the perfect sage, his life is worthless.

Similarly for the Aristotelian scholar, deeply engaged in philosophical wisdom. If he takes substantial intrinsic attitudinal pleasure in the fact that he is engaging in this sort of thing, then his life is going well for him. If not, not. The activity itself is not the source of value on my view. Rather, it is the enjoyment it provides.

So, in the end, we have to say that almost any sort of life—even the life of the magazine publisher—might be a good life on some forms of attitudinal hedonism.

In some discussions of the Good Life, we find allusions to the doctrine of the autonomy of the individual. Roughly, the idea behind this doctrine is that each individual has (or should have) the freedom to determine for himself what will make his life good in itself for him. Paternalism violates this doctrine. If a paternalist tells you that you must achieve health, wealth, and honor in order to have a good life, he leaves you no freedom to determine for yourself what will make your life go well for you. Preferentists, on the other hand, might seem to have a view consistent with this doctrine of autonomy. It might also appear that attitudinal hedonists could endorse it, too. For these views seem to imply that it is entirely up to the individual to determine what will make his life go well for him. In the one case, this would follow, since what is good for an individual depends upon what he wants; in the other case, since what is good for him depends upon what he enjoys. Different people will want and enjoy different things. Thus, these doctrines may seem to avoid paternalism. They do not dictate to the individual. They do not identify certain things and then tell the individual that his life goes well only if he achieves those preordained goals.

But, of course, it is not quite so simple. For in the case of preferentism, the axiologist *does* inform the individual of something that he must achieve in order to have a good life. The preferentist tells the individual that he must achieve the satisfaction of his desires. Otherwise, he says, it does not matter what he does or gets: he will not have a good life. Similarly for the attitudinal hedonist. He "preordains" what things the individual must achieve in order to have the Good Life. He declares that the individual must achieve *enjoyment*. So it is not clear that preferentism and hedonism are consistent with the doctrine of the autonomy of the individual. Like any version of the Objective List Theory, these views specify "from on high" what will make the life of another go well for that other. In this respect, they leave no freedom to the individual to decide.

It might appear that preferentism and attitudinal hedonism are consistent with a slightly weaker form of the principle of autonomy. For the preferentist can say that it is up to the individual to decide what he will prefer. And the attitudinal hedonist can say that it is up to the individual to decide what he will enjoy. Thus, while these views dictate in general terms what the individual must achieve in order to have a good life, they at least give him the option of determining the content of those things.

But even this seems wrong. For it is doubtful that we have much freedom to determine for ourselves what we will desire, or what we will enjoy. I happen to enjoy the taste of cold beer and salty peanuts. Although I have tried, it just does not seem possible for me to stop enjoying these things, or to start enjoying the tastes of sushi and white wine. Although IAH implies that what is good for me depends upon what I intrinsically enjoy, it does not seem to grant me any outstanding amount of freedom, since I have little control over what I will enjoy.

In then end, then, I remain puzzled by the doctrine of the autonomy of the individual. I am not clear whether my views are consistent with it, and I am not clear whether it matters.

10.3. *Unresolved Puzzles*

There are puzzles and problems that one might hope to see solved in a book about pleasure and the Good Life, but which have not been solved here. Indeed, they have not even been mentioned here. Let me briefly acknowledge some of them.

a. *Infinite worlds and lives.* I like totalism. That is, I like the idea that the value of a complex thing such as a world or a life is the sum of the values of certain selected items within that life or world. Totalism makes it possible to engage in axiology. If we were 'life holists' maintaining that the value of a life is an emergent property, not functionally dependent upon the values of the fundamental value-bearers therein, then it would be hard to explain why any life has its value. At best we could struggle to describe a really good life, and then hint that the value of another life is to be assessed in some highly intuitive way by appeal to the extent to which it resembles the ideal life. That would be unfortunate.

But totalism breaks down in the case of lives containing infinite supplies of fundamental value-bearers. The sums do not come out. I do not know how to set this right.

b. *Repugnant conclusion.* Totalism also runs into trouble in cases involving huge (but finite) supplies of small pleasures. No matter how good a life full of intense, long-lasting, well-directed, well-deserved pleasures might be, we can always imagine another life full of an enormous number of barely noticeable pleasures. Totalism implies that the latter life is better. Parfit[3] has drawn attention to the repugnancy of this sort of conclusion. Although I have suggested a solution elsewhere, I have to admit that I do not know how to set this right.

c. *Origins, bases, etc. of desert.* Several variants of the view sketched here make essential use of the concept of desert. This appears first in the notion of the pleasure (pain)-worthy object. I said that such objects 'deserve to be objects of pleasure (pain)'. It appears again in the concept of the pleasure (pain)-worthy subject. I said that such subjects deserve to experience pleasure (pain). To spell out these versions of the theory in their full glory, one would need to explain in detail what makes an object deserve to be an object of pleasure (pain). One would also need to explain in detail what makes a person deserve to be a subject of pleasure. I have not completed either of these jobs (but I have said some words about them elsewhere[4]). Thus, I acknowledge that the present work is incomplete. I hope someday to get closer to completion.

d. *Epistemology.* Finally, the skeptical reader may wonder what makes me think I know so much about these things. He may question my epistemic credentials. What authorizes me to pontificate as I have? At present, I prefer not to answer this question. Perhaps I have moral intuition. Perhaps I am just emoting. Perhaps I find myself in reflective equilibrium with these thoughts. Perhaps I just take pleasure in writing them down and offering them to you.

---

[3] Perhaps following McTaggart.   [4] See 'Adjusting Utility for Justice', sect. 4.

BIBLIOGRAPHY

Adams, Robert, *Finite and Infinite Goods: A Framework for Ethics* (New York and Oxford: Oxford University Press, 1999).

Alston, William, 'Pleasure', in Paul Edwards (ed.), *The Encyclopedia of Philosophy* (New York: Macmillan Publishing Co. & The Free Press, 1967), vi. 341–7.

Aristotle, *Nicomachean Ethics* (Indianapolis and New York: Bobbs-Merrill, 1962).

Baldwin, Thomas, *G. E. Moore* (London: Routledge, 1990).

Bentham, Jeremy, *An Introduction to the Principles of Morals and Legislation*, (1789); reprinted in *British Moralists*, edited with an introduction by L. A. Selby-Bigge (Indianapolis and New York: Bobbs-Merrill, 1964).

Bigelow, John, John Campbell, and Robert Pargetter, 'Death and Well-being', *Pacific Philosophical Quarterly*, 71, 2 (1990): 119–40.

Brandt, Richard, *Ethical Theory: The Problems of Normative and Critical Ethics* (Englewood Cliffs, NJ: Prentice-Hall, Inc., 1959).

—— 'Overvold on Self-Interest and Self-Sacrifice', *Journal of Philosophical Research*, 16 (1991): 353–63; reprinted in J. Heil (ed.), *Rationality, Morality, and Self-Interest: Essays Honoring Mark Carl Overvold* (Lanham, Md.: Rowman & Littlefield, 1993), 221–32.

—— *Morality, Utilitarianism, and Rights* (Cambridge: Cambridge University Press, 1992).

—— *Value and Obligation: Systematic Readings in Ethics* (New York: Harcourt, Brace & World, Inc., 1961).

—— 'Hedonism', in Paul Edwards (ed.), *The Encyclopedia of Philosophy* (New York: Macmillan Publishing Co. & The Free Press, 1967), iv. 432–5.

—— *A Theory of the Good and the Right* (Oxford: Clarendon Press, 1979).

—— 'Two Concepts of Utility', in Harlan B. Miller and William H. Williams (eds.), *The Limits of Utilitarianism* (Minneapolis: University of Minnesota Press, 1982); reprinted in *Morality, Utilitarianism and Rights*, 158–75.

Brannmark, Johan, 'Good Lives: Parts and Wholes', *American Philosophical Quarterly*, 38, 2 (April 2001): 221–31.

Brentano, Franz, *The Origin of our Knowledge of Right and Wrong*, ed. Oskar Kraus, English edn. ed. Roderick M. Chisholm, trans. Roderick Chisholm and Elizabeth Schneewind (London: Routledge & Kegan Paul, 1969).

Broad, C. D., selection from *Five Types of Ethical Theory*; reprinted in Richard Brandt (ed.), *Value and Obligation: Systematic Readings in Ethics* (New York: Harcourt, Brace & World, Inc., 1961), 50–6.

Carson, Thomas L., *Value and the Good Life* (Notre Dame, Ind.: University of Notre Dame Press, 2000).

Chang, Ruth, *Incommensurability, Incomparability, and Practical Reason* (Cambridge, Mass.: Harvard University Press, 1997).

Chisholm, Roderick M., 'The Defeat of Good and Evil', *Proceedings and Addresses of the American Philosophical Association*, 42 (1968–9): 21–38.

——'Objectives and Intrinsic Value', in R. Haller (ed.), *Jenseits von Sein und Nichtsein* (Graz: Akademische Druck- und Verlagsanstalt, 1972), 261–8.

——*Brentano and Intrinsic Value* (Cambridge: Cambridge University Press, 1986).

Cicero, Marcus Tullius, *De finibus bonum et malorum* (On Moral Ends), ed. Julia Annas, trans. Raphael Woolf (Cambridge: Cambridge University Press, 2001).

——*De natura deorum* (The Nature of the Gods), trans. and ed. P. G. Walsh (Oxford: Clarendon Press, 1997).

Conee, Earl, 'Pleasure and Intrinsic Value' (Ph.D. dissertation submitted to the University of Massachusetts, 1980).

——'A Defense of Pain', *Philosophical Studies*, 46 (Spring 1984): 239–48.

Darwall, Stephen, 'Valuing Activity', *Social Philosophy & Policy*, 16, 1 (Winter 1999): 176–96.

——*Welfare and Rational Care* (Princeton: Princeton University Press, 2002).

DePaul, Michael, 'A Half Dozen Puzzles Regarding Intrinsic Attitudinal Hedonism', *Philosophy and Phenomenological Research*, 65, 3 (November 2002): 629–35.

Diagnostic and Statistical Manual of Mental Disorders, 4th edn., ed. Michael First (Washington: American Psychiatric Association, 1994).

Diogenes Laertius, 'The Life of Epicurus', in *The Epicurus Reader: Selected Writings and Testimonia*, trans. and ed. Brad Inwood and L. P. Gerson (Indianapolis: Hackett Publishing Co., 1994), 3–4.

Epicurus, 'Letter to Menoeceus', 'Principal Doctrines', other writings, all in *The Epicurus Reader: Selected Writings and Testimonia*, trans. and ed. Brad Inwood and L. P. Gerson (Indianapolis: Hackett Publishing Co., 1994).

Fehige, Christoph, 'Instrumentalism', in Elijah Millgram (ed.), *Varieties of Practical Reasoning* (Cambridge, Mass.: MIT Press, 2001), 49–76.

——'Sympathy A Priori', unpublished manuscript.

——and Ulla Wessels (eds.), *Preferences* (Berlin and New York: Walter de Gruyter, 1998).

Feldman, Fred, 'On the Advantages of Cooperativeness', in Peter French, Theodore E. Uehling, Jr., and Howard Wettstein (eds.), *Midwest Studies in Philosophy*, Volume XIII: *Ethical Theory: Character and Virtue* (Notre Dame, Ind.: University of Notre Dame Press, 1988), 308–23.

——'Two Questions about Pleasure', in David Austin (ed.), *Philosophical Analysis* (Dordrecht: Kluwer Academic Publishers, 1988), 59–81; reprinted in *Utilitarianism, Hedonism and Desert*, 82–105.

——'Adjusting Utility for Justice: A Consequentialist Reply to the Objection from Justice', *Philosophy and Phenomenological Research*, 55, 3 (September 1995): 567–85; reprinted in *Utilitarianism, Hedonism and Desert*, 154–74;

also reprinted in Louis P. Pojman and Owen McLeod (eds.), *What Do We Deserve?: A Reader on Justice and Desert* (New York and Oxford: Oxford University Press, 1999), 259–70.

——'Mill, Moore, and the Consistency of Qualified Hedonism', in Peter French, Theodore E. Uehling, Jr., and Howard Wettstein (eds.), *Midwest Studies in Philosophy*, Volume XX: *Moral Concepts* (Notre Dame, Ind.: University of Notre Dame Press, 1996), 318–31; reprinted in *Utilitarianism, Hedonism and Desert*, 108–26.

——'On the Intrinsic Value of Pleasures', *Ethics*, 107 (April 1997): 448–66; reprinted in *Utilitarianism, Hedonism and Desert*, 127–47.

——*Utilitarianism, Hedonism and Desert: Essays in Moral Philosophy* (Cambridge and New York: Cambridge University Press, 1997).

——'Hyperventilating about Intrinsic Value', *Journal of Ethics*, 2, 4 (1998): 339–54.

——'Basic Intrinsic Value', *Philosophical Studies* 99, 3 (June 2000): 319–46.

——'Hedonism', in *The Encyclopedia of Ethics*, 2nd edn., ed. by Lawrence Becker and Charlotte Becker (New York: Routledge, 2001), ii. 662–9.

——'The Good Life: A Defense of Attitudinal Hedonism', *Philosophy and Phenomenological Research*, 65, 3 (November 2002): 604–28.

——'Comments on Two of DePaul's Puzzles', *Philosophy and Phenomenological Research*, 65, 3 (November 2002): 636–9.

Frankena, William, 'Value and Valuation', in Paul Edwards (ed.), *The Encyclopedia of Philosophy* (New York: Macmillan Publishing Co. & The Free Press, 1967), vol. 8, 229–32.

——*Ethics*, 2nd edn. (Englewood Cliffs, NJ: Prentice-Hall, Inc., 1973).

Freud, Sigmund, 'Three Contributions to the Theory of Sex', in *The Basic Writings of Sigmund Freud* (New York: The Modern Library, 1938), 569–71.

Goldstein, Irwin, 'Why People Prefer Pleasure to Pain', *Philosophy*, 55 (July 1980): 349–62.

——'Pain and Masochism', *Journal of Value Inquiry*, 17 (1983): 219–24.

——'Hedonic Pluralism', *Philosophical Studies*, 48 (1985): 49–55.

——'Pleasure and Pain: Unconditional, Intrinsic Values', *Philosophy and Phenomenological Research*, 50, 2 (December 1989): 255–76.

Gosling, J. C. B., and C. C. Taylor, *The Greeks on Pleasure* (Oxford: Clarendon Press, 1982).

Griffin, James, *Well-Being: Its Meaning, Measurement and Moral Importance* (Oxford: Clarendon Press, 1986).

Hurka, Thomas, 'Virtue as Loving the Good', in Ellen Frankel Paul, Fred D. Miller, Jr., and Jeffrey Paul (eds.), *The Good Life and the Human Good* (Cambridge: Cambridge University Press, 1992), 149–68.

——*Perfectionism* (New York: Oxford University Press, 1993).

Kagan, Shelly, 'The Limits of Well-being', *Social Philosophy and Policy*, 9, 2 (1992): 169–89.

——'Me and My life', *Proceedings of the Aristotelian Society*, 94 (1994): 309–24.

——*Normative Ethics* (Boulder, Colo.: Westview Press, 1998).

Kahneman, Daniel, *et al.* (ed.), *Well-Being: The Foundations of Hedonic Psychology* (New York: Russell Sage Foundation, 1999).

Kraut, Richard H., 'Desire and the Human Good', *Proceedings and Addresses of the American Philosophical Association*, 68, 2 (1994): 39–54.

Lemos, Noah, 'Higher Goods and the Myth of Tithonus', *Journal of Philosophy*, 90, 9 (September 1993): 482–96.

——*Intrinsic Value: Concept and Warrant* (Cambridge: Cambridge University Press, 1994).

Lewis, C. I., *An Analysis of Knowledge and Valuation* (LaSalle, Ill.: Open Court Publishing Co., 1946).

Lucretius, *De rerum natura* (On the Nature of Things), trans. H. A. J. Munro, in Whitney J. Oates (ed.), *The Stoic and Epicurean Philosophers: The Complete Extant Writings of Epicurus, Epictetus Lucretius, Marcus Aurelius* (New York: Random House, 1940), 69–217.

Lyons, David, *Forms and Limits of Utilitarianism* (Oxford: Clarendon Press, 1965).

Mill, J. S., *Utilitarianism* (1861) (Indianapolis: Bobbs-Merrill, 1957).

Moore, G. E., *Principia Ethica* (1903) (Cambridge: Cambridge University Press, 1962).

——*Ethics* (London: Oxford University Press, 1912).

—— 'The Conception of Intrinsic Value', in Moore, *Philosophical Studies* (London: Routledge & Kegan Paul, Ltd., 1960), 253–75.

Nagel, Thomas, 'Death', in Nagel, *Mortal Questions* (Cambridge: Cambridge University Press, 1979), 1–11.

Nozick, Robert, *Anarchy, State and Utopia* (New York: Basic Books, 1974).

O'Keefe, Tim, 'Cyrenaics', in *The Internet Encyclopedia of Philosophy*; http://www.utm.edu/research/iep/c/cyren.htm

Parfit, Derek, *Reasons and Persons* (Oxford: Oxford University Press, 1984).

Persson, Ingmar, 'Pain as a Sensory Quality', unpublished manuscript.

—— 'Feldman's Justicized Act Utilitarianism', *Ratio*, 9, 1 (April 1996): 39–46.

—— 'Ambiguities in Feldman's Desert-Adjusted Values', *Utilitas* 9, 3 (November 1997): 319–27.

—— 'Mill's Derivation of the Intrinsic Desirability of Pleasure', *History of Philosophy Quarterly*, 17, 3 (July 2000): 297–310.

Plato, *The Dialogues of Plato*, trans. B. Jowett (New York: Random House, 1937).

Rawls, John, *A Theory of Justice* (Cambridge, Mass.: The Belknap Press of Harvard University Press, 1971).

Rist, John Michael, *Epicurus: An Introduction* (London: Cambridge University Press, 1972).

Rosenbaum, Stephen, 'Epicurus on Pleasure and the Complete Life', *Monist*, 73, 1 (January 1990): 21–41.

Ross, Sir William David, *The Right and the Good* (Oxford: Oxford University Press, 1930).

Sacks, Oliver, *The Man who Mistook his Wife for a Hat and Other Clinical Tales* (New York: Summit Books, 1985).

Seligman, David B., 'Masochism', *Australasian Journal of Philosophy*, 48, 1 (1970): 67–75.

Sen, Amartya, 'Utilitarianism and Welfarism', *Journal of Philosophy*, 76, 9 (1979): 463–89.

Sidgwick, Henry, *The Methods of Ethics,* 7th edn. (1907) (London: Macmillan & Co. Ltd., 1972).

Slote, Michael, 'Goods and Lives', *Pacific Philosophical Quarterly*, 63 (1982): 311–26; enlarged and reprinted in Slote's *Goods and Virtues* (Oxford: Clarendon Press, 1983), 9–37.

Splawn, Clay, 'Updating Epicurus's Concept of Katastematic Pleasure', *Journal of Value Inquiry*, 36 (2002): 473–82.

Sumner, L. W., *Welfare, Happiness, and Ethics* (Oxford: Clarendon Press, 1996).

——review of Feldman, *Utilitarianism, Hedonism, and Desert*, Ethics, 109, 1 (October 1998): 176–9.

——'Something in Between', in Roger Crisp and Brad Hooker (eds.), *Well-Being and Morality: Essays in Honour of James Griffin* (Oxford: Clarendon Press, 2000), 1–19.

Thalberg, Irving, 'False Pleasures', *Journal of Philosophy*, 59 (1962): 65–74.

Velleman, David, 'Well-being and Time', *Pacific Philosophical Quarterly*, 72 (1991): 48–77.

Zimmerman, Michael, 'On the Intrinsic Value of States of Pleasure', *Philosophy and Phenomenological Research*, 41 (1980–1): 26–45.

——'Evaluatively Incomplete States of Affairs', *Philosophical Studies*, 43 (1983): 211–24.

——'Mill and the Consistency of Hedonism', *Philosophia*, 13 (1983): 317–35.

——*The Nature of Intrinsic Value* (Lanham, Md.: Rowman & Littlefield, 2001).

INDEX